THE ITALIAN ROMANTIC LIBRETTO

JOHN BLACK

THE ITALIAN ROMANTIC LIBRETTO
A Study of Salvadore Cammarano

THE UNIVERSITY PRESS

EDINBURGH

© J.Black 1984
Edinburgh University Press
22 George Square, Edinburgh

Set in Linoterm Trump by
Speedspools, Edinburgh, and
printed in Great Britain by
Redwood Burn Ltd, Trowbridge

British Library Cataloguing
  in Publication Data
Black, John, 19–
Salvadore Cammarano and
the Italian opera libretto
1. Cammarano, Salvadore
2. Opera—Librettos
I. Title
782.1′2   ML50.C/

ISBN 0 85224 463 0

Contents

v

150369

« CONTENTS »

Foreword

To spend a number of years studying the life and work of an Italian opera librettist may seem a very strange thing to do. Indeed, in the course of writing this book I have frequently been asked 'What is the point of writing about libretti? The music is the only part of an opera which matters – the stories are nonsense and no one worries about the words!' Another question has been 'What is the point of writing about a lot of long-forgotten operas anyway?' It is true that I have written an account of Salvadore Cammarano's contribution to Italian romantic opera, doing so, deliberately, without discussion of the music for which his work was designed, though without ever forgetting that the purpose of his work was to provide words for a composer to set to music. I began with the assumption that the study of the career of a librettist who worked for a number of composers, from the most famous to the now completely forgotten, would throw a new light – or, at least, light from a new angle – on operatic life of the period, and I hope that such an assumption has been shown to be warranted. Operas had to be decided upon, drafted and written, and then seen on to the stage, and at every stage the librettist had an essential role to play.

Nor is it true that all his operas are forgotten. Many of them have been staged in the last couple of decades as interest in the Italian romantic opera has grown, and others have been broadcast. Records are no substitute for a theatrical performance, but they are an invaluable aid to study and familiarization, and half a dozen or so operas based on Cammarano's texts are available on commercial recordings, and at least another dozen on a 'private – not for sale' basis. I believe that even more will come to the fore as singers and conductors explore some of the lesser-known composers. Certainly some of these operas have sunk without a trace, probably deservedly, but this is, and must be, true of all periods.

One of the greatest difficulties I faced in writing this study was the absence of any authoritative study of the romantic libretto. There are of course many scattered references to points of technique, particularly in books on individual composers, but no full treatment of 'themes and conventions' (to borrow a title from Muriel Bradbrook's study of Elizabethan tragedy). There is no book in English (and precious few in Italian) on the librettists of the nineteenth century, and nothing on the libretti that were written. Even the elements of of Italian versification seem a closed book to many who have written, in this country at least, on Italian opera. Consequently, the study of Cammarano's techniques which forms the second half of this book has had to stand on its own feet, and although I have attempted to sketch in the background while retaining a proper sense of proportion, the lack of an adequate frame of reference has made it difficult to assess success or failure. Several times I was tempted to break off this work in order to concentrate on a wider study, but decided not to be deflected from my purpose. The other possibility, to write about Cammarano's career without discussing his techniques, seemed to me to be an empty and profitless enterprise.

I have tried to make this book accessible and useful to the reader who is interested in opera, but has no special knowledge of the subject. To this end I have written it without footnotes, and have added a list of selected further reading, rather than an exhaustive list of references. I have also tried to write with an eye to readers who have little or no Italian, though they may have to skip Chapter 14, which defeated all attempts at simplification to this level.

In pursuing my studies I have received so much help and encouragement that in acknowledging my indebtedness to some I am liable to overlook others. I want to single out for special mention William Ashbrook; Jeremy Commons; Don White and Patric Schmid; John Allit; Professor Giovanni Aquilecchia and other members of the Department of Italian at Bedford College, University of London, Professor Inge-Stina Ewbank of the department of English, and the librarian and his staff, particularly Valerie Allport (Inter-Library Loans). I owe a particular debt to Dott.

Gabriella Carrara-Verdi, who with great kindness made available to me unpublished material from the Verdi archives at Busseto; and to Librarians/Directors for access to, and permission to use, materials in their custody, of the Lucchesi-Palli Library and the Conservatorio S.Pietro a Majella in Naples; the Cini Fondazione in Venice; the Museo teatrale of La Scala, Milan; the Conservatorio di Musica of Bologna. No words would be enough to thank the staff of the State Archives in Naples. Needless to say, while I have learnt much from them, and from many others, all the mistakes in the book are mine alone.

I am also very grateful to Mrs V.White, whose ability to convert my manuscript into impeccable typescript never ceased to surprise me, and to my old friend Archie Turnbull, Secretary to the Edinburgh University Press, the best midwife an author could want for his books. Most of all, this book owes its existence to the loving forbearance and encouragement of my wife, to whom it is rightly dedicated.

CHAPTER ONE

The Operatic Life of Naples:
Cammarano's Background and Early Life

Salvadore Cammarano was born into a theatrical family, well established in Naples. His grandfather, Vincenzo Cammarano, had arrived there from Sicily in 1764. He was then forty-four years old, and an accomplished actor in the comic tradition. He soon joined the company of Tommaso Tomeo, at the Teatro del Fosso, and five years later transferred to the newly-constructed Teatro di S. Carlino, which was to become the home of the Neapolitan dialect comedy. He stayed there for over thirty years, best known as an interpreter of Pulcinella, in which role he was much admired by David Garrick. He retired from the stage in 1802, and died seven years later.

With Vincenzo from Sicily came the two daughters of his first marriage – Domenica and Caterina, both of them destined for successful theatrical careers; his second wife Caterina Sapuppo, and their infant son Filippo. Following the family's move to Naples, three more sons were born: Giuseppe (who was to become Salvadore's father), Antonio (later to become a painter) and Michele (a tenor). Filippo followed in his father's footsteps, taking over the role of Pulcinella, but was more important as a writer for the dialect theatre, trying to remove from it the more farcical elements. His work included translations of Goldoni into Neapolitan dialect, opera libretti in the same tradition, and even the music for a farce. He dominated the theatrical life of Naples till he retired, in 1832, with a pension from King Ferdinando II. He died ten years later, after a period of ill-health, in reduced circumstances.

Vincenzo's second son, Giuseppe, embarked on a theatrical career at an early age, being given small parts at Teatro S. Carlino. Later his father recognized that his talents lay in a different direction and he was allowed to study painting. At the age of thirteen he was working with the scenery designer at the Teatro S. Carlo, Domenico Chelli. Some of his work caught the eye of King Ferdinand, who awarded him a stipend for five years to study in Rome. Within two years, bad health compelled him to return to Naples. In 1816, when the Teatro S. Carlo was being rebuilt after a disastrous fire, he was called in by the architect-designer Nicolini to decorate the auditorium. Nicolini singled out for special mention his drop curtain, which was used until replaced by a new one by Mancinelli in 1834. He is best known for the enormous painting in tempera on the ceiling of the auditorium. He died of typhus on 2 October 1850, at the age of eighty-four.

Giuseppe married Innocenza Mazzacane, and they had four sons: Salvadore, the librettist, who was born on 19 March 1801, was the eldest. He died on 17 July 1852, less than two years after his father. The next eldest was Luigi, who became a composer of opera – though not a very successful one – and who died of cholera in Naples in the summer of 1854. Giuseppe's two younger sons, Vincenzo and Giovanni, both became miniaturists.

This was the background into which Salvadore Cammarano was born. Although his name is often given as Salvatore, in later life he himself invariably wrote it with a 'd', probably out of pride in his calligraphy, and I think it proper to adopt his own preference.

Our knowledge of the circumstances of the life of Salvadore Cammarano, except for that which can be derived from his works, the scanty correspondence between him and the composers with whom he worked, and the references to him in letters from others, is largely derived from three sources – a long obituary notice by C. T. Dalbono in three issues of the journal *Poliorama pittoresco*, an obituary notice by Vincenzo Torelli in his literary paper *L'omnibus*; and a short entry in Martorana's *Notizie biografiche e bibliografiche degli scrittori del dialetto napolitana*, printed in Naples in 1874. Most other articles and entries in handbooks and the like can be traced back to these three sources, though there are some useful notes by di Giacomo, who was on friendly terms with Salvadore's eldest son Michele, himself a famous painter. The course of the librettist's life is but little documented, though a number of very interesting autograph manuscripts are preserved in the Biblioteca Lucchesi-Palli and in the Conservatorio S. Pietro a Majella, both in Naples. *L'omnibus* also includes not only a chronicle of events in the artistic life of the city, with notes and reviews, but a great deal of theatrical gossip from Naples and, indeed, from the whole of Italy.

Given the family background, Cammarano's career was inevitably pointed in the direction of the arts. Initially his father wanted him to be a painter like himself, and gave him his first lessons. The boy made rapid progress, winning many prizes from the Reale Accademia delle Belle Arti, and being awarded medals following public exhibition of his works. However, as a boy Salvadore naturally frequented the theatre and soon began to write plays; di Giacomo states that his first, youthful dramatic offering was *Priamo*, a tragedy in five acts, in prose. His literary teachers were G.Rossetti and the Abate Quattromani, who is said to have taken a particular interest in the boy. On the latter's advice, Giuseppe agreed that his son should be allowed to study further in dramatic literature. There was at that time in Naples a gathering called the Accademia Poeta Delfica; it had been formed in 1820 by a lawyer, Domenico Cascini, who was passionately fond of the theatre, and it met in his house. Salvadore Cammarano is said to have been assiduous in attendance at this Accademia, and some of his poems from this period still exist. No more is known of his formal education in the arts, except that at some time he attended Nicolini's classes in stage design, and that in 1830 he won second prize from the Reale Accademia delle Belle Arti for a plaster-cast.

In 1819, when he was eighteen, Cammarano's play *Baldovino* was produced at the Teatro Fiorentini. According to Dalbono, writing over thirty years later, it was not well received, but this did not prove discouraging to the author who had sufficient strength of character to profit from the experience by re-examining the faulty passages. I suspect that the author had a soft spot for this work, for on one autograph copy of a later tragedy, *Carlo Magno*, he wrote across the side of the title page, 'This is the pen with which I wrote out *Baldovino*'. Over the next twelve years or so, *Baldovino* was followed by other prose works for the

Fiorentini and S.Carlino theatres: *Un rittrato e due pittori; Si è spento il lume; Una festa di ballo; Due matrimonii all'oscura; La tomba e il veleno; Gioventù vieni ad apprendere; Torvaldo; L'eroina dell'amor fraterna;* and *Il figlio sconsciuto.* Dalbono writes of these works, none of which appear to have survived, that they all showed a tendency towards seriousness, suggesting a vein of melancholy which lay under the surface of his outward appearance. Only *Una festa di ballo* was revived from time to time during the 1830s.

Having set his heart on a career as a writer of opera libretti, Cammarano was faced with the problem of obtaining opportunities for his work to become known to the managers of opera houses and to composers who might wish to use it. The writing of opera libretti was a precarious business. An impresario would employ one or more 'poets', sometimes on a contracted basis with a salary, but often on a more casual basis. Consequently the librettist became part of the staff of the theatre and was responsible to the management. To take one or two examples: Felice Romani, the best-known librettist of the 1820s and 30s, had established his own career under a contract to the impresario of La Scala theatre in Milan, in 1814, which required him to provide six libretti each year (forty days being allowed for serious works and sixty for comedies) at a fixed salary of 3000 milanese lira a year. (For the sake of comparison, all money values will be recalculated in terms of the Neapolitan ducat, and this salary works out at about 800 ducats.)

Jacopo Ferretti, probably the most witty and polished librettist of the time, had a position in the Papal tobacco monopoly in Rome, but this was perhaps something of a sinecure since his literary output, both for the operatic stage and in a host of other forms, was prolific. Luigi Romanelli, a librettist of somewhat conservative, even old-fashioned, style, was Professor of Declamation at the Istituto Femminile di Milano and was the only librettist of the period to achieve a 'collected edition' – eight volumes of his texts were published in Turin in 1832. Gaetano Rossi, another member of the older generation of librettists, wrote 160 texts, mostly for Venice and went on turning them out till he died at the age of seventy-five. Like Romani, he was a professional 'house' librettist, and although a cruder worker than Romani he was more influential in guiding the influence of the new romantic sensibilities into the opera libretti.

However, most librettists were theatrical hangers-on of one kind or another, either amateurs or professionals. Some were lawyers with an interest in the theatre, like Salatino or Tarantini in Naples, or public servants like Bardari. More often they were professional actors and theatrical managers like Checcherini at the Teatro Nuovo in Naples or Calisto Bassi at La Scala, Milan.

During Cammarano's lifetime, Naples was the capital of the Kingdom of the Two Sicilies, which embraced the south of the mainland of Italy and the island of Sicily, and was the seat of the royal, Bourbon, government. It was a busy port and business and commercial centre, as well as being the administrative and military headquarters for the Kingdom. Its population rose from 350,000 in 1828 to 400,000 in 1843, and kept on rising till at the time of the first national census in 1861 it had reached 447,065. This continuing increase masks noteworthy contractions due to the severe cholera epidemics of 1836–37 and 1854–55, the first of which is well known to students of Neapolitan opera through the frequent references made to it in Donizetti's letters. As befitted a city of that importance, it had a thriving court-supported theatre specializing in serious opera and ballet. For many people interested in nineteenth-century Italian opera today, Naples means the S. Carlo theatre and the operas of composers like Donizetti and Bellini, with the operatic life centred round two or three shortish, star-spangled seasons. This image could not be further from the truth.

To begin with, alongside the Royal Theatres, there was a thriving operatic tradition, the musical equivalent of the Pulcinella performances which formed the staple diet of the little theatres of the city. Setting aside the theatres, either serious or lowbrow, in which spoken performances were the rule, there were no less than five theatres regularly giving performances of opera, and a sixth occasionally, during the period, roughly from 1835–50, in which

5

Salvadore Cammarano worked as a librettist. In contrast to cities of lesser size and importance, performances took place almost all the year round.

First, the theatrical year: this year-round activity was interrupted only by four short breaks, though there were, as might be expected, occasional unscheduled periods in which the theatres were closed, as, for instance, during periods of court mourning, or at the height of cholera epidemics. Another similar cause of unexpected closure was the failure for various reasons of the management – this affected in particular the lesser theatres, but was not unknown at the Royal Theatres as well. The regular breaks were: first, in Holy Week, from Palm Sunday to Easter Saturday, with the theatres re-opening on Easter Sunday, after a break of seven days. Second, for the Novena of S. Gennaro, for the celebration of the liquefaction of the blood; the theatres were closed every year from the Thursday before the last Sunday in April for seventeen days, re-opening on the second Sunday in May. Donizetti in his letters refers several times to this period as 'the eighteen days of silence', and the closure is often quoted as being of eighteen days, but a study of performance records shows that it was always a seventeen-day period. Third, for a period of sixteen days, from 10 to 25 September, regardless of the day of the week on which these dates fell, a closure also associated with S. Gennaro. Fourth, from 16 to 24 December, a similar nine-day closure ending when the theatres re-opened on Christmas day. There were also a few other days on which the theatres were all closed – e.g. Fridays in Lent and 16 and 17 January.

When these periods of statutory closure are taken into account, there were over three hundred days in the year in which performances of opera could be – and, indeed, were – given. The general picture shown by the examination of the records of performances is of continuous activity, and it is not very helpful to classify the periods separated by these closures as 'seasons' (carnevale, etc.), because the routine of the opera houses was taken up very much where it had been left off at the end of the previous period. Successful productions were carried over, though new works were obviously prepared during the closure periods, and often chosen to open the new period.

The various theatres were leased to impresarios, whose role it was to engage the singers and theatre staff, provide operas for performance, and so to manage the affairs of the theatre as to make a profit for themselves. The two Royal Theatres were also run by an impresario, but received a subvention from the Treasury. Naturally enough, the impresarios were anxious to maintain public interest and patronage, and to that end regularly introduced new operas, either especially written for the purpose or successful elsewhere but as yet not heard in Naples. Some of these new works were only performed once, including Vignozzi's opera *La Sposa*, the first of Cammarano's texts to be set to music. Even more never achieved five performances. Some favourite works, however, would remain in the repertoire of one or other of the theatres for many years, even decades.

Performances at the Royal Theatres included ballets given between the acts of the opera – often a ballet on a serious subject between Acts I and II and a comic one between Acts II and III. Frequently – and not just at the Royal Theatres – programmes were made up of isolated acts of different operas; for instance, on 2 April 1837, the performance at the S.Carlo consisted of Act I of Donizetti's *Gemma di Vergy*, Act III of his *Sordello* (i.e. *Torquato Tasso*) and additional ballet. Some short operas would be coupled with odd acts of other works, as when Nicola Gabrielli's very popular opera, *La lettera perduta*, not long enough in itself to sustain a full evening, was billed with Act I of Donizetti's equally popular *Il Furioso*, at the Teatro Nuovo on 20 February 1837. These are not isolated occasions: the use of parts of two or more operas to make up a full evening's programme was a normal, everyday occurrence, whatever we might think today of going to the theatre to hear, say, Act I of Donizetti's *L'ajo nell' imbarazzo*, Act II of Rossini's *Corradino* and Act II of Pacini's *Gli arabi nelle Gallie*, as at the S.Carlo on 18 February 1833. These three works are all so different in type as to defy any attempt at artistic unity, but they would be sung by and large by the same singers, and it was, after all, the singers that the audience really went to hear.

7

Audiences obviously expected to listen to longer performances than we do today. Works like *Norma* or *Roberto
Devereux* would nowadays be considered quite enough for
one evening, but were then almost always combined with
ballet or with odd acts of other operas. Perhaps the times of
performance gives us some clue to this; although performances at the Royal Theatres began some time between 7.30
and 9.00 in the evenings, the others commonly began in
the early hours of the morning, 1.30 or 2 a.m. being not
unusual. Several of the smaller theatres gave occasional,
and for periods regular, twice-daily performances, *di giorno* and *di sera*. Whatever timing these terms may conjure
up for the modern theatre-goer, *di giorno* performances
turn out to have begun at about 11.30 in the evening and *di
sera* at 1.30 or 2.00 in the morning. In these circumstances
it would not be surprising if performances at the S. Carlo
were so long that the audiences did not leave the theatre
till well after midnight.

For most of the period 1830–1850, there were five
theatres in more or less continuous use for opera. They
were, in order of importance, the two Royal Theatres (the
S. Carlo and the Fondo); the Nuovo; the Fenice; the Partenope. Occasional use was made of several other theatres,
including the S. Ferdinando and the Teatro alle Fosse del
Grano (where the first Neapolitan performance of Donizetti's *Lucrezia Borgia* took place in 1848, three days before it was first given at the S. Carlo). In a typical year, there
might have been about 120 performances of 30 different
operas at the S. Carlo; eighty performances of twenty-five
operas at the Fondo; 250 performances of thirty-five operas
at the Nuovo; 180 performances of thirty-five operas at the
Fenice; and eighty performances of twenty operas at the
Partenope. The use of the S. Ferdinando varied greatly from
year to year, but on average might have been twenty performances of ten operas.

These figures suggest that in a typical year there might
well be over 700 performances of some 150 operas, but
since some operas were performed in several of the theatres
in the same year, this does not mean that 150 *different*
operas were given. It was not unusual to find two or even
three theatres giving the same opera on the same evening –

the *locus classicus* of this being the evening of 11 May
1834, when the first Neapolitan performances of Donizetti's *Il furioso all'isola di San Domingo* took place simultaneously at the Fondo, the Nuovo and the Fenice. All in
all, the assiduous opera-goer living in Naples between
1830 and 1850 could have seen at least 750 different
operas, ranging from high tragedy to comedy and farce.

The two Royal Theatres – the S. Carlo and the Fondo –
were never both open on the same evening, except on rare
occasions when a Gran Festa di Ballo was mounted at the
former, and there would be an opera given at the latter. A
number of operas were played at both these theatres, using
the same cast, the theatres being, of course, under the same
management. Occasionally a production was transferred
from the Nuovo to the S. Carlo for an isolated performance
but none, as far as I am aware, from the other theatres.
Sometimes two of the lesser theatres came under the same
management, and works moved between them continu-
ously. The S. Ferdinando seems to have been used primar-
ily as an 'overflow' house for successful productions from
the Fenice or Partenope, though it was regularly used for
prose works and amateur productions.

Familiarity with the operatic repertoire of the Neapolitan theatres leads to the conclusion that the inhabitants, taken as a whole, preferred lighter works. The most
frequently performed composers over the period 1830
to 1850 were Vincenzo Fioravanti and Pietro Raimondi.
Most of Fioravanti's many operas were given at the Nuovo
and the Fenice; twenty-eight received their first performances in Naples. His greatest success was *Il ritorno di
Pulcinella dagli studi di Padova*, which was in the repertoire of the Fenice for ten years from 1838 and was played
regularly at other theatres, but *I due disperati per non
poter andar in carcere* was a close runner-up. Both *Il fol-
letto innamorato* and *La dama e lo zoccolaio* were very
popular. Pietro Raimondi's *Il ventaglio*, to a libretto by
Domenico Gilardoni, after Goldoni, was performed every
year for twenty years following its first production in 1831,
being played over 400 times in all. Other popular works of
his included *La vita di un giuocatore* and *La verdummara
de Puorto Andromaca*. He did not confine himself to

comedy, however, and nine of his fifty operas were first given at the S. Carlo. Other very popular works were Lauro Rossi's *La contessa villana* and Luigi Ricci's *Il diavolo condannato nel mondo a prender moglie*, which seems to have been almost indestructible.

On the more serious side, Bellini was by far the most frequently performed composer, and *La sonnambula* rivalled *Il ventaglio* in popularity – receiving 117 performances in 1834 alone, 67 of them at one theatre, the Fenice. Although Donizetti first came to Naples in 1822, later making his home there before leaving for Paris in 1838, it was not till about the time he left that his operas came to dominate the serious repertoire. His lighter works such as *L'elisir d'amore* were always well received. Similarly the great Verdi period did not begin till the very end of the 1840s. The truth is that foreign composers – that is, composers from outside the Kingdom of the Two Sicilies, or those who had not studied in Naples – usually found it very difficult to get a foot in the door of the operatic life of the city. Composers like Fioravanti and Raimondi were all very much in the tradition of Neapolitan comic opera, and wrote for an audience that knew that tradition at first hand. At the S. Carlo and the Fondo, works by Rossini were still very popular, as were those by Coppola, though to a lesser extent. Mercadante's operas were frequently performed, and he continued to produce new operas while enjoying the directorship of the Conservatorio S. Pietro a Majella till his death in 1870. Most of the composers – and this applies to all theatres, not just the royal theatres – have long since been forgotten; some 10–15 per cent of all the operas given in Naples in this period are known to us by their title only, the composers and librettists being now untraceable.

The repertoire was almost always contemporary, though some older works like Rossini's *Semiramide* or *Tancredi* were played from time to time, and *Il barbiere di Siviglia* was always popular, never a year going by without some performances. There was an occasional revival of works by Pergolesi, such as *La serva padrona*, or by Cimarosa (*Un matrimonio segreto*), and there was once a production of Mozart's *Don Giovanni Tenorio*, which ran for six performances at the S. Carlo in 1834, though nothing else by Mozart. Though most of the repertoire was ephemeral, the very popular works were kept on the list year after year. A few words on each of the theatres may help to set the scene for the operatic life of Naples. The *R. Teatro S. Carlo*, the major theatre for the performance of serious opera and ballet, adjoined the Royal Palace. The first theatre on the site was built in 1737 but was destroyed by fire on 12 February 1816. It is difficult to believe, but it was rebuilt, and re-opened on 12 January of the next year. The repertoire was fundamentally serious, though lighter works were not excluded – Donizetti's *L'ajo nell'imbarazzo* and *L'elisir d'amore*, Rossini's *Il barbiere di Siviglia* and Gnecco's *La prova di un opera seria* were all given there occasionally, and frankly sentimental works like Donizetti's *Linda di Chamounix* (which was very popular in Naples) were regularly included. It is notable that the vernacular comedies and farces of the 'Pulcinella' and 'Diavolo' variety were never included.

From the announcements at the beginning of the various seasons, from Cammarano's own staging directions and from other contemporary accounts it is possible to put together a good picture of the staffing of the S. Carlo and the Fondo in the 1830s and 40s. To cover performances at both theatres there would be between fifteen and twenty singers, ranged from the prima to the terza rank; a chorus of fifty, with at least another fifty non-singing extras available to swell out the crowd scenes; an orchestra of eighty (with an additional thirteen casual players, not under regular contract), made up as follows: 26 violins, 8 violas, 8 cellos, 10 basses; 4 flutes, 4 oboes, 4 clarinets, 2 bassoons; 4 horns, 2 trumpets, 3 trombones, 1 cimbasso (a narrow-bore equivalent of the tuba); 4 percussion. (No doubt the two harps were on the casual list.) The figures do not need to indicate that quadruple woodwind was always available; in other cities, and the same was probably true for Naples also, there were separate principals for opera and for ballet. In one of Cammarano's staging notes he makes room for a stage band of thirty players, in addition to on-stage trumpeters. The other salaried staff (at least in the 1840s) included one poet 'with responsibility for putting the works on stage', a chorus master and his deputy, a director of music, a director of ballet (Taglioni, on a special and highly paid contract), a Maestro al cembalo and a composer of ballet music. In passing we may note that the poet, director of music and the composer of ballet music were all budgeted for at the same salary. There were also twelve principal ballet dancers and a corps-de-ballet of eighty-four. The numbers of stage staff, wardrobe and scene-building staff are not known but, to judge from the budgets estimated for these activities, must have been considerable.

The *R. Teatro del Fondo della Separazione de'Lucri* (the Fondo) was built in 1779, near the famous Castelnuovo, to the designs by the Sicilian Francesco Seguro. It was inaugurated on 17 July 1779 with a performance of Cimarosa's *L'infedele fedele,* and was always intended for performance of musical works. It was rebuilt with a covered carriage-way in 1850, later being re-named the Teatro Mercadante. It was used for serious works of a smaller scale, for *semi-seria* and lighter works, in alternation with the S. Carlo, and also housed the Secretary-General of the Superintendency of the theatres.

The *Teatro Nuovo sopra Toledo* (the Nuovo) was built in 1724 on a very cramped site a little to the west of the main street, the Toledo (now the via Roma). Its narrow span permitted an audience of only about 450. It was burnt down in February 1861, but rebuilt and reopened later the same year with improved capacity. It was burnt down again in 1935 and rebuilt once more, this time as a cinema. It was the main home of the Neapolitan dialect opera buffa, and did not usually include more than an occasional tragic work in its repertoire. It seems to have been a popular theatre, to judge by the frequency of performances there. In the 1830s and 40s it used to have an orchestra of thirty players, probably all that could be squeezed into the pit, made up of 10 violins, 2 violas, 2 cellos, 2 basses; double woodwind; 2 horns, 2 trumpets, 1 trombone and one harp (no mention is made of percussion, but it is hard to believe that the theatre could have managed without drums and cymbals to keep the chorus in time). I have not seen any reference to the size of the chorus, but it could not have been large – when Mercadante's *La Vestale* was given there in 1841, the critic of the weekly journal *L'omnibus* complained that there was too large a crowd of extras on the stage for a small theatre.

Earlier that same year, the director of *L'omnibus*, Torelli, had written of a performance there that it went badly for lack of ensemble and direction – the orchestra, chorus and indeed the whole company was discordant, as if unprepared. On another occasion he described the orchestral playing as 'something horrible'. Clearly all was not always well at the Nuovo – and when in 1848 that theatre staged the first Neapolitan performance of Donizetti's *Maria de Rudenz* the same journal commented that, having specialized in light works it presumed to give a tragic opera but gave instead a parody.

The *Teatro La Fenice* was constructed in 1806, in some large stables belonging to the Duke of Frisia. It was always intended for opera, and many singers and musicians who later became famous started their careers there. In the 1830s it specialized, like the Nuovo, in dialect opera, but in 1841 *L'omnibus* was able to record that many famous composers were being heard there before reaching the S. Carlo, and suggested that the impresario had greater means for acquiring new scores. By 1842 the same paper commented that the Fenice was becoming one of the principal theatres of the capital, leaving buffoonery to those of lesser importance. I have not seen any reference to the numbers of singers or chorus, but one list of the orchestra quotes eighteen players. This theatre was rebuilt in 1930 but destroyed in 1943.

The *Teatro Partenope* was a graceful and well-designed theatre in Largo delle Pigne, now the Piazza Cavour. It was opened in 1828 to give 'prose works other than Pulcinella', but the impresario of the Fiorentini successfully protested and in 1830 permission was given for performance of opera. Its new career began on 11 May 1830 with Mercadante's *Elisa e Claudio*. After a period of serious works, it turned to buffo, and later moved back to serious again.

The *Teatro S.Ferdinando* was built in 1791 near the Ponte Nuovo, by Camillo Leonti. It was said to be beautifully designed – the best theatre in the city after the

S. Carlo – but it was unfortunately in an out-of-the-way location. It was occasionally used for opera, and was eventually destroyed in 1943.

The management of the operatic life in Naples was for thirty years in the hands of the impressario Domenico Barbaja, who was such an important figure as to deserve a short digression. He was born in extreme poverty in Milan in 1778, and began life as a coffee-boy in the gambling rooms in the foyer of the La Scala theatre. By blending cream with coffee or chocolate he created a beverage which immediately caught on and laid the foundations of a highly successful commercial career. In 1808 he obtained the concession for the gambling halls of the Royal Theatres in Naples, and the next year he became the impresario. He was responsible for overseeing the rebuilding of the S. Carlo after the disastrous fire of 12 February 1816, and also for much other building in Naples. His first great artistic achievement in Naples was to attract the young Rossini to the musical direction of the Royal Theatres with a contract which required him to write two operas each year. His direction continued to rely heavily on Rossini's operas even when he was able to call on local talent like Bellini or Mercadante, or on foreigners like Donizetti. He was equally successful in obtaining the services of great singers, and seems to have had an instinct for knowing what the public wanted, though he was totally uneducated in any formal way. He remained impresario at Naples till 1840, with only short breaks. From 1821 to 1828 he occupied a similar position at the Kärtnerthortheater and the Theater an der Wien in Vienna, and from 1826 to 1832 also at La Scala, Milan, in addition to his post in Naples.

Contemporary opinions on Barbaja's character vary: he clearly had a genius for making money, for which ends justified means. He was a lavish spender, and obtained the best money could buy for his theatres, while fleecing the people who worked for him. He was at the same time vain and bad-tempered, and a tyrant to his staff. For all that he was the outstanding impresario of his time. Bearing in mind the difficulties of communication and travel in an Italy divided and occupied by foreign powers, it must have required outstanding administrative ability to manage simultaneously opera-houses in Naples, Milan and Vienna, and he was clearly an altogether exceptional man. He died in 1841.

Barbaja usually had two or three official poets at the Royal Theatres, though they do not seem to have been employed full-time in that capacity. For years the house poet was Andrea Leone Tottola, who turned out over a hundred libretti between 1800 and 1830. Giovanni Schmidt was more or less contemporaneous with Tottola. He came from Livorno, and produced some forty libretti between 1800 and 1835. The composer Pacini has left an unforgettable vignette of him – he was a talented man, he wrote in his memoirs, but 'misery was his constant companion, so much so that his character, afflicting beyond description, only had to be seen to inspire melancholy'.

The most important of Barbaja's librettists of the years around 1830 was undoubtedly Domenico Gilardoni, about whose life and character virtually nothing is known, although he is mentioned in a letter by Bellini in a way which suggests he did not have an easy life. Despite his north Italian name, he wrote a great deal of Neapolitan dialect. It was his death in 1841 which left a vacancy for a librettist at the Royal Theatres. Indeed with the death of Gilardoni there was no writer of any consequence available for serious works, at a time when public taste was moving towards the full-bloodied romantic themes. In the mid-1830s, the only poet left on the books of the management was Andrea Passaro, a specialist in comic works.

The story of how Salvadore Cammarano came to be engaged in the Royal Theatres has often been told. It probably took place in the autumn of 1832. It seems that at the request of Salvadore's father, Giuseppe, the architect and stage designer Nicolini approached Barbaja with a recommendation for the young man, and secured an interview for him. Cammarano showed Barbaja a libretto he had written and which he had brought along in his pocket (it was in fact *Belisario*, which was later to be set by Donizetti in 1836). However, Barbaja roughly refused to read it, and the would-be librettist had to return it sadly to its place in a folder in his old writing desk. Although Barbaja refused point-blank to employ him as a poet, he did agree to sign him up as a *concertatore*, something akin to a combination of producer and stage manager, and Cammarano was to retain these duties for the rest of his life.

However, when the Prospectus for the forthcoming season was published on 31 May 1834 both Cammarano and Passaro are listed as *Poeti concertatori*, and in the following months we find Cammarano undertaking a number of duties in this dual role. Furthermore, when Cammarano's first printed libretto, *La sposa*, was set to music and performed at the Fondo, the smaller of the two Royal theatres, Cammarano is described in the preliminaries to the text as 'poeta drammatico e concertatore de' Reali Teatri'. Consequently there can be no doubt that by the middle of 1834, at the very latest, Cammarano was established in the joint role of librettist and stage manager. It may perhaps be significant that by this time Barbaja had been replaced as impresario by a 'Società d'industria e belle arti', although he was to return in 1836 – by which time Cammarano, with the triumph of *Lucia di Lammermoor* behind him, would have been in an unchallengeable position. The alternative hypothesis is that he was in fact appointed in the joint role from the start.

The role of the librettist (always referred to as the *poeta*) in the theatrical life of the period needs some discussion, though many of the important points have already been touched on. He was first and foremost an employee of the management, though this relationship was to change during the course of Cammarano's career, particularly under the influence of strong-minded composers like Verdi. The house poet had two main functions: first the touching-up of old works which were being re-staged, and second the preparation of new texts. Today we are used to a cast chosen to suit the demands of a particular opera, but in those days a basic set of singers were engaged for a season, perhaps only four or five; these, with resident singers for secondary parts, had to undertake the whole repertoire staged. Consequently all the operas chosen had to be adapted to the abilities of the singers, making extensive 'touching up' of the music a regular feature. If the original composer was available to help, so much the better. If he was not, the job was entrusted to the theatre's director of music or whoever else was able to do it. The singers, too, brought with them their favourite arias often from little-known or long-forgotten operas, and these, too, might have to be tailored to fit the text. Consequently a librettist was needed to make the necessary adaptations to bring the operas into line with the assembled company, to bring them up to date with changes in public demand, and to provide new scenes and words for new arias.

It would be absolutely wrong to imagine a librettist sitting down and devising a completely new plot for an opera and then turning it into acceptable verse. Nothing could be further from the truth. The librettists' practice was to take a successful play or a well-known story and adapt it to the requirements of the opera house, bearing in mind the company available and the wishes of the composer. Just as the letters of composers such as Bellini, Donizetti and Verdi make frequent mention of the titles of plays they have seen or heard about, with comments on their suitability for operatic treatment, so Cammarano used to keep lists of plays he had seen or read, with indications of their potential as bases for libretti. A constant flow of plays from all over Europe reached the Fiorentini theatre in Naples, either performed by visiting companies, especially those coming from France, or by the resident company, in which case they were usually translated into Italian (or, rather, 'adapted for use on the Italian stage') by actor-dramatists such as Luigi Marchionni, a member of the company for many years.

Libretti were not, then, original creations: they were adaptations of other works, usually without acknowledgement, there being no copyright laws or even courtesies to prevent it. Works used in this way included plays, novels, poems and historical subjects, and many of them were treated several times by different librettists for different theatres and composers. For instance, both Cammarano's best-known subjects, *Lucia di Lammermoor* and *Il trovatore*, had been used, unsuccessfully, by other librettists before he prepared his own texts, the former five times and the latter once. Similarly his *Il reggente* was not the first Italian version of the libretto Scribe wrote for Auber, *Gustave III ou le bal masqué*, and was not to be the last, since some fifteen years later Somma and Verdi returned to the same subject.

The librettist was also responsible – at least in Naples – for obtaining clearance of the work from the censor's office. Cammarano's normal procedure – and I have no reason to suspect that in this he differed from his contemporaries – was to write first a detailed synopsis of the plot. This often amounted to eight or ten closely-written pages. At the same time he wrote out a list of the distribution of arias, duets, etc., between the various characters: it was necessary for each important singer to get his or her due, and for arias to be distributed properly between the acts. The synopses often contain in narrative form phrases which recur in the final text, but the two tasks – the preparation of a detailed narrative sketch and the composition of the verses – seem to have been two quite separate activities.

The synopses were then submitted to the censor's office and, if approved, were then 'versified'. The completed text would then be submitted for approval, to see that no improper words or sentiments had crept in. The composer was usually involved at the synopsis stage, and where correspondence is extant it is obvious that some of them made extensive alterations to the dramatic structure. Verdi's letters are particularly interesting in this respect, particularly since at least in his collaboration with Cammarano he worked by correspondence. Donizetti preferred to discuss matters with his librettists in person, but he certainly recommended changes in the text of *Belisario*, which he saw first in the worked-up, not the sketch, condition.

In all these discussions we ought to remember what the word libretto means. We use it today as synonymous with the text of a work which the composer has set to music, and the stage directions necessary to a full understanding of the work, and I have been using it in this sense, and will go on so doing. Strictly speaking, however, this is not what a libretto was. It was not a literary document, and it did not seek to establish a text for all time. It was more a programme with the text of the performance included, and was designed to be read during the performance, since the house lights were not turned down when the opera began. The libretto usually began with a list of credits: the heads of the various production departments, wardrobe, stage machinery, illumination, scene-shifters, etc.; often (though not in Naples) the names of the principal orchestral players; frequently a preface, or a long historical note, by the author. Then, usually on the page facing the beginning of the text, a list of characters and the singers taking part. Somewhere in the preliminaries you find the name of the composer and sometimes the name of the librettist. For example, on page 3 of the original libretto of *Lucia di Lammermoor* there is a twenty-line foreword by the author. Underneath is printed in much smaller type: 'La poesia è del Sig. SALVADORE CAMMARANO / La Musica è del maestro Sig. GAETANO DONIZETTI, maestro onorario di S.A.R. il Principe di Salerno, e maestro di contrappunto e compositore nel R. Conservatorio di Napoli.' Then follows the text.

The amount of stage directions given depended very much on the author; Cammarano, being a highly practical man of the theatre, usually gave extensive directions and fairly detailed accounts of the setting. In addition to the text which was being sung there were *virgolato* passages, marked with commas at the beginning of every line, which were not being performed, either because the exigencies of the performance had led to them being cut or because the composer had never set them to music in the first place: they were printed because they helped the reader to understand the drama better. Frequently there is a note in the preliminaries, 'Some lines are omitted in this performance', which presumably protected the management from disappointed customers. Occasionally footnotes to the text are printed. Some librettists were fonder of this practice than others, and Cammarano only rarely used it.

Until the 1840s, libretti were printed for a particular performance by a printer who had, presumably, a concession from the authorities – in Naples for most of the period covered those for the S. Carlo and Fondo theatres were always printed by the Tipografia Flautina. By the end of the 1840s the control over both music and texts by strong-minded composers and publishers like Ricordi of Milan had grown to such an extent that authentic libretti were published with spaces where opera-goers could write in the singers' names for themselves. Naturally the list of theatrical credits disappeared, and the text began to achieve some sort of permanency, as did the music.

Consequently the libretto was an ephemeral document, but the variations in the text used between performances, and the usage of the period which sanctioned the inclusion of music from other operas – though this practice was on the decline during the 1830s and 40s – does prompt the question, what is to be regarded as the authentic text of an opera? It could be taken to be one of a number of documents. It could be first the text in the librettist's final fair copy (if we had it, which we seldom do); second, the same text as it came back from the censor, with offending words and phrases removed and others, matching the metrical pattern, substituted; third, the text as set by the composer, which may have been based on either the first or the second document – but the composer frequently played ducks and drakes with the text, leaving words out and adding expressions to suit the demands of the melodic line, particularly in the free verse *(versi sciolti)* of a recitative-like passage. Fourth, it could be the text as printed for the first performance, which is likely to be the text as approved by the censor, perhaps omitting some sections not required in performance, even though this text frequently does not match exactly what is heard in the theatre. For the purpose of this study I have taken the first printed text as the authentic version, and have based all comparisons, either with draft manuscript versions or with subsequent printed versions with this, since it seems to me to be the only standard applicable to all Cammarano's work.

CHAPTER TWO

1834–1837

La sposa — Ines de Castro — Un matrimonio per ragione —
Lucia di Lammermoor — Belisario — Eufemio di Messina —
L'assedio di Calais — Pia de' Tolomei

In June 1834 Cammarano was responsible for staging Donizetti's *Anna Bolena* at the S. Carlo, and wrote a few additional lines for it. This may have brought him valuable experience, but not much comfort, because the production was withdrawn after only three performances. *Anna Bolena*, despite its great success elsewhere in Italy and, by this time, a growing international reputation, was not often played in Naples – it had a run of nineteen performances in 1832, and eleven in 1833. It reappeared in 1836 for eighteen performances at the Fenice and Partenope theatres, and was not seen thereafter; it was not a work likely to receive wholehearted Bourbon approval, and was prohibited from 1840–8. On this occasion, Cammarano was clearly touching up an established production, and it is a little surprising in the circumstances to find him writing a note of the scenery needed, and another giving details of the costumes, in a form which clearly indicates instructions to the two departments. The autograph is clearly dated June 1834, so it must have been drawn up for the 1834 performances, which took place on 19, 20 and 22 July of that year.

The other work assigned to June 1834 is problematic. In the catalogue of the Conservatorio in Naples there is the entry under the name of Salvadore Cammarano:

> Gugliemo Tell. Scenario per il opera. [Sono le sole scene di quest'opera che il Cammarano nel giugno del 1834, tracciò per i Reali Teatri di Napoli.] m.s. 1834

Unfortunately the text – like ten or so other items under the same catalogue number – can not now be traced by the library staff and the matter must remain a puzzle till it is found. The difficulty lies in the fact that *Tell* was not performed at the S. Carlo in 1834 – or at any other theatre, either. Its sole production in Naples was in the previous year, 1833, when it ran for fourteen performances at the S. Carlo, with two additional performances of Act I and a third of Act I and II together. If Cammarano had sketched out scenes for the production of *Tell* in 1833, we would have an earlier date for the initiation of his poetical work at the Royal Theatres, and this would tend to discredit the traditional story of Barbaja's rejection of him as a poet. On the other hand, it may be that further performances were contemplated in 1834, and that Cammarano was given the job of revising it, adding new scenes where neccessary, in the same way as he had to do for *Anna Bolena.*

There is nothing difficult about the dating of his first performed work as a librettist, the text of *La sposa.* Submitted to the censors on 11 September 1834, it was approved on 29 October. It was set to music by Egisto Vignozzi, and was produced at the Fondo theatre on Monday, 3 November 1834, with a distinguished cast which included Tacchinardi-Persiani, Crespi, Salvi and Luzio in the main roles. It must have been of some chagrin to the budding librettist that it was never performed again after the first night. The composer is described in the libretto as a graduate of the Royal College of Music in Naples, and of the Academy of Music of Bologna, but very little is known about him today. The only other opera of his that I can trace came out in Venice the following year, and was a setting of Romani's old text *Elena e Malvina*, which had already been set by four other composers. *La sposa* is a slight piece of theatre, and it is one of the very few Cammarano texts for which I have been unable to discover the source. It reads as if it was based on a second-rate French *comédie-vaudeville*, and concerns Adele who, though about to marry Ernesto, confesses her love for Enrico, who was thought to have been lost in a shipwreck. He turns up, too late to stop the wedding; eventually Ernesto is revealed as Adele's long-lost brother and a suitable reconciliation takes place, the marriage not having been consummated. The most interesting feature of the text is the presence of a buffo Lord of the Manor, who lapses into Neapolitan dialect when addressing his villagers – the only

occasion when Cammarano uses dialect in any of his libretti. (Martorana's biographical note states that when this
same text was set by Giorgio Miceli in 1858, under the title
La Fidanzata, the dialect was replaced by standard Italian,
but this is not borne out by the printed libretto – the dialect
remains, although it may perhaps have been changed in
performance.) *L'omnibus* was represented at the performance of *La sposa*. Its reviewer commented on several pieces
that were applauded sufficiently for the composer to be
called on to the stage, and considered this a good omen for
the future of the work. He went on to say that the libretto
was written with much strength of feeling and was full of
new ideas, but that the comic situations were a mistake,
making the part played by Luzio (the dialect-speaking
landowner) into a true caricature, badly put together and
quite superfluous. On the whole, though, it was a judicious
notice, which Cammarano could have been forgiven for
finding encouraging – even though it did not secure the
opera a second performance.

Although *La sposa* was the first of Cammarano's texts to
be performed, it was not the first to be written. His libretto
of *Ines de Castro* was submitted for approval on 7 January
1834 and was intended for the composer Giuseppe Persiani. Permission was not forthcoming till over a year
later, and the opera was first given at the S. Carlo on 28
January 1835, with the famous Malibran as the eponymous
heroine. Persiani (1804–1869) was described at that time
as 'maestro di capella della scuola del Real Conservatorio
di Napoli'; he was a composer of some considerable gifts,
who had begun his operatic career some ten years previously, and whose best known works were *Danao re d'Argo*
(Florence, 1827) and *Eufemio di Messina* (Lucca, 1829),
both of them with libretti by Romani. He had married the
famous prima donna, Fanny Tacchinardi, who thereafter
hyphenated his name to hers. She was singing in Naples in
1834 and 1835.

The story of Ines de Castro, the unhappy fourteenth-
century mistress of Don Pedro, son of Alfonso IV, King of
Portugal, had frequently been treated on the stage before,
as play, opera and ballet. Cammarano starts off his libretto
with a preface (a common enough practice) in which he

tells his readers that knowing the narrow limits of his ability he had thought it prudent to consult other works on the same subject – the tragedies by de la Motte and Berto-lotti and certain ballets which carried the name of the victim; also de Greppi's Don Pietro, though there is no evidence in the libretti that he took anything from it; and, lastly, the sketch of a tragic drama, well put together, by a very worthy friend of his own.

This friend was Giovanni Emanuele Bidera, a lawyer of an Albanian family who was born in Palermo in 1784 but who had settled in Naples. In the 1820s he had a number of plays produced at the Fiorentini, and was the author of a book on the art of declamation. He was best known for his descriptions of the customs and surroundings of Naples, and in 1834 he began a short career as a librettist with the text for Donizetti's *Gemma da Vergy*; *Marino Faliero* was to come in 1835. He retired to Palermo in 1848 and died there ten years later. Whether he had sketched out an *Ines de Castro* for his own use is not now known, but Cam-marano certainly prepared sketches of subjects against a time when they might be required, and it would not be in the least surprising if Bidera did the same. The libretti of *Ines* is often quoted as being by Bidera and Cammarano, but the circumstances of the collaboration gave rise to some comment at the time. The report of the performance in *L'omnibus* says 'The libretto is by Bidera, his the plan, his the distribution of pieces, his the words, which were put into verse by Cammarano; and because the libretto is being praised it is right that the praise should be shared between the two, and not given only to the last-named who in the preface to the libretto has not made known the part played in it by Bidera, who is perhaps the friend vaguely mentioned there'. *L'omnibus*, and its owner Vin-cenzo Torelli, was at the centre of the literary and café society of Naples, and its explanation of the origins of the libretto of *Ines* can almost certainly be taken as accurate. The performance was rated as highly successful, but the opera ran for only nine performances before being taken out of the repertoire the following March. *Ines* was never again played in Naples, which is very surprising, because it proceeded to go the rounds of the Italian theatres, with the heroine sung by Malibran, Tacchinardi-Persiani, Ungher, and others.

Ines proved to be Cammarano's most frequently set libretto, being used five times by different composers. The next setting was by Filippo Marchetti, for performance in 1840 at the Teatro Sociale, Mantua. In 1841, Pietro Antonio Coppola's setting was given in the Teatro S. Carlos in Lisbon. The next two settings were of the same text, using the title *Don Pedro di Portogallo*, first by Luigi Gibelli, for the Teatro Sociale in Novarra, 1849, and finally by Riccardo Drigo, for the Teatro Nuovo in Padua, 1868. All these versions differ slightly from the original in the scenes used and while Gibelli's *Don Pedro* eliminates several characters, the Drigo setting is based not on the text used by Gibelli but on the original *Ines*. The version of *Ines* given by Persiani in Paris in 1839 (with his wife in the title-role) departs most widely of all from the original, but the Italian operas usually had to be padded out for performance in Paris.

Right at the end of his life Cammarano turned back to his first successful libretto when (in 1851) he needed a text for Pacini. He was working on *Il trovatore* at the time, and was, I suspect, already ill. He took hold of *Ines* and rewrote it as *Malvina di Scozia*. The changes are perhaps sufficient for it to be allowed to stand as a libretto in its own right, and it will be discussed later. Whenever Cammarano was in doubt about having a libretto permitted for performance, he used to transfer the action to Scotland (perhaps this was considered so far-flung and outlandish a country that any degree of treason could be perpetuated without threatening the security of the Bourbon occupancy of the throne or the moral welfare of the people). We know from Pacini that the plot of *Ines* was not permitted by the censors under its original title (it had been prohibited in 1839 and 1842), so perhaps the neglect of *Ines* in Naples, as well as the need to transfer the action to Scotland, indicates that the subject was not looked upon with favour in royal circles. Thus, Torelli wrote in his obituary notice in *L'omnibus*, Cammarano opened and closed his career with the story of Ines – not strictly true, but it made a good story.

The next work on which Cammarano was engaged (it being tacitly assumed in the absence of evidence either way that putting operas on the stage of the S. Carlo and the Fondo, and touching-up other people's libretti were continuing, bread-and-butter activities) was a two-act *melodramma, Un matrimonio per ragione*, set to music by Giuseppe Staffa and performed at the Fondo on 8 July 1835. This libretto again carries a preface by the author, and from it we may sense that he still had not found complete artistic self-confidence. It is worth quoting in full:

> A comedy-vaudeville by Eugène Scribe, *Le marriage de raison*, has provided me with all the threads of this work; the small changes and the many condensations which are to be met with were forced on me by the very difficult requirements of our native drama. If I have retained in this work some of the many beauties with which the very distinguished French author enriched his vaudeville, and if my indulgent fellow-citizens do not consider it unworthy of being put before them, I have fully achieved the ends I had in view.

Giuseppe Staffa (1807–77) was a minor Neapolitan composer whose operatic career stretched from 1828 to 1852, during which he wrote seven operas, all of them for Naples. *Un matrimonio per ragione* was, in fact, the most successful of them all, actually reaching six performances, with a cast which included Tacchinardi-Persiani and Ronconi (who had to play a man with a wooden leg). It was revived, briefly, at the Teatro accademica di S. Severino in 1840. In the audience on the first night was Donizetti, and a week later he wrote to a friend in Paris 'At the Fondo, Staffa, the young Neapolitan who lived for a long time in Paris, gave an opera *Le marriage de raison*! Had the libretto been warmer, I bet that in many places he would have been more impassioned . . . Nevertheless, three pieces were applauded!' The critic of *L'omnibus* said much the same thing: the libretto lacked warmth, but the verses were excellent.

Le marriage de raison was in fact by Scribe and Varner, and is a neat situation comedy, with some social moralising thrown in, about a young man who wants to marry the ladies' maid. His father persuades him of the disadvantages of such a match, and arranges for the girl to marry a retired sergeant (with a wooden leg, the original having been lost in the service of the son). The dénouement rests on that hoary old device of what the young man heard when he was hiding behind a screen, and all ends happily. There is so little action in it that it is hard to imagine why it was ever thought of for an opera. In the process of conversion into a libretto the play lost all the virtues of delicacy and social comment it had; the father's advice to his son and his own life story are – wisely – sacrificed and we are left with the bare bones of a rather trivial story. But in one other respect the reviewer was right; the verses do show the flowing quality and the technical metrical competence that was to become the hall-mark of Cammarano's mature work. His verses *sound* well, and to this extent they are a gift to a composer sensitive to the sound of the words he was setting.

Donizetti's reference to the libretto of *Un matrimonio per ragione* is of particular interest since in the same letter he goes on to say that he has already finished work on *Lucia di Lammermoor* (the last page of the autograph full score is dated 1835 July 6, in Donizetti's hand), and with *Lucia* he began a three-year collaboration with Cammarano. The first mention of *Lucia* came in a letter of 18 May 1835, when Donizetti wrote 'The delay of the poem for the S. Carlo, which is going to be the *Sposa di Lamermoor* of Walter Scott makes it difficult for me to accept your kind offers for August . . . the worse for me . . . but the fault is the poet's.' Donizetti was in fact under contract to write an opera for production at the S. Carlo in July, and the arrangement was for him to have the libretto, already approved by the authorities, four months in advance. Obviously he was having difficulties in getting his text in time – difficulties which all composers of the period were forever complaining about.

In this instance the fault may not have been entirely Cammarano's, for ten days after this letter Donizetti found it necessary to write (on 29 May) to the Society managing the affairs of the Royal Theatres in pretty forthright terms. The letter tells us so much about the way in which new operas came about that it is worth quoting in full:

After I have explained in the clearest possible terms in my letter of the 24th of this May the reasons which induced me to write *Lucia di Lammermoor,* I don't know how you can seek to blame a long indecision in my choice of a subject for a delay in staging my opera in July. Permit me to tell you with my usual candour: you ought to recollect that among the terms of my contract is one which requires you to give me the libretto, approved by all the authorities, not later than the beginning of last March, while it was only a few days ago, following my repeated and urgent requests, that you put the poet Sig. Cammarano at my disposal. I quickly came to an understanding with him about the subject I mention above. You ought to remember that when, a few days ago, I myself put into your hands the synopsis, on which the performers were listed, not only did you not disapprove of my choice, but you yourselves sent it to the censors, from whom it came back with the outline of the action approved, a formality which you might well have overlooked, bearing in mind the urgency, which has frequently got us out of such difficulties. Thus the delay is not of my doing, so that I would be within my rights to protest many times over, were I not to have faith in your own honesty.

Time goes by, and I assure you that I cannot stay any longer in such uncertainty, since I have other commitments. Therefore either be good enough to authorize the poet Sig^r Cammarano to get busy without delay on the text for *Lucia di Lammermoor,* which has already been seen and approved by the censors, in which case I can commit myself to finishing the work by the end of August, without insisting on the four months permitted in my contract; or, alternatively, to allow me to put my affairs in order, going back to my rights under the terms of the contract and cancelling every way out which I offer in my earlier letter of the 25th of this month or in today's.

Apart from the light Donizetti's letter throws on the way operatic business was conducted, and his refusal to be pushed around by a dilatory management, there is a great deal of interest in the letter. He had apparently written on the 25th May about *Lucia;* Cammarano had been allocated to him 'a few days ago', but he had already produced a synopsis, which Donizetti had himself handed in: it had been to the censor's office and back; and now, four days later, he was demanding action, or else. On 18 May he had told his friend that the fault for the delay in the libretto of *Lucia* lay with the poet, so it is clear that he must have been in contact with Cammarano for more than just a few days.

As it happens, Cammarano's original synopsis for *Lucia* is still extant, 8½ pages of close tidy writing giving the details of the plot as we are familiar with it today. It is not dated, but an interesting feature is that at the time he wrote this synopsis, Cammarano had it in mind to call the opera *Lucia Asthon*. On 18 May, Donizetti referred to it as the *Sposa di Lamermoor*, a direct translation of Scott's *The Bride of Lammermoor*. By the 29 May he was using the eventual title, *Lucia di Lamermoor* (the autograph full score has *Lamermoor*; the double 'm' had crept back in, however, by the time the libretto was set up for the first performance). So when did Cammarano write his synopsis? It is not the copy presented to the censors, as it does not have their signed permission on it. (Donizetti's remark that the dramatic action had been permitted merely indicates their acceptance that the full text would also have to be submitted later.) I strongly suspect that either Cammarano had been working on Scott's story as a basis for an opera plot for some time and had progressed sufficiently with it to enable him to produce a detailed synopsis at fairly short notice, or that he had been given the task of writing for Donizetti long before the 'few days ago' Donizetti mentions on 29 May; in any case on 25 May he was blaming the poet for the delay. Perhaps Donizetti and Cammarano had reached their own understanding on collaboration.

Once the synopsis had been approved, Cammarano had still to reduce the narrative sections to the eleven- and seven-syllable lines of *versi sciolti*, and to provide formal verses for arias, cavatinas, concerted numbers, choruses, etc. He must have worked quickly to keep ahead of Donizetti, since the whole score was completed by 6 July, five weeks after his letter to the authorities. It was quite against the rules for the composer to set the text before it had been approved, but this was the case; the libretti was submitted for approval on 10 August, and was returned, no changes being asked for, on 12 September. Donizetti was clearly happy about Cammarano's work, for on 6 June he wrote to a friend in Milan asking him to explore the possibility of a contract with the Fenice Theatre in Venice, and adding 'The poet should be Sig^r Cammarano, the poet of the Royal Theatres in Naples, so that we can save time'.

Production of *Lucia di Lammermoor* had been expected on 20 August, but the management of the Royal Theatres was in difficulties, and had not, in fact, submitted the libretto by this date. It was not until the S.Carlo reopened after the usual September closure, on the 26th, that the first performance took place. Its success is well-known, and it ran for twenty-two performances before the middle of the following February. It subsequently grew steadily in popularity, though initially it seemed to make headway only slowly. It was, however, launched on a triumphant Italian and international career, and, for half a century or more, not a year passed without a production somewhere in the world. It certainly became Donizetti's best known tragic opera – and for many generations of opera-goers, perhaps his only tragic opera.

The libretto of *Lucia di Lammermoor* has a number of unusual features, not least the feeling of anti-climax in the last act which, though almost a structural feature of Italian romantic opera, is accentuated by the early disappearance of the heroine and her replacement in the last scene by the tenor. In many ways it is a tenor's opera, not a soprano's, despite the famous passages for the soprano, and Duprez, in his memoirs, claims credit for suggesting to Donizetti the treatment of the final aria, when, in the second stanza, the melody is transferred to the cellos, the voice breaking through with short, broken lamentations. The broken lines of a dying or despairing heroine are, in fact, a typical finger-print of Cammarano's style, and will be discussed in Chapter 12; it was not an original concept, being used in a number of earlier texts (often associated with madness).

Meanwhile there was the matter of the opera for Venice. By October, Donizetti was in direct negotiations with the impresario, Natale Fabrici, but difficulties arose over the choice of librettist. It seems from Donizetti's letter of 24 October that Fabrici had suggested that he should have the

services of the local poet Beltrame. It would be difficult
to fall in with this suggestion, Donizetti wrote, for two
reasons: first because Cammarano had already begun
work on the libretto, and second because he had never had
the good fortune to come across any of Beltrame's verses,
and it would be rash to work with a poet so far away, when
neither knows the style of the other. He might find this
unsatisfactory, and he might fall out with Signor Beltrame,
with whom he would need an unending series of conversa-
tions if together they were to weave (*tessere*) a libretto. He
had already talked to Cammarano, but Beltrame was in
Venice, and he couldn't talk to him, and he himself would
be arriving in Venice too late to make any changes in the
libretto. Perhaps Fabrici could make it all right with Beltrame . . .?

Pietro Beltrame wrote only two or three libretti, none of
them for a major composer, and was at this time still in his
late teens. Interestingly he was the author of a *Fidanzata
di Lammermoor* which had been set by Alberto Mazzu-
cato, and performed at Padua in 1834, later being given also
in Milan. Consequently Donizetti's remark that he knew
none of Beltrame's verses leads me to believe that this
earlier setting was not known to Cammarano and Donizetti when they were working on their own *Lucia* earlier
that year.

Donizetti's letter – which is in his most tactful vein –
does highlight the attitude taken by managements, that
the choice of librettist should be left in their hands, and not
to be in the gift of the composer – not an unreasonable
attitude when it came to dealing with the intricacies of the
censorship, when local knowledge would be invaluable,
but one which made proper collaboration between composer and librettist quite impossible if the composer were
not going to write the opera *in situ*. The need for innumer-
able discussions between composer and librettist shows
how far the writing of operas had progressed from the days
when the management simply handed down a text to the
composer and expected him to get on with setting it.

Having settled the matter of who was to write the libretto for Venice, the choice of a subject remained, and
Donizetti was able to inform the management on 12 Nov-

ember that he had settled for *Belisario*. Cammarano had obviously brought out the text he had written in 1832, and the copy that survives has all Donizetti's marginal notes and comments on it. Some of the changes which they found it necessary to make in it will be discussed later, but by and large little needed to be done to it. Perhaps they should have made more extensive revisions, since the text creaks badly at the joints and the last act, in particular, is dramatically poor, with the arrival of new characters and unprepared incidents, the plot turning on the threadbare expedient of a long-lost-son-identified-by-a-cross-round-his-neck.

One mystery about *Belisario* should be disposed of, the identification of the source, about which Cammarano himself was mistaken, though it was not his fault. In a preface printed in the first, but not in every contemporary, edition, he wrote: 'The basis of this work . . . is a tragedy of Holbein, which the worthy dramatic artist Marchionni has adapted for the Italian theatre'. This Luigi Marchionni was an interesting character, a regular player of parts large and small at the Fiorentini theatre till he lost his teeth (and with them, presumably, his voice) in 1849; he died in 1852. He translated and edited very many plays for performance at the Fiorentini. He came, like Cammarano, from a theatrical family, his sister Carlotta being a famous actress. He certainly did write a version of *Belisario* for Naples, which was first given in 1830, though not printed till 1846, and in it he states, indeed, that it is 'imitato da Holbein'. But although Franz Ignaz Holbein (1779–1859) wrote a number of successful plays there is no record of a *Belisarius* amongst them. In fact the source of Marchionni's play was the *romantisches Trauerspiel* in five acts by Eduard von Schenk, *Belisarius*, first produced in Munich in 1820, and frequently revived. (I am indebted to Dr Peter Branscombe for suggesting that I should examine Schenk's play.)

Donizetti's contract with the Venice impresario Fabrici was signed on 25 July; by this time *Lucia di Lammermoor* was complete and Cammarano could presumably get down to work on *Belisario*, though the question of the librettist was not finally settled till after 24 October. As Donizetti left Naples for Milan and Venice about the third week in November, for him to say on 24 October that Cammarano had already begun work on the libretto was probably a considerable understatement – though of course the libretto had been virtually ready for several years. *Belisario* was produced at the Fenice theatre in Venice on 4 February 1836, with great success, and it soon established itself in the popular repertoire. It was first seen in Naples on 18 June 1837 – it usually took about eighteen months for an opera first produced elsewhere to reach Naples – and it was given there regularly till 1842, after which it seems to have declined in public favour. After the early 1840s it was still revived occasionally in Italy and in other countries.

About the time he was working on *Belisario*, or perhaps after he had finished it, Cammarano was asked by Persiani to revise an earlier opera of his – *Eufemio di Messina* – which was then performed five times in January and February 1836. The preface Cammarano wrote for the libretto is worth quoting in full, as it is very revealing about his approach to revisions of this nature:

> As long ago as 1830 Maestro Persiani clothed with music a drama by Felice Romani called *Eufemio di Messina*: having to give this work in Naples, and having to adapt it for the present company, he considered it necessary to modify it, as a result of which it was also necessary to rewrite the text.
>
> Having been asked to carry out this editing, and urged on by pressing reasons, not least the friendship which binds me to Sigr. Persiani, I set to work, and I have not only made more than a few changes in the first act of the drama, but have almost entirely rewritten the second.
>
> I have thought it essential to make all this clear, while if from one point of view the libretto could not be adorned with the name of Romani from the other my own scruples would not allow me to arrogate to myself part of someone else's work.

Considering that Romani's libretto only consisted of two acts, Cammarano virtually provided Persiani with a new text. It must have involved him in almost as much work as a completely new one.

Meanwhile in Naples the Society that had undertaken to manage the Royal Theatres finally gave up in March 1836. Neither the S. Carlo nor the Fondo opened after the Easter break, and matters did not improve until Barbaja agreed to return. He signed a four-year lease on 4 June and the S. Carlo re-opened on 6 July with a work called *Manfredi trovatore* which Florimo states as having an anonymous librettist and music by various composers. A fortnight later came *Norma* and *I Capuleti ed i Montecchi* – two certain money-spinners by Bellini; then two other certain successes – Donizetti's *Parisina* at the S.Carlo and Rossini's *Cenerentola* at the Fondo. Obviously, things were returning to normal, and Barbaja could begin to plan for the future.

Whether or not Cammarano was paid for the time the theatres were closed we do not know; presumably not, for one of the reasons that Barbaja returned was to provide employment for the many people who had been thrown out of work by the failure of the previous administration. Over the summer the only new work to be produced at the S.Carlo was Raimondi's *Isabella degli' Abenati*, which had a libretto by Sapio, then on the threshold of an unimportant career as a librettist for composers of the second and third rank.

However, on 23 July *L'omnibus* announced that Donizetti was writing a big new work for the S.Carlo, which would perhaps be called *L'assedio di Calais*, as well as one for Venice, which would be *Pia de' Tolomei*; in both of these he was going to use libretti by Cammarano. Although negotiations began first for the latter, it was not the first of the two to be performed, so it is convenient to deal with *L'assedio di Calais* first. Presumably the contract for this work was agreed after Barbaja returned in early June, and the first mention of it comes in a letter from Donizetti to Ferretti; the letter is undated, but the text makes it plain that it was written after the introduction of *Norma* to the S.Carlo on 19 July. While he expected that the opera would be performed in September, by 8 September he was writing that it was down for performance on 19 November – an important date, the *giorno onomastico* of the Queen Mother, a court occasion which always involved a visit to the S.Carlo, with a work which was required to have a happy ending, sometimes specially adapted for the occasion, though this convention was occasionally ignored.

L'assedio di Calais, with the *ballo integrale* in the third act, which Donizetti set so much store by, was particularly suitable for such an occasion – not only did it have the requisite happy ending, but one which glorified the role of the (English) queen. The opera was very well received, the king congratulated the composer, but the cholera emptied the theatre. Donizetti's own view was that the third act of the opera was weak, as the ballet dragged back to the action; he thought of revising it but never had occasion to do so.

Cammarano's sketch for *L'assedio di Calais* and his draft libretto (with some of Donizetti's scrawls on it) are still extant, but are not dated. While the ultimate source of his libretto was de Belloy's famous tragedy *Le Siège de Calais,* first given in Paris in 1765, which was in the repertoire of the Fiorentini theatre during the early 1830s, the basis of Cammarano's text was a long ballet scenario with the same title by Louis Henry (Milan, 1827). It is a remarkable libretto, the closest Cammarano ever got to real poetry, particularly in his description of the embattled city and the heartfelt pride of its citizens. The scene that he chose for the end of the second act finale, in which the citizens step forward in turn to volunteer for places among the doomed six, is magnificent. *L'omnibus* wrote that the plot was wonderful, and that the author was to be praised for the way he had handled it, and for the good versification, adding that it was a pleasure to have such fine sentiments instead of the usual ignoble ones.

L'assedio di Calais has had a disappointing stage history; there were eighteen full performances over the following twelve months or so, and eleven more without the third act. A few more in 1838 and 1840 were all the opera ever received.

We must now turn back to the end of April 1836, and the negotiations which Donizetti was then opening with the impresario Lanari for an opera for Venice – negotiations which were eventually to lead to the production of *Pia de' Tolomei.* Again, Beltrame pressed his services on the composer, but Donizetti was anxious to involve Cammarano, who was to be paid the 'usual 100 ducats' for his libretto. Donizetti received about twenty-four times as much as the librettist, which does not seem unreasonable. Lanari wrote to Donizetti on 17 May 1836: 'I very much hope that our good friend Cammarano is satisfied with 100 ducats – which he accepted from the Society of "Industria e belle Arti" (which was at that time running the Royal Theatres in Naples) which was not generous to anyone: he can be assured that on top of that payment he will have my gratitude. Nevertheless, for his fee also I am leaving the contract blank'.

On May 31, Donizetti returned the completed contract, adding, 'Cammarano will write for you for 100 ducats. He suggests to you *Pia*, a subject very suitable for your company'. By 14 June he could write that Cammarano was already at work, and that as far as the management were concerned there need be no difficulties – the subject being free from plotting and licentiousness would not run into trouble with the censors. There were, however, to be problems which composer and librettist had not foreseen, in that they had to find a suitably large part for the mezzo-soprano, as laid down by the Superintendant of the theatre. Eventually Cammarano had to redraft his plot in order to expand the part of Pia's brother to make an acceptable *musico* part (what we might today call a 'trouser role') for her.

By mid-August, Lanari was pressing for a libretto – or at least a synopsis–for *Pia de' Tolomei*, though he recognized that they were both busy with *L'assedio di Calais*. He also wanted Cammarano to send him a note of the wardrobe and costume designs; he proposed to have everything made specially for the performance and it would be cheaper to have them made in Livorno, where he was writing from, than in Venice.

Having seen *L'assedio di Calais* safely on the stage, Donizetti set out for Venice, only to find that the Fenice theatre, where *Pia* was to be performed, had been destroyed by fire on 12 December. The performance was transferred to the Apollo theatre, where it was given on 18 February 1837.

Cammarano prefaces his outline of the plot of *Pia* with some lines from Dante (from Canto 5 of the Purgatorio), and with a short extract from the fifth book of Villani's

Croniche fiorentine relating to events of 1260. These same lines from Dante are quoted at the beginning of Sestini's long descriptive poem of 1822, which is usually given as the source of Cammarano's plot – it certainly inspired many tragedies in the 1820s and 1830s. In fact Cammarano's plot departs from and expands Sestini's treatment at a number of places; Sestini provides only the barest outline for a dramatic treatment. In particular, the layout of the last act, where Pia's husband, having banished her to his castle in the malaria-ridden Maremma for her supposed infidelity, tells her gaoler to put her to death unless his orders are countermanded by a certain time, is sufficiently remote from Sestini's to lead to strong suspicions that Cammarano may have found it somewhere else. The possibility that it might be an original idea should be resisted except as a last resort in dealing with Cammarano or his fellow librettists. In fact, internal evidence suggests that he was working from a play, also called *Pia de' Tolomei*, by the young Neapolitan dramatist Giacinto Bianco, which was performed for the first time, with great success, at the Fiorentini Theatre on 19 April 1836 (the ubiquitous Luigi Marchionni made a much-praised appearance in the part of the husband Nello).

Pia has had a chequered and not very happy stage career. A week after the first performance, Lanari reminded Donizetti that he promised to rewrite the first act finale, which had not pleased the audience. This finale is not well constructed, partly as a result of the expansion of the plot to accommodate a larger part for the mezzo-soprano. Consequently Cammarano was asked to re-work it, and when he and Donizetti sent the revisions to Lanari on 6 May, he wrote a covering letter:

> My dear Sigr. Lanari,
> Here is the finale as you want it: I hope it will go well. Bear in mind not so much the number of lines but the particular difficulties I have had to overcome in meeting your requirements, when it should please you to recompense me. I'm waiting for confirmation of what Sigr. Donizetti is writing to you on my behalf.
>
> Your Sincere friend,
> Salvadore Cammarano.

In a note on the same sheet of paper, Donizetti asks Lanari not to be stingy (*meschino*) when it comes to payment, which explains Cammarano's last sentence.

The revised version of the first act finale was first given in Sinigaglia in July 1837, and was repeated in Lucca in the autumn and in Rome the next spring. These four performances – Venice, Sinigaglia, Lucca and Rome – had for the most part different singers, and the three Pias were amongst the leading sopranos of the day: Tacchinardi-Persiani in Venice, Tadolini in Sinigaglia and Lucca and Strepponi in Rome. Ghino was sung by Poggi in Venice and by Moriani in Sinigaglia, Lucca and Rome. Of the principals, only Ronconi (as Nello, Pia's husband) sang in all four productions. If the opera failed to please, it certainly wasn't because of inadequate casting.

When *Pia* reached Naples in September 1838, an even stranger adaptation was perpetrated, in that the opera was given a happy ending, Nello returning in time to prevent Pia's death and to win her forgiveness ('O, Dante!' was Donizetti's comment). Most unusually, the libretto printed for the Naples performance prints both versions of the last act, with an explanatory note:

> The management for its own particular reasons was persuaded to seek a happy outcome for this drama. The reason for this change should not be attributed to anyone else. However, for those who hold this to be an affront to history, the author, following some wise advice, is reprinting the final act, as it was given in the original version and in the printed versions from Venice, Sinigaglia, Lucca and Rome.

It is hard to believe that Cammarano would have had anything to do with this revision, but the note above does say that *the author* is reprinting the original version, and this can only mean Cammarano. More convincing, the Naples libretto prints *for the first time* a preface which is to be found in Cammarano's original autograph libretto but not printed in any previous version of the text. It can only have been set up in print from material supplied by Cammarano himself.

Pia never caught on in Naples. The review in *L'omnibus* noted that it was not one of Donizetti's best operas, and continued: 'Once Cammarano's *Pia* finished in the same way as Dante's and Sestini's, but now she lives on in the consoling arms of husband and brother, so that she can sing an "aria finale" (which Donizetti has written for Ronzi de Begnis). In writing this libretto of *Pia* Cammarano has known how to treat the subject with a great deal of interest, and has made a very good job of it'. The review ends with a plea to the management to stage the opera with more care – the scenery for *Pia* was 'horrible'. Of this production, more later.

There is in the library of the Conservatorio S. Cecilia in Rome a copy of a libretto of *Pia* which shows that it was set again, in 1852, for performance at the S. Carlo, by the King's director of military music, Federico-Guglielmo de Liguoro, apparently by royal command. The libretto prepared for that purpose was the Naples printing of 1838, though without the happy ending and the management's disclaimer. There were a few small changes of wording in the text, mostly to eliminate mention of Guelphs and Ghibbelines. There is a further reference to this setting in the files of the Superintendent of Theatres, and it adds that due to illness of the principal performers time ran out and the work was not performed.

CHAPTER THREE

1837–1838

Roberto Devereux — Maria de Rudenz — Poliuto —
Censorship and the censors

Apart from modifying the first act finale of *Pia* to Lanari's specification for the performance in Sinigaglia, Cammarano was involved in the early months of 1837 in the preparation of libretti for Donizetti, one for performance at the S. Carlo, for October 1837, and the other required under the terms of the contract with the Fenice theatre in Venice for the following January. Despite these commitments, he did undertake to write a libretto for Persiani: *L'omnibus* recorded on 7 September that Persiani had signed a contract with the Italian Theatre in Paris for an opera, which was to be *Teresa Foscarini*, with words by Cammarano. Nothing came of this project, perhaps because the theatre was burned down the following January, and no more is heard of *Teresa Foscarini*, though Regli in his *Dizionario biografico* mentions it amongst texts left by Cammarano without ever having been set to music.

Consequently during 1837 Cammarano was working actively on two libretti: *Roberto Devereux* for Naples and *Maria de Rudenz* for Venice. Because Donizetti was living at that time in Naples – it was the terrible year for him in which his wife died – there is no correspondence dealing with the origins of *Roberto Devereux*; presumably they were in regular contact and could meet whenever they found it necessary. Cammarano's detailed synopsis of the libretto is not dated, nor is his fair copy of the final text – he did not usually add dates, and often the only way of ascertaining when a text was written is if it has the censor's approval on it, since this was always dated – so that the only clue available is Donizetti's statement that he was expecting to begin rehearsing the opera in September. This would suggest that Cammarano was working on the libretto sometime between April and July. It was submitted for approval on 30 August and was allowed on 24 October, subject to corrections being observed. By early October Donizetti was reporting that rehearsals were being postponed, probably because of the delay at the censors. *Roberto Devereux* was eventually performed at the S. Carlo on 28 October (not 29 October, as is often given – and certainly not 2 October, as listed by Loewenberg). It must have been in rehearsal before formal authority to proceed had arrived. *L'omnibus* thought Cammarano had done his work well, adding that he had drawn on an old play by 'Tomasso Corneille', on Ancelot's drama *Elisabeth d'Angleterre* and an old libretti by Romani, *Il conte d'Essex*, which had been set by Mercadante and performed with little success in Milan five or six years previously. In 1834, Donizetti had hoped that Romani would revise *Il conte d'Essex* for him, but he was unwilling to do so. Donizetti had obviously remembered the subject, and presumably suggested it to Cammarano.

Roberto Devereux was one of the best libretti that Cammarano ever wrote, and a great improvement on Romani's earlier handling of the same source. It was certainly the best he had written up to that time, if for no better reason than that for the first time he was working from a first-rate model, Ancelot's very well constructed five-act verse drama of 1829. Claims that he relied on Romani's libretto are entirely unfounded; a close study of the texts show that all the material used by Cammarano, plot, incident and illusions, are to be found in Ancelot, except for two minor references which in any case are not derived from Romani and may well be original. The remarks by Romani's widow in her biography accusing Cammarano of plagiarism are usually taken to refer to this libretto – though there is no indication that this is so, and there are other occasions where Cammarano worked over Romani's texts. In relation to Ancelot's play, both librettists stand in the same position. To the extent that nearly all libretti were based more or less closely on a play or other model, usually without acknowledgement, a charge of plagiarism could be levelled against all librettists; to the extent that several librettists used the same source – by no means uncommon, for well over half of Cammarano's sources were used by other librettists as well – charges of copying another's work could easily be levelled. Romani accused Cammarano of lifting whole scenes, and his widow called him a great literary pirate – but in *Il conte d'Essex* and *Roberto Devereux* both librettists did precisely the same in fashioning a libretto out of Ancelot's tragedy. There is nothing to suggest that they were not independent, and the only difference is that Romani's version is hurried and loosely put together while Cammarano's is much more carefully worked out and altogether tauter.

The only blemish on an otherwise excellent text is a furious outburst at the very end by Queen Elizabeth, an old-fashioned type of rondo-finale that was foreign to the spirit of the Donizetti romantic tragedy of the late 1830s. Cammarano possibly ended the opera in this way because while he had learnt how to conclude a tragedy with a dying protagonist, he did not yet know how to manage any other ending. Roberto has died on the block, and Elizabeth had not received the token with which she expected to save him; she is enraged, and to this extent the final outburst is dramatically justified. To some extent this is a failure of his source, though Ancelot ends on a line concerning the succession to the English throne, quite effectively, since the political situation is closely discussed in his play: Cammarano takes over the line ('Dell' anglica terra sia Giacomo il Re') but as he had removed all the political element the remark, even if heard in the theatre, must have been meaningless. When, later in his career, he was to use plays, usually ones of French origin, which ended with a striking gesture and curtain-line, he was able to use it effectively, and was not afraid to translate it into Italian verse and let it stand. At this stage in his career I suspect he felt a need to bring down the final curtain on a tragedy with either a pathetic death scene or a display of pyrotechnics.

The performance of *Roberto Devereux* was highly successful, and Donizetti's letters about it contain the first known reference to Cammarano being called on to the stage to receive applause – unusual for a librettist at that time. The opera got off to a slow start as a result of the illness of the baritone Barroilhet, but was given six times before the end of the year, and twenty-two times in 1838.

Thereafter it became a firm favourite in Naples, being given in nearly all the theatres over the years. It soon went the rounds of Italy, and was played all over Europe in the 1840s and 1850s. It is a sign of the careful watch that the authorities kept on theatrical performances that on 15 September 1838, nearly a year after the first performance, they wrote to Barbaja requiring him to observe the corrections that had been made to the text.

The commission for Venice caused Donizetti a great deal of trouble, not only the result of his – and his librettist's – inability to enter into day-by-day discussion with the impresario and the Venetian censor. The contract for an opera for early 1838 had been signed in February 1837, at the time of the production of *Pia de' Tolomei*, so that Donizetti and Cammarano had plenty of time in which to plan and write their opera. When Lanari acknowledged receipt of the revised Finale of *Pia* he expressed the hope that they had thought of a good subject for their new opera. He repeated this on 25 August, asking Cammarano to prepare two versions, one for three and the other for four principal singers.

On 19 September, Donizetti wrote that he had chosen for the subject of his opera a play (by Lockroy and Badon) *Un duel sous le Cardinal de Richelieu.* This was a typically well-made piece that had first appeared in Paris in 1832, and had been playing in Italy under a number of different titles. It was a plot that Bellini had in mind, but he died before he could use it, and it attracted a number of other composers as well. Donizetti considered it a dramatic subject, with tragic and comic possibilities that would be useful to him in preparing for an opera for the singers Ronconi and Ungher. Although Lanari was pressing for a synopsis of the new opera, and for a note of the costumes needed, Donizetti had to report ten days later that Cammarano had run into difficulties with the first act, and that he would have to find another subject. He didn't know what subject he might use, and he had not seen Cammarano to find out what he might be doing about it. On 5 October he was still without a subject and on 7 October he wrote that he still hadn't received a comma of the libretto.

However, in mid-October they did have a project to put

forward: on 13 October the impresario Lanari wrote from Bologna that he had glanced through the synopsis for *Maria de Rudenz,* and that he hadn't altogether liked what he had read. The president of the Fenice theatre agreed with Lanari that it was too grim and obscure a plot, and Cammarano was urged to remove some of the corpses from it, for unless he did so it would not be acceptable. However, by 21 November any problems must have been solved as Donizetti had his work in hand, though he was not happy with it.

It has to be said that *Maria de Rudenz* was one of the most obscure libretti Cammarano ever wrote – perhaps because of the pressure he was under to produce a text in time for Donizetti to fulfill the terms of his contract, but also because he inherited many difficulties from the source. This source was a five-act play *La nonne sanglante* by Anicet Bourgeois and Maillan (based remotely on the episode of the bleeding nun in Lewis' *The Monk*). It is a gothic horror play, not at all well constructed (though no doubt gripping in the theatre if well acted). A very late point of attack necessitated a great deal of preliminary explanation. Cammarano still further delayed the point of attack, and did not have room for much explanation, which accounts for the obscurity of his text.

Cammarano seemed to have a bad conscience about this work. In a later printing of the libretto he confesses in a preface:

> For reasons which it would be irrelevant to mention here, I was obliged some years ago to adapt for the lyric stage a foreign drama *La nonne sanglante.* Those who know the crude and gloomy happenings in that play will readily appreciate that I wanted to tone down its outlandish horrors, and if I hadn't been able to succeed in my purpose (and perhaps no one could) these few words will serve to indicate how much I abhor this bloodstained northern genre.

The truth is that as a model for an opera this play was altogether unsuitable, and the libretto is nothing but unrelieved gloom, with complicated and uncertain motivation and a holocaust for an ending. Well might Lanari and Count Berte be worried about the subject, and when the opera was produced at the rebuilt Fenice theatre on 30

January 1838, critical and public reaction was to prove their theatrical instinct all too right. The critic of the *Gazzetta di Venezia* had this to say:

> The public is fed up with all those crimes which are permitted for no good reason on the stage – it's always daggers, poison, tombs and death, over and over again . . . And here is one which seems nothing more than a parody, a caricature of the whole genre.

There are, to be sure, effective scenes and good curtains, with a very fine closing scene for Maria, where Cammarano returns to his speciality of pitiful broken lines, but his remark that perhaps no one could have succeeded in turning *La nonne sanglante* into an opera suggests that he knew very well where the fault lay. As it was, the opera was a failure, being taken off after two performances, despite the presence in the cast of Ungher, Moriani and Ronconi. It was played – again twice only – in Naples at the Nuovo theatre in 1848, and occasionally in a few other cities, but it never caught on. A performance had been projected for the Nuovo in August 1842, but on 3 August Cammarano wrote to the Superintendent of Theatres seeking his protection. The proposed performance had fallen foul of the censor Royer, who required so many changes in the text that Cammarano considered that his rights as author had been compromised. In any case he had ceded the rights in the text to the Impresario of the Royal Theatres. The Superintendent wrote a minute that on the return of the libretto from the censors he would look at it and make a decision: if the changes were extensive, he would uphold Cammarano's objection – if they were of little consequence, he would not act against the performance. As no performance took place, it is reasonable to assume he took Cammarano's side in the dispute.

Following the completion by June of a libretto for Mercadante, to be discussed later, the rest of 1838 was mainly taken up with Cammarano's collaboration with Donizetti for an opera intended for the opening of the autumn season at the S. Carlo. It is not clear what opera they had originally intended to write for that purpose, although there are reasons to surmise that it may have been the mysterious *Gabriella di Vergy*, since the libretto of that work contains

verses which had originally been set by Donizetti in
Roberto Devereux, but later discarded. (See the notes
accompanying the Opera Rara recording of this opera.) The
whole correspondence dealing with the origin and development of the opera, which *was* written, though not in the
event performed, has been put together in an as yet unpublished article by Jeremy Commons, which he has with
great generosity allowed me to quote.

The story of the substitution of *Poliuto* for the opera
originally contemplated begins with the French tenor
Adolphe Nourrit, who left France to try his fortune in Italy
and travelled from Turin to Rome with Donizetti, and
then on to Naples. It so happened that Barbaja had no tenor
under contract for the autumn season and by the end of
April Nourrit had been engaged. However, on 30 March
Nourrit, perhaps in happy anticipation of an engagement,
wrote to his wife that he planned the plot of an opera for
Donizetti. (When Nourrit died, by suicide, in Naples in
March 1839, an obituary notice in *L'omnibus* stated that
he had written a drama for which Donizetti had written
the music – we should remember that *Poliuto* had not then
been performed – and added a footnote, perhaps an after-
thought inserted at proof stage when the author was
assailed by doubts, that he could guarantee only that
Nourrit had given Donizetti the *plot* of an opera.) If the plot
was Nourrit's – it was based on Corneille's drama *Polyeucte* of 1640 – the versification was certainly Cammarano's, and two different fair copies in his autograph still
exist. Unfortunately, neither are dated, but on 8 May Donizetti reported that Cammarano was silent, as usual, and
'pacing St Francesco' for his verses. This remark refers to
Cammarano's habit, referred to in his obituary notices, of
seeking inspiration by walking up and down the semi-
circular colonnade in front of the church of St Francesco,
which had been built (by Barbaja himself) on the western
side of the square at the side of the Royal Palace, a couple of
hundred yards from the S. Carlo. Whatever Donizetti may
have said about Cammarano's silence on 8 May, a note on
the first page of the autograph full score shows that he
began composing the music two days later, on 10 May, so
by that time he must have had some text available to him,

even if the libretto was not complete.

But this was only the start of the trouble. In the middle of June, the Superintendent of the Royal Theatres reminded Barbaja that he had not submitted the libretto for the censor's approval, and that he was therefore in breach of his contract. Barbaja must have written to Cammarano about it, since his reply – found by Jeremy Commons in the archives of the office of the censors – is still extant. It is a dignified and important letter, worth quoting in full:

Signor Don Domenico Barbaja,

I am replying briefly to your anything but brief letter. The title of the drama I am writing is *Poliuto*; the principal artists who will be taking part are Sig^a Ronzi, Sig^r Nourrit and Sig^r Barroilhet. I cannot confirm accurately when my brain-work will be brought to an end: I will need about twenty days to finish the aforesaid drama. I cannot give you any decision from the new censors about the work because all my appointments with Sig^r Royer have fallen through, as he himself was waiting for instructions from his superiors before taking up office. But I am told that he has now started work and this morning I shall take my sketches to him. By this time my libretto for Sig^r Maestro Donizetti would have been already finished, but you should remember that one condition you laid down was that you needed only a small part for the tenor, and then with the engagement of Sig^r Nourrit this condition was totally changed, and I found I had to look for a new subject: as a result, the last thing I should be blamed for is a delay, which is of no advantage to me if it wastes precious time. I am in the right in this; and if I don't hurry my work it is because I have too much pride in it, and too much zeal for your management, and immense respect for the public – and you, better than any other person, know that I decline tempting offers so as not to betray my principles, principles which should surely bring me praise rather than reprimands. Hence in future I ask you to be more fair with your

Sincere friend
Salvadore Cammarano

From home, 16 June 1838.

One of the many interesting features of this letter is that Barbaja did not know what subject Cammarano was working on – and presumably had not realized that it had not been approved by the censors. The delay in Royer taking up his duties is explained by there having been a complete change in personnel in the censor's office following the King's action in dismissing all the previous incumbents. It also makes clear that it was the duty of the librettist to seek appointments with the censors, but the official channel of communication was from Barbaja to the Superintendent of the Theatres and from him to the censors. Obviously the censors were not faceless bureaucrats, but were willing to meet the librettist in person for discussions.

Barbaja accepted the case Cammarano put forward for a delay of twenty days, and in reply to the Superintendent confirmed the truth of what Cammarano had said. On 8 July, he wrote again, informing him that Cammarano had been as good as his word, and had delivered the libretto to him within the twenty days allowed. It was duly sent to the censors on 10 July. Donizetti was clearly half expecting trouble, since on 11 July he commented that the censors were pulling a long face at it. Correspondence between Barbaja and the authorities continued, with Barbaja putting pressure on them to approve the work. It is clear that Royer forwarded the libretto with a favourable recommendation to the Minister for Internal Affairs but it was not till 11 August that the Minister wrote 'When the reports of the censorship was delivered to His Majesty together with the lyric tragedy called *Poliuto* intended for the S.Carlo theatre, His Majesty deigned with his own sacred hand to declare that the histories of the Martyrs are venerated in the Church and are not presented on the stage'. This decision was communicated to Barbaja the next day.

Evidently the decision to prohibit *Poliuto* was taken by the King, in the face of a recommendation from the censor Royer that it should be allowed. Word got round Naples that this had happened, and the French music publisher Cottrau, who lived in Naples, wrote home to his firm in Paris 'The production of *Poliuto* at the S.Carlo has been prohibited; the King decided that the character of the work was too religious for a theatre. The ceremonies of the church, he said, should remain in the church'.

This left Barbajo without an opera to open the theatre after the September closure. Attempts to graft a new story on to the music – as had been done four years earlier with *Maria Stuarda/Bondelmonte*–came to nothing, and Donizetti later cut his losses by having Cammarano's libretto reworked by Scribe in a form suitable for performance in Paris, where it duly appeared as *Les Martyrs*. The original version was not produced in Naples till 1848, when it was very successful. Barbaja sought – and received – permission to mount *Pia de' Tolomei* instead of the new opera his contract required, and it was thrown onto the stage in a hurry. The libretto went to the censors on 27 August, and came back, approved, on 11 September. The designs for the costumes were approved on 10 September, though Ubaldo's clothes were not to be either black or brown and the coat of arms to be worn by Buccini (as Rodrigo) was to be longer. There was no time to get approval for the costumes themselves or the scenery, and the Superintendent's office attended the dress rehearsal on 29 September for this purpose. The first performance was on 30 September.

When the libretto of *Poliuto* was first printed in 1848, Cammarano wrote in a preface that he hoped that the audience would recognize that he had kept in mind the higher moral purpose of the work, the highest requirement to be laid on an author. *Poliuto* is certainly one of his very best libretti, being well laid out (perhaps thanks to Nourrit), and very clear throughout, with excellent motivation and development, with only one blemish, the instant conversion to Christianity of Poliuto's wife Paolina. The libretto touches on a number of themes which Cammarano was to return to at different times in his career – the inflexible institutional cruelty of the ecclesiastical establishment, for instance, and the clash and interplay between ecclesiastical and secular authority.

Be that as it may: *Poliuto* was prohibited in the middle of August 1838. Barbaja was left with no opera, Donizetti with a score he was able to use the following year, and Cammarano with an unused and, it would seem, unusable libretto; all that pacing up and down in front of S. Francesco had been in vain. He too, like Donizetti, cut his losses, and in the course of the next year or two he used the best of his verses in other works he was engaged on, notably in *La vestale*, which he wrote for Mercadante, and, to a lesser extent, in *Saffo*, for Pacini; some turn up, too, in *Il reggente* and *Il proscritto*. When *Poliuto* was eventually performed in 1848, after the death of the composer, Cammarano was in a dilemma; the first two works were amongst his most popular and most frequently performed so that his verses had become very well known. He solved his dilemma by extending his preface to *Poliuto* with the words:

> N.B. Some verses in this libretto, which I thought to be condemned to oblivion, have put in an appearance in other works of mine: one obvious way was for me to substitute other verses for those I have referred to, but that could have proved detrimental to the music: and out of respect for the music, and for the distinguished if unhappy friend who wrote it, I have left the poetry as it was in the original, appealing to the indulgence of the public.

Poliuto marked the end of Cammarano's collaboration with Donizetti, though there were occasional proposals for further operas, but it was not the last of his libretti that Donizetti set to music. Donizetti himself left Naples for Paris in October 1838. It had been a memorable period of collaboration, for *Roberto Devereux* and *Poliuto* can certainly be counted among Cammarano's best work, and the overwhelming success of *Lucia di Lammermoor* had at one stroke put him in the first rank of contemporary librettists. Not much is known about the personal relationship between the two men, although Donizetti spoke of Cammarano in one letter as a 'good fine man', and di Giacomo describes the hard-working and inspired librettist as the composer's devoted friend. He goes on to quote a postcard from Cammarano to Donizetti, which he dates as belonging to the time they were working on *Poliuto*, and which suggests an intimate, teasing relationship:

> I'm enclosing the aria (meaning the piece, not the substance we breathe!) It's fresh, even reaching warmth. I waited for you at the 'Café delle due Sicilie' till 2 o'clock. I ordered coffee twice and dropped off to sleep twice. The Finale seems to me to have come along not too badly: we will read it together: four eyes are worth more than two – even eight counting my glasses and calculating your eyes as being worth

four. This evening I'll go to the theatre at about 7. Come and
find the impresario, who is fuming. He would move you to
pity, if he deserved it.

The fate of *Poliuto* calls into question the working of
that very important institution, the censor's office. Much
of our knowledge on this subject is based on the work
of Jeremy Commons, still largely unpublished, although
other clues are to be found in letters and books relating to
the period, and all the papers are available in the State
Archives in Naples. We must begin by ridding ourselves of
whatever preconceptions we may have about the work of
the censors, who to us may suggest a group of stern-faced
police inspectors, trying vainly to hold in check a movement towards political liberalism aimed at the overthrow
of an antediluvian Bourbon autocracy, prohibiting any text
which might be thought seditious and striking out any
word like 'liberty' which might put ideas into people's
heads. There was, indeed, a repressive side to their work,
but it seems to have been directed more to the spread of
moral rather than political subversion, against the violence of the emotions, particularly the free-thinking loose
morality that spread outwards from Paris, the centre of all
that was rotten in Europe.

The censors had, in fact, a double responsibility for the
oversight of the theatrical life of Naples, as exemplified in
the instructions given by the minister of Police, the
Marquis Delcarretto, to Francesco Ruffa on his re-appoint-
ment as one of the censors in 1835:

> A commission of three censors (*Revisori*) examines from
> today onwards all theatrical productions, whether new or
> in the repertoire, from a double point of view: as literary
> productions, in which it is responsible to the Ministry of
> Internal Affairs; and as theatrical performances, in which it
> is responsible to the police.

Delcarretto elsewhere qualifies this distinction by placing under the authority of the Police political, religious
and moral aspects, leaving literary content to his colleague. At least one member of the commission of three
censors was appointed by the Police, but joint responsibility of this type is always inimical to administrative
efficiency: the panel of censors had to make decisions in

relation to different criteria, and, when their own delegated authority might seem to be insufficient, had to submit minutes on difficult cases to two separate authorities. While each libretto was read separately by the literary and the police censors, it is not unreasonable to assume that they worked in close co-operation with each other. Certainly both their signatures were required for approval, and these could come through at different times. As a result of this system, delays were inevitable, and no doubt extremely frustrating for the impresarios, who had to work through the Superintendent of Theatres in all matters involving the censors, though the librettists were often called in by the censors for direct discussions. No doubt the censors' life was not made easier by the habit of librettists to submit their work for approval at the last minute, or even later. There was an absolute rule – usually overlooked – that a libretto had to be approved before the composer could start work on it.

On the literary side of their work, the censors, who were men of literary experience themselves, seemed to view their task as one of educating the public away from violence and declining moral standards. They saw it as their responsibility to take their authors by the hand, and by improving their work so to inspire their beneficial effects on the community. At the same time it was necessary to remove doubtful concepts – for instance, the original libretto of Cammarano's *Roberto Devereux* shows several instances of 'onor' (honour) crossed out by the censor and 'amor' (love) substituted – a nobleman's love could be impugned, but not his honour. The report which two of the censors signed in February 1837 is outstanding in its approach to the constructive side of their function:

> [The censorship] as far as it is in its power has kept on
> encouraging young authors, approving their output when it
> has discerned in them signs of talent which provide hope for
> better things: and it has noticed with pleasure that it has not
> been unsuccessful in its attempts to direct their steps away
> from the present fashion of contaminating the stage with
> representations of atrocious misdeeds, coldly premeditated.
> Already, thanks to its watchfulness, more than five young
> men can be counted, all capable of weaving together a melo-

drama with melodious verses based on a well constructed plot; in this number we would single out Salvatore Cammarano for serious dramas, and Giurdignano for those usually described as of mixed type.

Who then were the men who were employed in these sensitive and difficult offices? At the outset of Cammarano's career there were three, of whom one, the Marchese Puoti, does not seem to have participated in the day-to-day business of the office. The two whose signatures appear on documents are Giulio Genoino and Francesco Ruffa. Genoino, known to Donizetti specialists as the librettist of his early farce *La lettera anonima,* had been a priest but had moved towards literature and librarianship. He was a well-known author of comedies, some of which were in the Neapolitan dialect, and is reported to have been active in protecting and encouraging young authors. In 1834, when Cammarano took up his duties at the Royal Theatres, Genoino was fifty-six. His colleague Francesco Ruffa was forty-two. Ruffa began life as a lawyer but after moving to Naples began to write poetry and plays. His ideas on drama and the dramatic art must have been very advanced for the time: Jeremy Commons writes that he believed that tragedy must always search for truth . . . 'compassion is awakened by the misfortune of just men' . . . and that our anger is directed against the triumph of cruel men – 'From such a beginning I deduce that those tragedies in which depraved men triumph with impunity and wise men are destroyed are the best adapted to confirming the spectators in virtue, since more than any others they can arouse our wrath'.

In 1838 the censors' office was re-organized, and a period of increasing severity was ushered in. Genoino was replaced by the Abate Gaetano Royer, whose name has already cropped up in relation to *Poliuto.* Adamo Alberti, the impresario of the Fiorentini theatre, has left an unforgettable picture of what happened:

A new censorship was formed, consisting of Sig^r Filippo Cirelli and the notorious Abate Royer. Oh how ruinous it was! No longer were any interesting productions allowed. Everything was prohibited and finally the point was reached when they struck out the word 'eziandio' [likewise].

Matters got so bad that he had to see the Minister of Internal Affairs and, by playing on his vanity, got him to instruct the censors to be more moderate in prohibiting theatrical productions. 'Thus for the moment two great disasters were warded off, the cholera and the Abate; they continued to pester us, but to a lesser degree.' Cirelli's name soon disappeared from the papers of the censorship, but returned in the next re-organization, of 1848. Royer remained as the Interior Ministry censor, and Ruffa as the Police censor throughout the period 1838–48.

The role of the censors can now be assessed in a clearer light. They had to guide the authors whose work they read into the right channels; this meant interviews and discussions, and no doubt piles of manuscripts to read (they must have blessed Cammarano, whose handwriting is a joy to read, unlike that of some other librettists). They had to see, correct and approve all new works coming up for performance, and to approve all older works coming back into the repertoire. There are many extant libretti signed as being part of the regular repertoire and approved for performance as long as existing changes were adhered to, with each page initialled by the censor, whether there were any alterations or not, and they had to approve new scenes. Above the censors were the two Ministers, Internal Affairs and Police. And above the ministers was the King, who was perfectly able and willing to take a strong line on his own.

The administrative arrangements for the day-to-day management of the theatres was in the hands of the Superintendent of Theatres and Spectacles, whose office was in the Fondo Theatre. His jurisdiction extended to the discipline of the personnel – he could fine or imprison them by administrative fiat; the oversights of contracts and author's rights; the running of the theatres and (through a network of out-posted officials) the control of performances. All correspondence with the censors passed through his office and was handled with notable efficiency and expedition. For much of Cammarano's time the Superintendent was Marchese Imperiale, who handled a prodigious amount of work and whose minutes remain an object lesson of administrative practice.

CHAPTER FOUR

1839–1840

Elena da Feltre — I ciarlatani — Il conte di Chalais —
La vestale — Cristina di Svezia

With the departure of Donizetti for Paris in October 1838, after the prohibition of *Poliuto*, and with Bellini dead, there were only two composers of sufficient stature to step into the breach, Mercadante and Pacini, and the latter had produced no new operas for five years. The years in which the early operas of Verdi were to sweep across Italy lay ahead, although there were plenty of lesser composers whose operas could be produced to fill the prospectus.

Cammarano's next libretto was the first of eight he was to write for Mercadante; collaboration between the two had been proposed in 1836 when Mercadante was engaged to write an opera for Paris, but the contract had fallen through. The subject then chosen had been *L'orfana di Brono ossia Caterina de' Medici* (after a romance by Michele Mauro), and at the very end of his life Mercadante returned to the libretto Cammarano wrote for him, after the latter had been dead for some years. The new work, on a different subject, was intended for performance in January 1839. Mercadante had begun his career in Naples in 1819, with an opera *L'apoteosi d'Ercole*, with a libretto by Giovanni Schmidt. Others of his early Neapolitan operas had libretti by Schmidt or by Tottola. In 1831 he had set Romani's libretto *Zaira* (previously set two years earlier by Bellini) for the S. Carlo, and the new commission was to be the first for Naples for eight years. It is therefore interesting to see that he did not return to Schmidt for a libretto, although in 1839 he was still on the list of the official poets for the Royal Theatres (the others for that year, in addition to Schmidt and Cammarano, were Bidera and Passaro). His decision to turn to Cammarano was a wise one: Schmidt's texts, putting on one side the wretched quality of his verses, were out-of-date, and not in keeping with the emotional energy that marked the late 1830s. The mature works of Mercadante's middle period were very much of this new type, and he had rethought his own technique to develop a strong personal style that departed from convention and focused attention on immediate emotion. *Il guiramento,* often considered his best opera, and certainly the one most frequently performed, had appeared at Milan in 1837, and in the following year *Le due illustri rivali,* in Venice. Later, a few months after the opera for Naples, came *Il bravo* in Milan. All these three operas had texts by the veteran librettist Gaetano Rossi, and like most of his texts they are long, crude but workmanlike. Cammarano's texts were never long (until he found himself having to cope with Verdi's compression) and, interestingly, the one he was to write most resembles the directness and thrust of Rossi.

Cammarano's opera for Mercadante was *Elena da Feltre,* and was presumably intended for the autumn season. Schlitzer states (in his article *Mercadante e Cammarano*) that the synopsis had been sent to the composer in March or April. The libretto was submitted for approval on 12 June 1838. The Superintendent of Theatres quickly received approval from the Ministry of the Interior, but there is no record of similar approval from the Police, and it was probably this that held up progress. Barbaja wrote enquiring about the libretto on 14 July, but it was 19 December before he was able to write again, having heard that it was by then approved, and asking for the return of the text so that it could be printed. He received it, approved subject to corrections, the next day. Approval must have been anticipated, since on 13 November the Superintendent had approved the costume designs, all, that is, except the prima donna's, which she had previously worn in *Pia de' Tolomei.*

The first official news of the opera came on 1 December, when *L'omnibus* announced: 'Mercadante is giving us *Elena da Feltre,* with a libretto by Salvadore Cammarano'. Storm clouds were, however, gathering, and Barbaja should have been alerted by a letter from the Superintendent asking him to have ready at the dress-rehearsal on 29 December a reject copy of the libretto for the censor Ruffa to write in, since he was going to be present. The first performance was on 1 January 1839, and the next morning the storm broke. The Superintendent sent a letter to Barbaja marked 'Very Urgent'; at the instance of the Minister for the Interior and of the Police the censors had brought him a complaint against Cammarano, as the poet of the drama *Elena da Feltre*, given the previous evening. Following the line 'Qui m'atterro a' piedi tuoi' ('I throw myself at your feet'), Cammarano had continued 'Qual mi prostro innanzi a Dio' ('As I prostrate myself in front of God'), but the censors had objected to the last line, and Cammarano promised to write something less sacred. He had not done so, and while the line objected to had indeed been removed, no new line had been substituted (reference to the printed libretto confirms this; there is a line missing from the rhyming sequence). What was worse, the singer (Barroilhet) had sung the offending line, not once but twice, loud and clear. It wasn't Barroilhet's fault, as he only sang what was in his part, but Cammarano's. Therefore Cammarano was to betake himself immediately to the censor Ruffa to agree on a substitute line, whereafter it was his (Cammarano's) responsibility to change the words in the singer's book and in the prompter's, and to see it was correctly performed.

This was not all, for in the Superintendent's correspondence day-book there is an entry summarizing a letter sent on 2 January 1839: 'To Sig. Barbaja. Cammarano fined —— ducats, a penalty on the same for having to be called before Sig. Ruffa to change a line in *Elena da Feltre*'. Unfortunately the amount of the fine is not given in the entry. Evidently the censors had good reason to attend the dress-rehearsal, but it was a pity that Barbajo and Cammarano did not take the hint.

Mercadante seems to have been very pleased at the results of his collaboration with Cammarano, judging from the evidence of a letter from him to Cammarano (printed by Schlitzer) which reads:

> *Elena da Feltre* is, for my part, completed and delivered. I do not know to whom I can better recommend it than to the author of the drama. The more I worked on it, the more I was satisfied with the good way the plot was worked out, the sense of proportion, the poetry and the energy of it. You will

be indulgent with me if I have misunderstood some things, and I am convinced that I have done as well as I know how and can deserve your particular esteem. Permit me to ask you to superintend the performance and staging, not allowing any alterations, omissions or mutilations, since I believe it is already short enough. As I have used a style of free expressive recitative, you should ensure that the singers take an interest in their roles. Sigifredo must be a good bass of the first rank, or the first act finale will be ruined, and that is where the great interest of the second and third acts originates. I am certain that you will want to help with this with the same enthusiasm with which you wrote the book, and I send you heartfelt greetings.

Mercadante had good reason to urge Cammarano to give his attention to the singing and the production. *I normanni a Parigi* and *Emma d'Antiocchia* had both been done very badly at Naples, and the composer wrote also to a friend in the city, asking him to keep a watchful eye on the preparations for *Elena da Feltre*, as Schlitzer reveals in the same article. In the event, he need not have worried: the new opera was done with a very good cast, and was done very well. He wrote again to the same friend, expressing his gratitude to Cammarano for the care he had taken over the production.

The views that Mercadante expressed about *Elena da Feltre* in his letter to Cammarano are confirmed by the critic of *L'omnibus*, who wrote 'Mercadante has written to his friends: "*Elena* is the best I know how to do, and if it doesn't please, the fault is mine, because the libretto is the best ever". Mercadante is right; the book is excellent, well organized, with most beautiful verses, a most interesting plot'. It is difficult today to agree with this praise of the plot of *Elena da Feltre*, and critics of it were not lacking at the time. Domenico Anzelmi, a future censor, who wrote a great deal of theatrical criticism, both for *Il Lucifero* and for *Il Giornale delle due Sicilie*, and whose notices, though long-winded in the extreme, usually contain a very sharp assessment of both drama and music, took a very different view from *L'omnibus* in his article in *Il Lucifero*. He proceeded to pick holes in the plot, not so much as we might expect for the weakness of the motivation at certain pivotal moments in the development of the drama, but for the

unacceptable moral situation in which Elena is caught, in
the working out of the contrast between filial duty and
love. How can we put up with a victim (he asked) who was
so generous in filial compassion but was not to have any
comfort, not even in her own death agony? Who was not
allowed to have the disillusioned but repentent Guido at
her side? Who was not allowed one word to make her death
less terrible? Who had to breathe her last breath in the
arms of Ubaldo, of a lover so deservedly hated, of he who
brought about her ruin? Surely this is the triumph of
bullying and injustice rather than filial love?

Elena da Feltre was first performed on 1 January 1839,
and not 26 December 1838 as stated by Loewenberg (on
that evening there was a performance of another opera by
Mercadante, *Il giuramento*). It cannot be claimed as a great
success, as it only ran for nine nights, and was not repeated
at Naples after this initial production. It seems that the
public never took this work to their hearts; it was played at
a number of theatres over the next five years or so, but after
that it was revived only very occasionally.

The source of *Elena* remains a mystery. When Anzelmi
summarized the plot in his notice in *Il Lucifero,* he refers
to the heroine as Elena degli Uberti, a designation she is
also given in the libretto. There is a play with this same
title, *Elena degl' Uberti,* by Francheschi, but it does not
seem to have been performed till 1851, and although the
two have a number of points in common, all they may
indicate is a common source.

Cammarano's next libretto was a work of a totally different genre, one of his very few comic works, *I ciarlatani.* It
was written to be set to music by his brother Luigi, and was
based on a *comèdie-vaudeville* by Scribe and Alexandre,
Les empiriques d'autrefois, first given in Paris in 1825 but
popular with touring companies. This light-hearted French
play was also used by Calisto Bassi as the plot for a two-act
libretto, for Panizza, and both operas appeared the same
year. Cammarano designated his work a *scherzo melodrammatico,* and it is in one act. It is the only libretto by
Cammarano to contain long sections of prose between the
musical numbers, but although Neapolitan dialect in
these sections would have been in keeping with the tone of

the work, he did not use it.

I ciarlatani was Luigi Cammarano's first opera, and enjoyed a great success at its first performance at the Fondo theatre, on 15 April 1839. *L'omnibus* called the libretto 'very witty', and *Il Lucifero* commented that the plot of this *scherzo melodrammatico*, tangled up and then untied with great skill by Salvadore Cammarano, had inspired the musical talents of his brother Luigi, and the evening was brought to a conclusion with the two brothers being called on to the stage together to receive the greatest reward for their labours they could wish, the applause of their fellow citizens. Although *I ciarlatani* was very popular in Naples, being repeated every year for the next five years, and occasionally thereafter, in the S.Carlo and Fenice theatres as well as in the Fondo, I have found no evidence that it was ever played elsewhere.

1839 was a busy year for Cammarano, for on 22 June *L'omnibus* reported that he had written a new drama for the S.Carlo theatre, called *Un duello sotto Richelieu*, for which Maestro Giuseppe Lillo had written the music. The production of this opera was delayed by the illness of the prima donna, Sig^a Palazzesi, who was to sing the role of Maria di Rohan. When it was finally performed, on 6 November 1839, it appeared under the title *Il conte di Chalais*. The French play on which this libretto was based was a justly famous three-acter by Lockroy and Badon, *Un duel sous le cardinal de Richelieu*. The authors were well-known actors and playwrights, Lockroy playing much the same role in the theatrical life of Paris as did Luigi Marchionni in Naples. It was the same subject as Donizetti and Cammarano had been working on two years previously, in 1837, for the contract for an opera for Venice that had eventually led to the composition of *Maria de Rudenz* and which had then been abandoned because Cammarano had run into too many difficulties with the first act. He clearly had not forgotten the project and, as he was to do on future occasions, brought it out again when a suitable opportunity arose, finished it and offered it to another composer. Eventually Donizetti was to set it himself. It had, not surprisingly, run into difficulties with the censors.

The play *Un duel sous le cardinal de Richelieu* fascinated a number of composers besides Donizetti, not excluding Bellini. At the same time that Cammarano and Lillo were working on it in Naples, it was being used for a libretto in Milan, with music by Federico Ricci. The first printing of that libretto was anonymous, but it was said to be by dall' Ongaro, Gazzoletti and Somma (the last named being the furure librettist of Verdi's *Un ballo in maschera*). This version was produced at the Scala theatre on 17 August 1839, but it is not likely to have been known to Cammarano, who was working on his own text in June. A comparison of the two texts does not suggest anything in common other than the dependence on a common source. The play deals with the turbulent life and loves of Marie de Rohan-Monbazon, duchesse de Luynes and subsequently duchesse de Chevreuse, and the political upheaval of the times. Behind the plot broods the unseen presence of Cardinal Richelieu, his fall from power and his reinstatement in the king's favour. Being packed with effective situations and incidents, it clearly lent itself to operatic treatment. The weight of the story is carried by Maria and the two noblemen who love her, the count of Chalais and the duke of Chevreuse (to whom she is secretly married at the beginning of the opera), so much so that in the second and third acts scarcely anyone else of any significance even appears on the stage.

The structure of this libretto, with its growing concentration on the three main characters, and the rapid ending, needs to be matched by fine music if the interest of the audience is to be sustained till the end. Perhaps Guiseppe Lillo was not yet up to the task; he was twenty-five years old at the time, having seen his first opera produced at the Conservatorio S. Pietro a Majella in 1834. Since then he had had considerable success at the Nuovo theatre with *Il giojello* (to a libretto by the lawyer-poet Leopoldo Tarantini) in 1835, and in 1837 the S. Carlo had put on thirteen performances of his *Odda di Bernaver*, for which he had used a libretto by Bidera. Interestingly, a libretto entitled *Carlo Magno* intended for Lillo was prohibited in 1837, since it contained sinister political illusions. Whether this has any connection with Cammarano's earlier play of the same name cannot now be ascertained. It is often reported that *Il conte di Chalais* failed, a judgement apparently based on a remark by Donizetti when contemplating using the text himself, but that is not the contemporary judgement. Certainly it was not an outstanding success, and was never given outside Naples, but it received twelve complete and four part performances. *L'omnibus* referred to Lillo's composition as 'happy' and Anzelmi in *Il Lucifero* reports enthusiastically on its reception. He ended by congratulating Cammarano and Lillo for the glory they would reap from this most beautiful opera (and the baritone Barroilhet for the dignity which he brought to the final scene by the way he had taken the part of Chevreuse). In praising Cammarano's verses he did complain that mellifluous lines about how the sun had shone on his life are not really appropriate to the situation when a man had just been convinced of the infidelity of his wife. This is typical of Cammarano: faced with a situation when an outburst of anger might reasonably be expected, his characters are more likely to be overcome with sadness or self-pity. Though he dealt often enough with violent emotions and incidents, his verses are rarely violent but tend more to the reflective: this was one reason why he was sought after by composers. Incidentally, Ricci's opera on the same subject did not fare as well in Milan as Lillo's did in Naples. Though well received (despite, said the Milan critic, a wretched libretto) it was taken off after four performances.

The next step in the history of the operatic treatment of Maria di Rohan came in June 1840, less than a year after the production of Lillo's opera, when Donizetti was in touch with the impresario Jacovacci about an opera for Rome, and wrote to him – 'As to the libretto, I know of a good one by Cammarano which didn't have much success because of the music by Maestro Lillo. If that is true, could you get hold of the libretto, submit it to the censors, see if it suits your company and then send it to me?' Donizetti does not mention his earlier interest (or the difficulty Cammarano had with the first act) but he had clearly not forgotten the possibilities inherent in the story. However, the proposal came to nothing. Two years later, he needed an opera for a contract for Vienna, and he remembered the subject again. He sent for a copy of Cammarano's text, read it and 'called in a poet to make some small adjustments' to it. The changes that were made for this setting were not made by Cammarano and were almost certainly never authorized by him – probably not even known to him.

The changes made in Cammarano's text were not large and did not in any way affect the structure of the play. Donizetti's setting was given in Vienna on 5 June 1834, with the title *Maria di Rohan*, and received thirteen performances that year. It was revised, and additional material added, for performance in Paris, where it opened on 20 November the same year, and again added to for Parma in May 1844. It reached Naples on 11 November 1844, under the confusing title *Il conte di Chalais*, and ran for twenty performances. It was occasionally revived in Naples, but it went on to become one of Donizetti's most popular operas in Italy, and in Europe generally, holding the stage longer than any other tragic work except *Lucrezia Borgia* and the evergreen *Lucia di Lammermoor*. The end result of the various changes which Donizetti had made to Cammarano's original libretto left him with a text certainly no better and in places much worse than the one originally given to Lillo, but *Maria di Rohan* justified Donizetti's instinct, and it was a pity that he and Cammarano had not persevered with the project in 1837. A further projected use of this libretto – by the composer Pacini – will be mentioned in the next chapter.

To conclude the discussion of *Maria di Rohan* it is interesting to record the views of Felice Romani on the subject; the famous librettist was by this time editor of the *Gazzetta piedmontese*, and no longer writing libretti. He wrote:

> A tragic and heart-rending subject, wherein there is weeping, screaming and howling; where to the big drum is added the bell, and to the bell the pistol shot; where love is unhappy; where jealousy casts its coils around; where all is secrecy and sadness and where there penetrates neither a ray of happiness or a gleam of light.

It is hard to believe that Romani had forgotten some of the libretti which he had written himself only a few years previously, such as *Lucrezia Borgia* or *Ugo conte di Parigi*: but in essence his remarks are to the point, and his own works had always a measure of balance and even restraint, reflecting his own classical literary sensibilities. These newer works were more abrupt; they dealt with strong emotions at a more personal level. While the Neapolitan censors were much stricter than those of the northern plains, they would have approved of Romani's literary postulates, if not of some of the subjects he himself chose for his libretti.

While Cammarano was waiting for Lillo's *Il conte di Chalais* to be produced at the S.Carlo, he was in discussion with Mercadante for an opera to follow *Elena da Feltre* in their collaboration, which Barbaja had commissioned. Cammarano offered him the outline of a libretto based on Dumas' dramatic trilogy, *Christine, ou Stockholm, Fontainbleu et Rome,* which dealt with that formidable bluestocking Queen Christine of Sweden, and which had appeared first in Paris in 1830. On 8 August 1839 Mercadante wrote at length to him about this project. The letter is long, but so full of interest that it is worth quoting in full:

> I have received the outline of the plot of *Monaldeschi o Cristina di Svezia,* and I have studied it carefully – and also the various pieces in your beautiful poetry, and I am full of praise for the layout of the plot and the way it is worked out, and its theatricality. But the plot does not altogether please me, nor the characters, as I must try to tell you with all the frankness which should exist between artists, between friends. The plot is monotonous, without much variety of colour or of characters, almost all of whom are loathsome, of little potential musically. Monaldeschi is a bad subject; besides moving towards marrying Guilia, he does not love Cristina, only the throne; then he is a hypocrite – he would be the tenor. Cristina is of very little interest in the first part, and in the second and third she manages to become a very Medea, red with jealous fury, with vengeance – quite unsuitable for Spech [Salvi-Spech, the soprano who was intended to sing in the opera]. Sentinelli – the baritone – the most hateful man in the whole work, pretends to be fierce, is dominated by the sole passion of revenging the death of his sister, long ago, and is not moved to pity, not even by the final disgrace of his nephew who is just the same, hateful. Giulia is a cold part. The young boy on the stage; these children on the stage always make people laugh and distract their attention.

The same plot was suggested by Romani and by Rossi and I rejected it, just as Bellini had rejected it – and for the same reasons.

That's all I need to say. You will understand it a hundred times better than me, and your usual enthusiasm and friendship will not keep me in suspense longer. Reach a decision and let me know. When I make a request, and have it written in to the contract that the good Cammarano should provide the libretto, I mean that it would be written expressly for me, and Cammarano knows what suits me, what I require, and what is pleasing to me – as he did with *Elena*.

Moving emotions, not violent ones, with a variety of styles, of forms, opportunities for smooth and forceful singing, orchestral colour, original and unconventional chorus pieces, large-scale ensembles, not furious but singable. In *Elena* the only loathsome, shocking part is Boemondo, but he is a second tenor, who hasn't much to sing and is therefore not wearisome.

I have made you my confession of faith, making it clear in all friendship that the style of *Cristina*, like that of *Maria de Rudenz*, does not appeal to me, although it would be treated well in your hands; and it only remains for me to beg you to choose another plot along the lines of those you sent me, such as *Nabucco*, *Lara*, or *La peste di Firenze*. That done, my dear Cammarano, write a libretto especially for me, I beseech you, I entreat you; help me, gratify me and the trouble you have been to till now over *Monaldeschi*, over the censorship, the lost time, it shall be a pleasant duty for me to recompense. I want to have from you an opera which will go the rounds of all Italy, as did *Elena*, which will give room for imagination and novelty. Be of good heart, take courage, we will press forward together for our own good, for that of the management and for the honour of our country.

This is a remarkably revealing letter. It was indeed true that Bellini had refused the subject when Romani had offered it to him – the difficulties, or at least some of them, emerged in the bitter polemics that surrounded the production of *Beatrice di Tenda* at Venice in 1833; Romani eventually wrote it up for Thalberg in 1855, his last libretto. The reference to *Nabucco* is particularly interesting, as it probably antedates Nicolai's rejection of the same subject in favour of *Il proscritto*, laying the way clear for Verdi's acceptance of it a couple of years later. *Lara* was a popular subject; it had already been treated by Bidera for the composer Ruolz in Naples, and Tarantini's version for Lillo was to appear in 1842. *La peste di Firenze* (Sestini's *Ginevra degli Almieri*, 1821) was another popular basis for operas. The most interesting feature of the letter is not so much the regard in which Mercadante evidently held Cammarano, but the reasons he gave for rejecting *Cristina* – he realized he could not retain the sympathy of the audience with characters whose behaviour was so inhuman. It didn't matter having one double-dyed villain, provided he could be an unimportant second tenor without very much to do, but not if he were to be one of the main characters. Moreover, the role of Cristina simply did not suit the soprano who had been engaged – not for her the role of a Medea: so in consequence they would have to look around until they found a subject which met his wishes. It is interesting to note the contrast Mercadante made between *Cristina* and *Elena de Feltre* – he clearly did not share Anzelmi's view of the moral turpitude surrounding the important characters of the latter opera.

Mercadante clearly knew himself well, his gifts as well as his limitations; he needed a plot he could set in his own way, which was smoothly moving (in later life it became slow moving, almost to an extreme) and free from emotional excesses. He knew that Cammarano *could* produce a libretto in the style he needed, and in due course he received one which fitted his gifts to perfection, and one with which he expressed himself as 'contentissimo'.

This was *La vestale*, which was to become one of his most popular works and which was produced at the S. Carlo for the first time on 10 March 1840. The story of the vestal virgin who let the sacred flame go out while she was occupied with a young man, and who was buried alive as a punishment, had been used by de Jouy in his libretto for Spontini's famous opera of the same title, which was one of Barbaja's earliest introductions to Naples. Cammarano's text was not based at first hand on this earlier opera, although it closely follows the same story, but on a play that Luigi Marchionni had written some fifteen years previously. This was based on the Spontini opera, though developed and added to in a number of significant ways.

When Spontini's opera had been written in 1807, it was not possible to represent the tragic end of a heroine on the stage – even though the death was preceded by a dignified descent into the fatal tomb, with the slabs sealed behind her. Consequently de Jouy had to have recourse to a *deus ex machina* in the shape of a fire-ball to provide an excuse for her pardon and release. Even in 1823, the libretto that Romanelli wrote for Pacini avoided the 'strong' ending, and a vision of the goddess Vesta was called upon to put everything right. Even later, the true ending to the story might have been forbidden on the operatic stage of Naples, since it was not till after 1830 that a heroine might be put to death in full view of the audience. However, in 1825 Marchionni was able to write – in prose – a version for the Fiorentini theatre which restored the proper ending, in which Emilia is buried alive. He added an attempt at armed rescue by her lover, which came too late to save her. In this he was anticipated by Vigano whose ballet on the same subject was first produced in Milan in 1818, and included both the entombment and the subsequent armed uprising.

La vestale is on any count one of Cammarano's best libretti, though it suffers in places from excessive condensation, and it admirably fulfilled Mercadante's requirements. It treats with very human understanding the position of Emilia, who had become a vestal virgin when her *sposo* had been reported to have been killed in battle. When he returns victorious, it falls to her lot to crown him with the laurel wreath, and a clandestine meeting is arranged in a hurried aside. The use of the word *sposo* obviously caused trouble; *sposo* can mean either fiancé or husband, and the implication of the latter in relation to virginity was, I suspect, unacceptable in some places, and *sposo* was struck out and *amor* or *anima* substituted. There are in fact two distinct versions of the text, the second, without *sposo*, being perhaps more widely used. There was also a truncated version of the final scene which was occasionally used, the opera ending as Emilia goes down into the tomb amid universal cries of 'Oh horror', omitting Decio's attempt at rescue, his attack on the High Priest and his suicide on Emilia's tomb.

The first night of *La vestale* was very successful. At the

end of Act II all the company, including the poet, was called on to the stage twice, and this was repeated at the end of the opera. *L'omnibus* liked the libretto, and the verses, which established Cammarano as an excellent librettist who did not seem to know how to do anything badly. The ending of the opera did not please the critic; as he had already praised the burial of the Vestal Virgin, it was presumably Decio's intervention which upset him.

La vestale ran for some fifty performances at the S. Carlo in 1840 and 1841, evidence of great success. It was then produced at the Nuovo, although this theatre was too small for it, and it was performed in other theatres in Naples before returning to the S. Carlo in 1845. By this time it had been established as a popular favourite all over Italy, indeed throughout the whole of Europe. For thirty years or so it was usually to be found in the repertoire in one or other of the theatres in Italy. It ran into trouble with the censors in Rome, and was played there first with a modified libretto, as *Emilia*, and later as an oratorio with the title *San Camillo*.

Mercadante's rejection of *Cristina di Svezia* did not persuade Cammarano that *Cristina* was an unsuitable subject for an opera. Throughout his career there are instances of plots rejected by one composer being offered to others, and often accepted; Cammarano was not one to waste an idea once he had begun work on it. So it was with *Cristina*, which was accepted by Alessandro Nini and produced with his music at the Teatro Carlo Felice in Genoa on 6 June 1840. Unfortunately, Cammarano was late in completing the text for Maestro Nini, and it is usually ascribed to Cammarano and Saccherò. What has happened is made clear in a footnote to the printed libretto:

> N.B. The libretto was to have been written by Sig^r Cammarano alone; not being able to finish it at the proper time as a result of unforeseen circumstances, M^o Nini asked Sig^r Saccherò to write the third part, without altering Cammarano's intentions.

In other words, Saccherò was to work from Cammarano's detailed prose synopsis. This was unfortunately the worst possible division of labour, for although Saccherò was a good constructor of plots, many of his verses are crude and ugly. The third act of the Genoa *Cristina* contains expressions which Cammarano would never have used, and which would have horrified the Neapolitan censors. (See Chapter 12 for a discussion of Act III of this libretto.) The completion of *Cristina di Svezia* was almost Saccherò's first work for the operatic stage; he worked mainly in Milan, but spent part of 1844 as an official poet at the Royal Theatres in Naples, during which time he wrote the libretto of *Caterina Cornaro* for Donizetti, a most interesting text which displays his sure sense of the theatre as well as his weakness as a poet.

Alessandro Nini was then at the outset of a short but by no means unsuccessful career. His output links with Cammarano in a number of interesting ways; his first opera had a libretto by Beltrame, *Ida della Torre*, a version of the *Bride of Lammermoor* story. His second, and his greatest success, was *La Marescialla d'Ancre*, with a libretto by a real poet, G.Prati, based on Vigny's play, which Cammarano was to use seven years later. In 1843 he wrote a *Virginia* to a libretto by Bancalari, greatly inferior to the one which Cammarano wrote for Mercadante. *Cristina di Svezia* was not very successful, being given only six times, though always to applause, and was, I think, never revived.

However, the libretto was used again, in a version with the third act written by Cammarano, and with the finale of the first act rewritten. A comparison of the two third acts, as we will see, reveals the quality of Cammarano's work, when contrasted with that of another librettist working from the same detailed synopsis. The new version was set by Lillo, and produced at the S. Carlo on 21 January 1841. It had only marginally better success than Nini's version in Genoa, being played seven times before being lost from sight. *L'omnibus* commented that the music was passable, and the work was received neither well nor badly. Three years later the text was again set to music, this time by Fabrizi, and given in Spoleto.

The difficulties of this libretto were the very ones which Mercadante had complained of, and which justified his rejection of it. It is both monotonous and crude, with scarcely a redeeming feature. If either Nini or Lillo had been more experienced composers, it is possible that they, too, would have rejected it, though they might have been swayed by the recommendations of an experienced librettist. From Cammarano's point of view, it was a plot saved and used again, though we do not know what were the unforeseen circumstances which prevented him from finishing it on time in the first place. Librettists were notoriously late with their work, and it may have been simply his inability to work to a dead-line rather than anything else which led Nini to entrust the text of the final act to the inexperienced Saccherò. By and large, Cammarano did not write many libretti for other theatres, except for established composers he had worked with in Naples. As he had once told Barbaja, he turned down many tempting offers if he could not do justice to his work. Probably he needed constant prodding if he was to produce his texts for the time they were needed.

CHAPTER FIVE

1840–1844

Saffo — Luigi Rolla — Il proscritto — La fidanzata corsa —
Il reggente — Ester d'Engaddi — Ruy Blas — Il ravvedimento

1839 saw Cammarano collaborating for the first time with Mercadante; 1840 saw him begin a collaboration with another of the leading composers of the time, Giovanni Pacini. Cammarano was to write five libretti for him, and of these the first, *Saffo*, was to become his best known and best loved libretto in Naples. Giovanni Pacini was a composer of unrivalled fluency (we have Rossini's word for this, and he should know!) and he had enjoyed great popularity up and down Italy. Between 1813 and 1867 he wrote about seventy-five operas – the total depends on how his works are classified and how many 'revisions' are counted in. Of these *Saffo*, often considered his most important work, comes almost exactly half-way. Up to *Saffo* his most popular work had been *L'ultimo giorno di Pompei*, to a text by Tottola, which had been given for the first time at the S.Carlo in 1825, and which was regularly revived there until the mid 1840s. He had given up composing operas in 1834 to devote himself to teaching.

The first mention of *Saffo* came in *L'omnibus* of 12 November 1840, when it was noted that this opera was to be expected, and that with it Maestro Pacini was making a return to the inferno of theatrical life after an absence of seven or eight years. Pacini tells in his memoirs (which are generally rather unreliable, particularly where dates and lists of operas are concerned) that in June 1840 he had returned to his home in Lucca; the following account is a paraphrase of what he then related about the origin of *Saffo*. He received a message inviting him to return to Naples, where a new libretto by Cammarano would be earmarked for him. He accepted the invitation, signed the contract and received the synopsis of the plot from the poet, together with the verses of the introductory section.

He got down to work with enthusiasm, in a way which he found it impossible to explain; but as he proceeded with the composition, inspiration deserted him to such an extent that he left for Naples with the clear intention of asking Cammarano to provide him with a different libretto, on the grounds that he was certain that he could not set *Saffo* in such a way as would receive approval.

Pacini continues that he reached Naples at the end of September and hurried round to see his friend the celebrated poet, and outlined his idea, with which Cammarano was greatly surprised. Vincenzo Flauto, as administrator of the Society which was then running the theatres, called him to a conference with Cammarano. Flauto himself was prepared to agree, on condition that Cammarano had no objections. For his part, Cammarano was willing to fall in with Pacini's wishes, but said that he would first like to hear the two pieces which Pacini had already set to music. Pacini tells us that he thought it only right to agree to this suggestion and they set off for his house, where he sat down at the piano and began to sing through the introduction. When he reached the line 'Di sua voce il suon giungea' (which comes from Alcandro's aria in Act I, scene I) Cammarano became pale, obviously deeply moved, and would not let the composer finish, throwing his arms around his neck: 'Maestro' said Cammarano, 'for heaven's sake carry on with your work; you will present Italy with a masterpiece'. Pacini felt a voice within him saying, 'get on with it, get on with it'. He claimed that he wrote the whole opera in twenty-eight days, and that the long final scene (certainly a masterpiece) was created in two hours (we should note that we do not know what he meant by 'created' here; presumably a sketch of melody and an outline of the harmony only; any more of this long scene would have been physically impossible in such a short time).

Saffo was performed for the first time on 29 November, so that if Pacini had indeed arrived in Naples at the end of September with only the introduction written, and if a few days – perhaps as much as a week – were lost in discussion with Flauto and Cammarano about the choice of a subject, it is likely that his story of completing the opera in twenty-eight days is correct. It seems probably that even so he was

held up by Cammarano's failure to complete the versification in time, since on 10 November, only two weeks before
the opera was first seen in public, Pacini wrote to Cammarano: – 'Our friend Flauto is insisting on having the
book: I beg you to send it to him and have a copy made for
me, so that I can hurry on and finish my work. Time flies!'
Flauto also wanted a note of the costume designs – so it is
clear that they had left things pretty late. It is an interesting commentary not only on the 'brinkmanship' of operatic composition, but also on the speed with which the
operas were thrown onto the stage. In fact, the libretto was
finished in time to be submitted for approval on 12 November, and it came back, approved subject to corrections,
on 26 November.

There were nine performances of *Saffo* in what was left
of 1840 and twenty-seven in 1841, and it became a very
popular opera at the S. Carlo. It quickly obtained successful performances all over Italy and, soon, internationally.
Critical opinion held that Cammarano had arranged the
old fable very well, and that he had shown himself a judicious writer and poet.

The precise source on which Cammarano drew for the
libretto of *Saffo* remains uncertain. There were many plays
about Saffo and her fatal leap from the cliffs of Leucade,
and it was a popular topic for ballets, but none that I have
examined seems to give a model for Cammarano's treatment of his heroine, and, in particular, for her participation
at the wedding of Faone and his new love, or for the long-
lost-daughter motive. A newspaper review of Beltrame's
Saffo, which was played at the Fiorentini Theatre in the
mid-1830s shows that this play contains just such elements, and although I have not found a copy of the text, it
was almost certainly the source. The source is certainly
not the play by Grillparzer, as is often stated.

Saffo became one of the most popular operas of the
period, and held the stage in Italy for many years, despite
the unevenness of the music and the occasional obscurities
of the libretto. The latter contains one of the most effective opening scenes that Cammarano ever wrote, though
Pacini failed notably to exploit it as he might have done.
The librettist most skilled at writing neat opening scenes

and expositions was unquestionably Romani, and in this respect *Saffo* compares with the best of his, such as *Parisina*. It also contains some of Cammarano's most mellifluous verses (some originally intended for *Poliuto*) and in later years became the text to which his new works were compared and by which they were judged. For instance, seven years later, the text of *Merope* was deemed to be 'worthy of the author of *Saffo*' – not the author of *Lucia di Lammermoor* or *La vestale*, be it noted. The theatrical literature of the period gives the strong impression that the people of Naples took *Saffo* very much to their hearts, and remembered Cammarano with particular affection for his part in it. To his contemporaries, Cammarano was the author of *Saffo*.

With *Saffo* out of the way, Cammarano still had two tasks before him. The first was the revision of *Cristina di Svezia* for Lillo to set to music, as already related. This version was performed for the first time at the S. Carlo on 21 January 1841. The second work on which he was engaged was a libretto for another well established composer, Federico Ricci, for performance in Florence. This was *Luigi Rolla*, which was brought out at the Pergola theatre on 20 March 1841.

Federico Ricci, who came from a Florentine family, was born in Naples in 1809, and is remembered today chiefly for his part in the music of the highly successful *Crispino e la comare*, which he wrote in collaboration with his eldest brother Luigi to a libretto by Piave (Venice 1850). While Luigi was thought of as continuing the established buffo tradition, Federico was of a more serious bent, and his music provides evidence of more solid workmanship. His first opera appeared in 1835, and twelve more followed over the next fifteen years or so, including the popular *Il prigone d' Edimburgo* (Trieste, 1838; libretto by Rossi) and *Corrado d' Altamura* (Milan, 1842; libretto by Saccherò, probably his best). He then moved to St Petersburg to become Maestro di Bel Canto at the Imperial Conservatorium of Music, and his later operas were written for performance outside Italy.

Luigi Rolla, with Moriani (to whom the score was dedicated) Stepponi and Ronconi was warmly received in Florence, it being considered that Ricci was very fortunate to have an artist of the calibre of the famous tenor Moriani to launch it for him. It was the last opera of the Quaresima season at the Pergola, but despite its success it was quickly forgotten, receiving only occasional revivals in the late 1840s. The libretto was based on a very popular play by Lafont, *Le chef d'oeuvre inconnu*, first produced in Paris in June 1837. Later that same year Lafont's play was given in Naples at the Fiorentini theatre in an Italian version prepared by Luigi Marchionni, and was quickly established in the regular repertoire. It is a well constructed if rather far-fetched story of a young sculptor who is in love with a high-born lady, and whose masterpiece is touched up without his knowledge by Michelangelo; he wins a competition with it, but dies before he can be crowned with the laurel wreath and claim his bride. It was a play which attracted several composers, and in 1841 – the same year as Ricci's opera was performed in Florence – two more versions were staged in Naples, one with libretto by Giachetti and music by Mabellini (at the S.Carlo) and another by Rubino and Sarmiento (at the Fondo). The Cammarano/Ricci version was not performed in Naples.

It is easy to see why Lafont's play appealed to librettists and composers; the starving love-sick sculptor, his loyal brother, the faithful girl, her relentless family and the golden touch of the great artist are all good ingredients for emotional display. There is, however, a fatal lack of dramatic action at the level needed in opera, and Cammarano's text – though much more serviceable than either of the other two mentioned – cannot be rated as a successful vehicle for operatic music. Its worst flaw is that where dramatic tension is required Cammarano had to fall back on sentimentality, and the tragic edge is blunted.

In 1841 there was a further project for a Cammarano/Pacini opera, but it came to nothing. Pacini was to write an opera for the Fenice theatre in Venice, and on 14 June he wrote to the management enclosing a copy of a text by his librettist. A week later he wrote again, saying that he would not expect them to object to his choice of poet, Sig^r Cammarano being a dramatic writer 'of much fame' and, as would be seen, the subject wasn't sacred, nor Roman, nor Grecian, nor mythological. It was, in fact *Il conte di Chalais*, under a different name, *Maria contessa di Rohan*. On 30 June it was accepted for the Carnevale and Quadresima seasons of 1841/2, and approved by the Venetian censors on 25 July, but no more was heard of it. The manuscript libretto – still in the archives of the Fenice – is a hastily written copy of the printed text of Lillo's *Il conte di Chalais* (not of Cammarano's autograph, which differs from the printed text in some small particulars). Nowhere in the correspondence does Pacini mention that it had already been set by Lillo, and the fact that he had the text copied out instead of sending a printed copy suggests that he was anxious not to give the Fenice reason to believe that they were being presented with a second-hand libretto.

Over the summer and autumn of 1841, Cammarano was at work on a serious opera for his brother Luigi, of which more later. In December of that year, Coppola's *Ines de Castro* came out in Lisbon, but it is unlikely that he knew about this, let alone was consulted. However, later in the year he was again involved in collaboration with Mercadante, and the opera they wrote together – *Il proscritto* – was produced at the S. Carlo on 4 January 1842.

It is likely that Cammarano was at work on the libretto in the autumn of 1841, so that Mercadante could have finished the music early in December. It was certainly submitted for approval on 31 October, and was allowed on 13 December. Preparations for production could then have proceeded during the December closure. There was no preliminary announcement of the opera in *L'omnibus*, as is often found, but the review which appeared after the first night was critical in tone. Despite the beauty of the verses, wrote *L'omnibus*, this was not one of the best libretti of the poet Cammarano, who now already enjoys an Italy-wide fame, and the choice of this subject for an opera for the S. Carlo was a mistake. In fact, Mercadante's opera ran for thirteen performances, so that it cannot be rated as a total failure; but as far as I can ascertain it was never performed again, either in Naples or elsewhere.

The remark about the mistaken choice of subject needs an explanation. *Il proscritto* was based on a very well put together but impossibly stagey play by Soulié and Dehay,

Le proscrit, first produced in Paris on 7 November 1839. It deals with the secret return of an outlawed Bonapartist gentleman at the time of the royalist revival, just as his wife, thinking her husband dead, is about to marry a member of the opposing party. Eventually, torn between love and duty she kills herself, and the play ends with an almost unbelievable curtain line, the husband saying to his rival – 'Dead or alive, Sir, she belongs to me still' (which Cammarano took over in direct translation – 'Spenta o viva è mia tuttor' – as the ending of his own text). The play is full of fairly stock but effective dramatic situations, though there is little attempt at characterization or development. It is a theatrical piece, not a dramatic one, and striking situations and curtain lines do not make an opera.

For all that, *Le proscrit* certainly appealed to the impresario of the Scala in Milan, who commissioned a libretto based on the subject from Gaetano Rossi, offering it first to Verdi who – rightly – rejected it. It was thereupon set by Nicolai, who turned down *Nabucco* in its favour. It duly failed, being withdrawn after one single performance on 13 March 1841. The subject was then taken up by the Neapolitan librettist d'Arienzo, to be set to music by Aspa, and their version was performed at the Nuovo on 2 September 1841. It ran on into 1842, achieving seventeen performances altogether – in other words, it was still running at the Nuovo when Mercadante's opera opened at the S. Carlo. (It would be nice to be able to report that operagoers had a choice of either version on the same night, but unfortunately they never coincided!) The d'Arienzo/Aspa opera is totally different to the crude text turned out by Rossi or the much more polished or credible Cammarano one. D'Arienzo, a successful librettist of the second rank, managed to remove the political element, and added a group of low characters who lapse frequently into Neapolitan dialect (although he retained the Grenoble, 1817, setting of Soulié and Dehay's play), and he so pares down the role of the heroine that she displays none of the dignity nor the anguish of the original. Furthermore, he manages to contrive a happy ending.

Since Cammarano made no attempt to defuse the political element of the play, he obviously thought it prudent –

or was advised – to alter the setting and the time of the action. The French revolution and its consequences were rather too close for comfort in Bourbon Naples of the 1840s. What better place than Scotland? And at the time of the hated Cromwell, *Il Protettor*? It is, to be true, not one of his best libretti: the nature of the subject was against him – a domestic drama set against a political background with only superficial confrontation arising out of situation not character did not lend itself to operatic treatment. It is one of Cammarano's least interesting pieces, though worse ones have survived when coupled with outstanding music.

There is some critical disagreement as to the reception of *Il proscritto* on its first performance. The *Gazzetta Musicale* of Milan reported that 'faithful to our rule of not bothering about theatrical notices, we omit reference to the number of times the famous composer, the poet and the singers were called out to the proscenium'. The success this journal reported did not last and subsequent performances were poorly received, only the first act obtaining some applause. On the other hand, the Naples correspondent of the *Revue et Gazette musicale* of Paris, whose dispatch was printed on 23 January, reported that the first night was coldly received, but that the opera was successful on subsequent evenings. He added 'the libretto has been much praised, something rare south of the alps'.

Neither Aspa's nor Mercadante's opera lasted long in the Neapolitan repertoire, but it was not many years before another *Il proscritto* was announced for the S.Carlo. This turns out to be none other than Verdi's *Ernani*, then on its triumphal rounds of Italy.

The story of Cammarano's next libretto, *La fidanzata corsa*, which was written for Pacini and which was eventually performed in December 1842, goes back to the time when *Saffo* was given in Naples, breaking the composer's seven-year-long silence, at the end of 1840. In January 1841 Pacini wrote to the impresario Lanari 'as you know, I am contracted to write two new works for Naples, the one an opera buffa for the Teatro Nuovo, *Il nano misterioso*, which I must send off in July next; the other, in November, for the S.Carlo, will be *La vendetta corsa*'. Transcriptions of Pacini's correspondence have generously been put at my disposal by Jeremy Commons.

The Nuovo opera, under the title *L'uomo del mistero* and with a libretto by Andreotti, was produced in November 1841, and enjoyed a long and successful run. The S. Carlo opera had to wait; on 22 March 1842, Cammarano wrote to Pacini, in reply to enquiries Pacini had been making of the Neapolitan impresario Vincenzo Flauto. He knew that Pacini had another *Saffo* boiling in his veins, Cammarano wrote, but he himself needed time, without which he was good for nothing. '*La fidanzata corsa* which has taken root so strongly in your thoughts is certainly not a subject I consider unsuitable for you, but first I must bend it to the shape of musical drama, and to the abilities of our company . . .' He didn't want to hide from Pacini that he was still busy with another work, but he would soon be free to work for him '. . . Therefore have faith in me, dear Maestro, and in my honesty, and remember if inspiration is in short supply that is not so for the good intentions of your sincere friend'.

Three weeks later he wrote again, a much more formal letter on behalf of the management, reminding Pacini of the terms of the contract under which he was to have an opera ready for staging in early November. He was to have part of the libretto four months before that, and the rest from time to time so that he would have it all two months ahead of the time of production. He assured Pacini that he would have at the promised time the libretto which he considered himself fortunate to be writing for him, and he hoped for another success like that of *Saffo*.

The arrangement under which the composer received the libretto bit by bit – and not necessarily in the right order – was not perhaps such a disadvantage as might appear at first sight, as the composer would have had the detailed synopsis of the plot, and would know how the various pieces fitted together. Given the timetable suggested in Cammarano's formal letter, Pacini was due to receive the completed text by early September, and on 5 August Cammarano wrote to him again, asking when he might expect him to arrive in Naples so that they could work together on the two large-scale pieces (the finale of the second act and the scene of the vendetta). For the moment, so as not to waste time, he was busy with the two arias, Alberto's and Rosa's.

The libretto was submitted for approval on 25 October 1842, and returned, approved, on 10 December. A week later the Superintendent wrote a sharp note to the management reminding them that composers were not to begin work on a text until it had been approved – a regulation that was honoured more in the breach than in the observance. The opera was given on 10 December 1842, by a strong cast headed by Tadolini and Basadonna, and the notices were enthusiastic, though the run was interrupted by the illness of Basadonna. It ran for forty-three performances over the next three years, and was produced widely in Italy and abroad. The critics complained – not without reason – of the obscurity of parts of the plot, and *Il Lucifero* added that the ending, however atrocious it might be, was beyond reproach as it developed out of the personality of the characters and not from the author's contrivance. The same critic added that the opera house had long lacked a libretto with a well-organized plot which would hold the attention of the audience to the last word of the final scene, and that is precisely what Cammarano had provided '. . . although it was not an original idea (how few are such ideas?)'.

All the reviews of the period focus attention on Cammarano's ability as a writer of verse, and this is indeed one of the things that mark him off from most of his contemporaries. In addition to the talent for verses, he had a profound understanding of the theatre and with it a sense of a good plot. *La fidanzata corsa* is derived from a three-act French play by Ducange, *La vendetta ou la fiancée corse*, first produced in Paris in 1831 and in Naples, in Italian, at the Fiorentini in 1833 (where it enjoyed a continuing success). It is a highly melodramatic story of Rosa, whose betrothal and forthcoming marriage to Alessi will put an end to a long-standing and bloody feud. But Rosa has fallen in love with Alberto, the local representative of the occupying power. When Alberto claims Rosa as his bride, Alessi, true to Corsican ideals of honour, shoots her, as the final curtain falls. The French play is set in Corsica during the directorate but Cammarano, either on his own initiative or under guidance from the censors, put it back to the sixteenth century, and the occupying power, instead of France, is Genoa. Despite its shootings and other crudities, Ducange's play was a very good basis for an opera libretto, and Cammarano made the most of it. It provided him with good strong theatrical situations to exploit, and plenty of the 'violent love' that composers were always on the lookout for. It is a dramatically effective libretto, and it is a pity that the neglect into which Pacini has now unjustly fallen means that we are unlikely to see this opera on the stage.

In his letter of 22 March to Pacini, Cammarano admitted that he had been too much occupied with other work to be able to give his undivided attention to *La fidanzata corsa*. In fact, he must have had a particularly busy year, for in addition to two other operas, both of which appeared in the February of the following year (1843) (*Il reggente*, for Mercadante, at Turin, and *Ester d'Engaddi*, for Peri, at Parma) he was working on a project for Donizetti.

The new opera for Mercadante probably occupied Cammarano during the first part of the year, for on 16 June Mercadante wrote to him:

> I thank you with all my heart for the revised first act finale. For charity, do not speak to me about getting someone to help you, and of your worries – I know that for you it is a strain to be short of time, but you should not be discouraged, and least of all abandon me.

The tone of this letter suggests that Cammarano was under pressure to finish more work than he could comfortably manage, and was even asking Mercadante to intercede on his behalf in order to find someone to help him. The opera they were working on together – *Il reggente* – was based on Scribe's *Gustave III ou le bal masqué* (a libretto he wrote for Auber in 1833). It dealt with the assassination of the King of Sweden during a masked ball in the Royal Opera House in Stockholm on 16 March 1792. It is a story familiar to opera-goers through Verdi's treatment of it (*Un ballo in maschera*) some fifteen years later, and had already been used by Rossi as the basis of his libretto *Clemenza di Valois*, set to music by Vincenzo Gabuzzi, and performed in Venice in 1841. As long before as 1834 Bellini had proposed it for an opera for Naples (if the censor would allow it; perhaps if the King were not to be killed!), in the same letter as he toyed with the idea of *Un duel sous Richelieu*. It was, of course, a ready-made opera text, but it required to be ruthlessly condensed from the five-act Parisian grand-opera format. As was to be expected, Rossi went about his task crudely and moved the setting to Arles at the time of the crusades, providing a prolix and totally imaginary introduction to set the drama in its 'historical' environment.

Cammarano would probably have been justly concerned over a plot which turned on a royal assassination had the opera been intended for Naples. Indeed, it is unlikely that the Bourbon censorship would have contemplated permitting it. It was intended for production in Turin, but even so he thought it advisable to move the time and place from the Sweden of only forty years previously. There was, of course, one safe location – Scotland – and the time chosen was 1570. The King of Sweden was transformed into Il conte Murray, Regent of Scotland, and the treacherous minister Ankarstroem into Il duca Hamilton. One of the two scheming noblemen became Lord Howe, the other Lord Kilcardy (a corruption, perhaps, of Kirkcaldy?) and at the end of the opera the Regent is planning to send Hamilton as Ambassador to the court of Elizabeth 'sul Tamigi'. The substitution of a regent for a King was a masterstroke: it enabled some of the political under-currents of the play to remain, while a figure of political authority existed whose death avoided spilling royal blood.

Il reggente was performed at the Teatro Regio in Turin on 2 February 1843, with great success, 'the libretto strewn with beautiful verses, and truly worthy of Cammarano'. It moved on to a number of other cities, though it was some years before it was again produced in Turin, and not surprisingly it was never produced in Naples. The libretto of this opera gives rise to some textual difficulties, in that the text printed for the first performance, which may be accepted as the 'firm' version, differs from most later versions, which include up to three additional scenes at the beginning of the second act. These scenes certainly read as if they could have been written by Cammarano, and were set by Mercadante for the Trieste performance of November 1843, according to a note in the autograph full score.

The other work which appeared in February 1843 was Peri's setting of *Ester d'Engaddi*, written for the Ducale Theatre of Parma, and warmly received there. Achille Peri was born in Reggio Emilia in 1812, and had begun his career as an opera composer two years previously in his home town, with a setting of Calisto Bassi's libretto *Il solitario*. *Ester d'Engaddi* was his second work, and he went on to compose a total of ten operas before 1862; he died in 1880. His best known work was probably the *melodramma biblico, Guiditta*, to a libretto by Marcello (Milan, 1860). Cammarano based his *Ester d'Engaddi* on Silvio Pellico's well-known drama of the same name – a magnificent study of the persecution of a woman wrongly believed to be unfaithful to her husband (in circumstances very close to Pia, except that it is her exiled father, not her brother, who appears to have compromised her) and of the relentless cruelty of the ecclesiastical establishment in forcing her through a ritual ordeal – the drama being heightened by the ritual cup having been poisoned by a disappointed rival for her love. It is a slow-moving libretto, but well put together and clear in motivation, perhaps rather deficient in its range of dramatic situations. Five years later Pacini turned to the same subject, but with a much inferior libretto by Guidi (Turin, 1848). Cammarano's libretto is not lacking in poetry, and in the hands of a major composer might have fared better. As it was, it was revived only very rarely, and soon dropped out of sight.

The most interesting of the various projects which Cammarano was engaged on in 1842 was the one which came to nothing, his renewed collaboration with Donizetti, who had just accepted appointment as Hofkappellmeister in Vienna. Donizetti returned to Italy in July 1842, reaching Naples in August, where he proceeded to negotiate a contract with the Royal Theatres for an opera to be produced in October 1843. The librettist was to be Cammarano. At the end of the following January (1843) he wrote to a friend that the opera for Naples was going to be *Ruy Blas*, moved to another location.

Some explanation of this choice of subject is necessary,

since on the face of it *Ruy Blas* (like most of Hugo's work) would seem to be a prime suspect for Bourbon censorship. In fact, it had already been seen in Naples, although under highly unusual circumstances and in a mutilated form. Adamo Alberti, for many years the impresario of the Fiorentini theatre, tells in his autobiography how in 1839 one of his actors, Luigi Belisario, played a trick upon the censors. Knowing that *Ruy Blas* would not be permitted, he rearranged the play under the title of *Falco Melian* and obtained approval for it without its identity being recognized. The public applauded mightily, knowing the name of the original author. This was the play that Cammarano seized upon three years later; he worked up a synopsis of the plot (removing any of the political element that might have been left) and submitted it to the censors under the title *Folco d'Arles*. It is hard to believe that the censors were by this time in any doubts as to the origins of the plot, but Cammarano's treatment was evidently judged to have purged it of any objectionable matter, and it was signed as permitted by Gaetano Royer on 5 September 1842 – the same Royer, it will be recalled, whom Alberti had denounced as being as bad as the cholera when it came to closing down his theatre.

Donizetti later sought to be released from this contract, as he no longer wished to travel to Naples to oversee the production. In February 1843 he asked a friend to enter into negotiations with the management on his behalf, emphasizing that this was not to hold back Cammarano's work, which he understood to be going ahead in accordance with the terms of the contract. Flauto, the impresario of the Royal Theatres, was clearly unhappy about this, and reminded Donizetti of his obligations in no uncertain terms. There must have been some further disagreement about the libretto, either from Donizetti's point of view or the censors'; more likely from Donizetti's, as when Flauto wrote to him in the middle of May, finalizing agreement, he wrote: 'We will therefore say no more about Cammarano's libretto. Let your opera be *Catarina* [*sic*] *Cornaro*. But when shall I receive the score so that I can have it approved by the censors?'

Donizetti had in fact already begun work on this opera in

Vienna, but had put it on one side when Lachner's opera on the same subject was announced for performance there in November 1842. He clearly thought it would be quicker to complete this work for Naples, have it produced in his absence in January 1844, and thereby fulfil the terms of his contract with the minimum of trouble to himself. The libretto of *Caterina Cornaro* was by Saccherò, and on examining it Flauto recognized a number of matters which the censors would not permit. However, the project went forward and the following November Flauto was able to report to Donizetti that Cammarano had had to make some alterations to Saccherò's text as required by the censors.

In the same letter Flauto proposed that Donizetti should write two more operas for Naples, for 1845 and 1846; the poet was to be Cammarano, whom he already had under contract. These suggestions, too, came to nothing, but the clear implication is that Donizetti and Cammarano had not fallen out over the *Ruy Blas* libretto, and would be prepared to work together again. In the event, Cammarano kept the 'approved' synopsis of the libretto up his sleeve, as was his usual practice, and, as we will see, brought it out again seven years later, when it was set by Nicola di Giosa.

1843 saw the appearance of only one new Cammarano libretto, *Il ravvedimento*. (Donizetti's *Maria di Rohan*, using the text he had written for Lillo some years earlier, came out in Vienna in June). *Il ravvedimento* was written for Cammarano's brother Luigi, and was the only serious opera that composer wrote. Though serious in style, it is not tragic, and all ends happily. It was written for the Fondo, and although it was submitted for approval on 31 December 1841, it was not performed until 16 May 1843, receiving three performances altogether. It is based on a play by Mélesville and Duveyrier, *Clifford le voleur*, which had first appeared in Paris in 1835, and in Naples three years later. Given in Italian at the Fiorentini theatre, it had enjoyed a long run. It did not make a successful libretto; it is all disguises, mistaken identities, long-lost sons, recognitions and repentances – all the stock-in-trade of the Parisian theatres. The scene was in Scotland (on this occasion *not* a Cammarano evasion) in 1746 and there is a tenuous historical background of events surrounding the Pretender, the dragoons of 'Cumperlandio' and the 'horrible battle of Culloden'. For the most part, all is confusion of identity and purpose, and the libretto is faulty in terms of construction and balance. It is doubtful if more skilled attention than Luigi Cammarano was able to bring to it would have done much with it.

In June 1843 there occurred the first of the circumstances which linked Cammarano to Verdi, then a young composer with two highly successful operas to his name, *Nabucco* (1842) and *I Lombardi* (1843). Verdi was negotiating with the management of the Fenice theatre in Venice for an opera, the contract which was to lead to *Ernani* (March 1844). He had run into the familiar difficulty of finding a suitable subject; *King Lear* and Byron's *The Corsair* were taken up but soon laid aside. Then his choice fell on another work of Byron's, *The Bride of Abydos* (*La fidanzata d'Abido*). 'I have written to Cammarano, to Solera, to Bancalari of Genoa', wrote Verdi – but none of them can have been willing to undertake the task, and Byron's play does not appear on any of the surviving lists of subjects which Cammarano made. Verdi finally agreed to work with Piave (for the first time and not without hesitations), and the subject chosen was Victor Hugo's *Ernani*, which Bellini had begun work on in 1830, but had quickly dropped.

Then in the middle of 1843, Pacini was in correspondence with Cammarano about a libretto for an opera he was to write for performance in Florence, which was not to appear till two years later, in the middle of 1845. Cammarano wrote to Pacini on 27 June 1843 (a letter forming part of the correspondence transcribed by Jeremy Commons):

> Here is the synopsis of the opera for Florence; if it reaches you late, you must not accuse me of negligence, but rather of zeal – yes of zeal. The synopsis of *Alzira* was already prepared when your letter took me off the subject, and I was not pleased, because after *Saffo* it would not be wise for me to take a risk again. I therefore began to think of other plots, and in order to satisfy Buccini, and so as not to compromise myself with Lanari who was under the firm impression that

we would be writing *Alzira*, I turned back to *Bondelmonte* – the same subject as he once suggested – and which has in truth a certain historical interest, particularly for performance in Florence. But does it have theatrical interest? And does it conform to the requirements of musical drama? This was the terrible difficulty I had to overcome.

He concluded the letter by promising to begin on the versification immediately.

It would be good to know why Pacini, experienced man of the theatre that he was, rejected *Alzira*, a plot which was soon thereafter to be accepted by Verdi without any quibbles, but unfortunately he does not refer to it in his memoirs. Cammarano's remark that after *Saffo* he was not taking any risks presumably means that while on the earlier occasion he was prepared to persuade Pacini to accept a particular plot, he was not willing to use his influence in that way again.

It was presumably 'the opera for Florence' (*Bondelmonte*) which gave rise to the following letter from Pacini to Antonio Ventura (Barbaja's nephew, and impresario of the Teatro Nuovo). It is dated 24 August 1843 and also forms part of the Pacini correspondence transcribed by Jeremy Commons:

At last I have seen your letters, and I'll begin by thanking you for the payment made to Cammeramo [*sic*] of 500 francs, of which I am waiting for the formal receipt.

500 francs was about 120 ducats, the sum that Cammarano had earlier been paid for a libretto. There is of course no evidence that this was payment for a libretto rather than some private debt, but the fact that it was paid through semi-official 'Barbaja' channels suggests that it was. If so, what libretto? Their earlier collaboration over *La fidanzata corsa* had been completed nine months previously, and one hopes that Cammarano would not have to wait so long for payment. But Cammarano wrote *that* text as part of his official duties under the terms of his contract with the Royal Theatres, so that Pacini should not have had to pay him himself. It is consequently almost certainly a reference to payment for the Florence opera; we know that the project was far enough advanced in June for Cammarano to offer to hurry ahead with the versification, and it

would not be impossible for him to have finished the text in time for him to be due for payment at the end of August; and since writing this libretto did not fall to him in his official capacity, payment by or on behalf of the composer would be expected.

Nothing else has come to light about Cammarano's life in 1843, with two trivial exceptions. The first of these is a letter, preserved in the Lucchesi-Palli library in Naples, addressed to him in December 1843 at his home address – unusually, since most letters were addressed simply to 'Sig^r Salvadore Cammarano, dramatic poet, Naples' or some such. From this letter we learn that he was living at No. 24, Strada S. Brigida, a street lying a couple of hundred yards to the north of the S. Carlo, just off the Toledo. His life was thus centred on the S. Carlo; a short walk northwards along the Toledo took him home; or a shorter walk to the west, to the pillared promenade of S. Francesco, where he used to seek inspiration for his verses; a similar walk eastwards, to the Fondo theatre, brought him to the offices of the administration of the theatres.

On a similar domestic note, in the same collection of letters, bound up under Cammarano's name, is a delightful note from Mercadante, dated 24 May 1844; it is not clear to whom it was sent, but its preservation in that particular collection, and its subject matter, suggest that the recipient may well have been Cammarano:

> My dear friend,
> I am asking you to do me the favour of lunching with me next Sunday at half past three, to spend an hour in the company of our friends Sig^r Ferretti and d'Arienzo – make it possible to extricate yourself from that very good man your father and grant me this favour.
>
> Yours affectionately
> Mercadante
>
> Wednesday 24 May 1844.

This letter points to a cordial relationship between the composer and the recipient; it also portrays the latter as a dutiful son who is expected to take Sunday lunch in the bosom of his family. Marco d'Arienzo was a prolific writer of libretti (including, it will be recalled, *Il proscritto* for Aspa) and he wrote three for Mercadante. The first of these, *Leonora,* was produced at the Nuovo in December 1844, so that it is likely that he and Mercadante were working on it at the time of the letter. The Ferretti mentioned could therefore well have been the librettist from Rome on a visit to Naples; he was an old colleague of Mercadante's, as the two had collaborated on a couple of operas thirty years previously.

Whether all this speculation is justified or not, it makes a pretty picture, far removed from the politics and the pressures of theatrical life, and is worth quoting if only to remind ourselves that while in a study of a period interest naturally focuses on the works of those under review, they had their own private lives to lead and their own personal interests to pursue.

CHAPTER SIX

1844–1847

Alzira — Francesca Donato — Il vascello de Gama —
Bondelmonte — Stella di Napoli — Orazi e Curiazi —
Eleonora Dori

After the short-lived production of *Il ravvedimento* in May 1843, there was a break of almost two years before Cammarano's next libretto found its way on to the stage. He remained on the staff of the Royal Theatres as Poet and Stage Manager (*Poeta e concertatore*). In the middle of 1844 he had to prepare Donizetti's *La regina di Golconda* for the Fondo theatre (it received a handful of performances at that theatre and the S. Carlo, beginning on the 30 May), and the list of costumes required of the wardrobe department in his handwriting is still extant.

The most important event of 1844 for Cammarano, though he probably did not realize it at the time, turned out to be the beginning of his collaboration with Verdi. Because they usually worked apart (there is no evidence to suggest that Cammarano ever left Naples), and because Verdi habitually kept letters he received, and copies of those he wrote, their collaboration is unusually well-documented. Verdi was an exacting task-master, even in the early years of his career, but at the beginning of their work together he treated Cammarano with unusual respect; later to this respect was added sincere affection.

The very first letter preserved in Verdi's letter-book (*I Copialettere*) is a reply, dated 21 March 1844, to Vincenzo Flauto, who had evidently raised with him the possibility of his writing an opera for performance in Naples. Verdi's most recent opera had been *Ernani*, which had appeared at the Fenice theatre in Venice in March 1844, and his reputation was established beyond any question. Verdi replied that for reasons which included 'the advantage of writing an opera to the text of the famous poet Sig. Cammarano' he would hasten to accept Flauto's offer. One of the provisions he laid down was that the text was to be in his hands, in Milan, by the end of 1844. Since it was common practice for contracts to allow a period of four months between receipt of a libretto and production, Flauto had probably suggested a performance in the spring or early summer of 1845.

Some months after replying in this vein to Flauto, Verdi had received a synopsis from Cammarano – the same *Alzira* which Pacini had rejected the previous year. On 23 February 1845 he wrote to Cammarano that he was very happy with the idea: in the hands of a Cammarano, Voltaire's tragedy, which he had read, would make an excellent libretto. Cammarano must have sent some sample verses along with the synopsis, for Verdi concluded his letter 'I beg you to send me promptly some more verses. It's not necessary for me to tell you to keep it short. You know the theatre better than I do'. This request for brevity was to prove troublesome; Cammarano was used to the way in which composers like Donizetti and Mercadante set his poetry to music, which in terms of words per minute was much more leisurely than Verdi's, whose style was more concise and propulsive. *Alzira* is the shortest of all Cammarano's serious libretti, and he may well have had these remarks of Verdi in mind as he wrote it. When the opera was produced it turned out to be unexpectedly short, and at the last moment Verdi had to produce an overture for it. Cammarano soon learned to write longer texts for Verdi than he used to write for other composers. On 18 April following Verdi wrote to Cammarano, 'I have received the Finale, which is marvellous [*stupendo*]. I am waiting for some touching up (as you promised me) and the outline, at least, of the final act'. Verdi seems to have been delighted with Cammarano's verses, for three days later his pupil Muzio wrote to Verdi's benefactor, 'the verses are very beautiful' and added as an example the opening lines of the Prologue.

The Finale which Verdi had received (on 16 April) was presumably that of Act I, for on the 25th he wrote to Flauto that Cammarano was absolutely up to time; he had received the Prologue and all Act I, and was confidently expecting Act II to reach him the next day. For once,

Cammarano seems to have been on time, though his habit of sending his texts in dribs and drabs cannot have made things easy for his composers, particularly one like Verdi whose attention was directed to the dramatic sweep of the whole work rather than the emotion of the moment, and who liked to set a text in the proper sequence. The libretto was finished, and submitted for approval on 5 May. However, by the end of April Verdi was ill, and in dispute with the management. By 10 May he could write to Cammarano again, 'I have received the duet and the aria in Act II. How beautiful they are! You are succeeding excellently with your verses – how shall I do with the music? . . . However, press on with the final scene at your own convenience, or wait till I shall be in Naples, as you wish – but make it touching'. Two weeks later, the lines for Alzira's cavatina had arrived, and were adjudged extraordinarily fine, particularly the recitative of the opening section. Verdi added an interesting footnote: 'Forgive me one observation: do not three cavatinas in a row seem to you to be too many?' All this, of course, after the libretto had been formally submitted for approval.

The composition of the opera was delayed by Verdi's ill-health, and the unsympathetic attitude of the S.Carlo management did not help. However, by the end of June Verdi had arrived in Naples and on 30 July he could report that the opera was finished. Production was set down for 9 August, but was delayed to the 12th at the request of the scene designer Angelo Belloni who, according to Schlitzer, painted all five sets in ten days – an indication of the haste with which new operas were thrown on to the stage. Despite a first-class cast, which included Tadolini, Fraschini and Coletti, the opera never caught on. Public disapproval grew with each performance, and it received fourteen complete (and five partial) performances during the remaining months of 1845, thereafter dropping out of the repertoire. Torelli in *L'omnibus* praised the libretto for its gravity and the opportunities afforded the composer, but was disappointed by the music. Ventimiglia in *Il Lucifero* was more specific: Cammarano's Prologue was redundant, the two acts too short, so that only the skeleton of Voltaire's *Alzire* remained. Nevertheless the text contained some

beautiful moments and the verses were always praise-
worthy, though the composer had not always taken advantage of them.

Alzira was produced in Rome in November 1845, but
again failed. Verdi commented to the librettist Jacopo Ferretti that he had been well aware before the opera reached
the stage that it was structurally faulty, and that touching
it up would only make matters worse. Cammarano's view,
in a letter to Pacini a couple of weeks after the Naples
premiere, was succinct: 'It is music which cannot please'.

However, Cammarano cannot escape a share of the responsibility for the failure of *Alzira*. His libretto, apart from
the brevity and perfunctoriness, was not unlike others he
had written and was to write, but even for its time was
beginning to seem somewhat old-fashioned, and unsuited
to the cut and thrust of Verdi's early style – a problem that
was always to dog the Verdi-Cammarano collaboration. In
the background was the unaccustomed deference with
which the up-and-coming composer treated the established and experienced librettist – as evidenced not only in
his letters but also in his willingness to work on a libretto
he knew to be structurally weak. A glance at Verdi's previous librettists tells us why. His first opera was written to a
text by the irascible and opinionated Solera; it was Solera's
first attempt at a libretto, and there is good reason to
believe it was not all his own work. Verdi's second opera
was to an old text by Romani. Then came two more Solera
texts, followed by one – *Ernani* – by Piave, again a very
inexperienced librettist, it being his first independent libretto. By contrast, Verdi suddenly found himself in a new
situation, having been given the opportunity of working
with a poet of great experience and theatrical acumen, one
who over a period of ten years had been associated with
composers like Donizetti, Mercadante and Pacini. Verdi
was not a man to be in awe of anyone, but he certainly
entered on his collaboration with Cammarano in a respect-
ful vein, only permitting himself a mild query about
a string of cavatinas. Consequently he found himself
saddled with a libretto which, even if it had been good of its
type, was quite unsuited to his style and to his approach to
musical drama. Cammarano's libretti were geared to a

concept of opera which was reflective rather than dramatic, and even if he ever became aware of the way in which Verdi's developing musico-dramatic style was taking him, he may well not have been able to produce the type of text Verdi needed as a vehicle for his ideas.

It was about this time that Cammarano signed a contract with the management of the Royal Theatres, a copy of which has been preserved in the Lucchesi-Palli Library in Naples. It is not dated, but on internal evidence there are grounds for thinking it was written around 1844. Cammarano was to be paid 700 Austrian lire (about 140 ducats in Neapolitan currency) for a libretto for the S. Carlo theatre for that year; this was presumably *Alzira*. This was stated to be the same sum that Saccherò had received, and the only text of his which was first produced in Naples was *Caterina Cornaro*, in January 1844. He was to receive 50 ducats for the adjustments he had made to *Il proscritto* and *Francesca Donato* but it was noted that he had already drawn 40 ducats in advance. In the first year from Easter 1844, Cammarano was to write one opera, and two in each of the three following years. For these he would be paid monthly, at the rate of 40 ducats per month in the first year and 70 per month thereafter.

It is not clear from the document how the payment of 700 lire for the libretto mentioned at the beginning of the contract relates to the monthly payments referred to in the final section, but the overall picture is fairly clear. Cammarano was to receive a monthly salary, with the obligation of providing an agreed number of libretti each year. Work over and above this agreement, such as re-writing old texts, was paid for over and above the monthly salary; naturally any work he undertook for other composers or theatres was his own business and provided an extra bonus. No mention is made in this draft contract to Cammarano's duties as stage manager/producer, but in all the years which could be covered by this contract, his name appears – usually along with one or more others – in the Prospectus of the Royal Theatres as *Poeta e Concertatore*, so these duties were presumably taken for granted. The discovery that he had drawn some of the money due to him 'on account' confirms the many references over the years to his chronic shortage of money.

Just what adjustments had to be made to the libretto of *Il proscritto* are not now known, nor even which opera was being referred to. The Cammarano/Mercadante opera of January 1842 did not last long; nor did the d'Arienzo/Aspa work of the same period, and that was a Teatro Nuovo production in which the Royal Theatres would not have been involved. The other opera which was produced in Naples under that title was Verdi's *Ernani* (of March 1844), but this was not until the middle of May 1847, though an earlier production may have been intended. As it turned out, Cammarano did not produce the two libretti per year in the later years covered by this contract, but this was probably due to the deteriorating financial position of the management, and the political upheavals leading to the armed uprising of 1848, rather than to any failure on his part. Apart from *Alzira*, 1845 saw two operas to his texts staged at the S. Carlo, 1846 one, 1847 two and 1848 none.

Although the contract for *Alzira* was signed in the middle of 1844, Cammarano does not seem to have sent any sizeable portion of the text to Verdi until the following April. During these years two further libretti had claimed his attention. The first of these, already mentioned in connection with the draft contract, was *Francesca Donato*. This was an opera which Mercadante had written for performance in Turin in 1835, with a text by Romani. The story on which the libretto was based was taken from Byron's *The Siege of Corinth* (1816). Apart from a production in Barcelona in 1841, the opera does not appear to have been performed again until revived in Naples in January 1845. The issue of *L'omnibus* of 19 September 1844 carried an announcement that the new season at the S. Carlo was to include a new opera by Mercadante, and another old one by the same Maestro, *Francesca Donato*, which had been re-written; in fact the libretto had been altered in time for it to be submitted for approval on 23 September 1843, and had been allowed on 9 December. The entry in Florimo's catalogue gives the libretto as by Romani and Cammarano, while the manuscript full score in the Conservatorio S. Pietro a Majella in Naples is catalogued as having the third act by Cammarano, but this is rather deceptive. A com-

parison of the Turin libretto of 1835 with the Naples one of
1845 shows that in Act I Cammarano altered about twenty-
five lines, and added a new eight-line chorus. In Act II, he
altered about thirty-five lines, including some fairly extensive passages. In the first part of Act III he made only a few
small changes, but he rewrote the rest of the act almost
completely, restructuring the ending by providing a new
closing duet for Francesca and the renegade Alp and a new
final scene of greater dramatic strength (though perhaps
less credibility), with Alp escaping across a bridge as it is
blown up, taking him with it. There are some interesting
pointers to changes in public sensibilities, with patriotism
substituted for filial duty as a basis for personal motivation. Even in its revised format, however, *Francesca
Donato* was not successful, being performed only three
times.

The new opera which Mercadante wrote for this season
at the S. Carlo also had a libretto by Cammarano – *Il
vascello de Gama*, produced on 6 March 1845. It, too, was
unsuccessful, running for eight performances only and
never revived in Naples or, as far as I can ascertain, any-
where else. Never had so much spectacle been seen on the
stage, said *L'omnibus* – and not without good reason. Cammarano based his libretto on an involved five-act play by
Desnoyer, *Le Naufrage de la Meduse*, first given in Paris on
27 April 1839, itself based on an historical incident, when
the French naval vessel 'La Meduse' went aground on the
Banc d'Arguin off the African coast as it was on its way to
regain possession of Senegal, on 2 March 1816. The loss of
the ship was ascribed to the incapacity of the captain, an
elderly emigré; although 149 people managed to escape on
a raft, only fifteen of them were alive when the raft was
sighted. Desnoyer's play, with its elaborate staging, was
highly successful, and, needless to say, he had woven a
romantic tale of love and rivalry through the historical
events. Two years later, in 1841, the choreographer Hus
mounted a ballet at La Scala, Milan, which followed Desnoyer closely, though transferring the action to Siam. Cammarano, too, altered the time and the locale of the action –
which was still a little too close for comfort – this time not
to Scotland, as by now we might have expected, but to

Portugal in the sixteenth century. He had written the text in 1844, and it was submitted for approval on 30 October; it was allowed on 15 November. Although intended for the Carnival season, it was not ready in time. There were complaints about this, but the files of the Superintendency do not give the reasons for this delay.

The libretto suffers from excessive condensation, and cannot have been easy to follow. It contains too many coincidences and disguised identities, and there is a transparent 'long-lost-brother' motive, which, to give him his due, Cammarano handled rather better than Desnoyer. The most interesting feature of the libretto was the opportunity it gave for spectacle, as Anzelmi remarked in his review – the settings included the captain's cabin on a Moorish ship; a harbourside inn with the 'de Gama' in the background; the deck of the 'de Gama' at sea; the raft adrift on the ocean. These must have required no little ingenuity on the part of the scene designers and the stage hands – to say nothing of the storm at sea, with the mainmast struck by lightning, falling on and killing the Commandant as the curtain falls on Act II. Alas, Anzelmi mocked the clumsiness of the machinists, the vast proportions of the ship, which 'rode out the tempest with the stupefied immobility of the gymnosophist'. He did, however, find the now customary words of praise for Cammarano's verses, 'now pathetic, now brilliant, now imaginative and always smoothly-flowing' (*fluidi*).

For the next opera to be considered it is neccessary to return to the Pacini/Cammarano correspondence of 1843, to the letter in which Cammarano accepted Pacini's decision to reject *Alzira* and to settle on *Bondelmonte* as the subject of their collaboration. It was, of course, an obvious choice for an opera for Florence, being based on a famous episode in Florentine history, an episode to which, rightly or wrongly, the old chronicles of Florence ascribe the origins of the Guelph/Ghibbeline struggles. It was related how Bondelmonte was betrothed for political reasons to a girl of the Amedei family; how he jilted her for the daughter of Gualdrata Donati; whereupon the Amedei and their kinsmen planned to murder him in revenge. On Easter Sunday 1215, Bondelmonte, all in white and riding a white horse, crossed the Ponte Vecchio and was struck down and stabbed to death at the foot of the statue of Mars. Readers of Dante will recall two passages:

> O Bondelmonte, quanto mal fuggisti
> le nozze sue per gli altrui conforti!

> Ricordera ti anche del Mosca
> che disse, lasso! 'Capo ha cosa fatta'
> che fu il mal seme per la gente tosca.

This famous incident was used as the basis for many plays and ballets in the 1820s and 1830s; the best known was Carlo Marenco's rather disorganized five-act tragedy (Turin, 1827) and there is internal evidence to suggest that Cammarano was familiar with it. Surprisingly the story had not been used as a basis for an opera libretto, except for a hastily carpentered libretto needed when Donizetti's *Maria Stuarda* was prohibited in Naples in the autumn of 1834, a time when Cammarano had just come on to the payroll of the Royal Theatres.

Reduced to its essentials, the historical narrative of Bondelmonte is lacking in dramatic incident: there is only the jilting of the first girl, the marriage with the second, the plotting of revenge and the murder itself. The scale of the contrivances introduced – particularly for the second-act finale, where the first girl, driven out of her mind by Bondelmonte's behaviour, happens to be outside the church as he emerges from the wedding ceremony – count against it. There is, however, (at the end of Act 1) a magnificent confrontation scene between the two women, full of well-wrought dramatic irony, which is amongst the very best scenes Cammarano ever wrote, though where he found the model for this scene has yet to be discovered. When *Bondelmonte* reached Naples in the summer of 1846, the review in *Il Lucifero* was written by Domenico Bolognese, then twenty-seven years old and himself a budding librettist, who was to succeed Cammarano as *Poeta e Concertatore* on the latter's death in 1852. He singled out for special mention this scene between the two women, with one of them pouring out her heart without knowing that it is this same friend who is the object of Bondelmonte's new attachment. 'Some people' Bolognese went on 'reprimand Cammarano for certain situations which are repeated too frequently in his libretti – an image excessively bold, or insufficiently worked out, or lacking in poetry; but these can be forgiven a poet who writes a great deal, and who then cannot revise his work'. *L'omnibus* also praised the confrontation scene, and added that the libretto was well constructed, with the most beautiful verses which could only bring greater honour on the poet.

Despite the many contrivances and coincidences, *Bondelmonte* is fast moving, effective theatre, and the verses flow along smoothly. It was first performed at the Pergola theatre in Florence on 18 June 1845, soon becoming a very popular opera. It was played all over Italy (and, indeed, outside Italy) until about 1860, when it began to drop out of sight.

To review Cammarano's work during the years 1843–45: the libretto of *Bondelmonte* can be ascribed to the summer of 1843 ('I will begin the versification immediately' wrote Cammarano on 27 June, and he received a payment, probably for this text, in late August); the alterations to *Francesca Donato* also belong to 1843; the libretto of *Il vascello de Gama* occupied him in 1844; and he turned to the writing of *Alzira* in the early months of 1845.

A few days after the first performance of *Alzira*, Flauto wrote (on 16 August 1845) a rather pained letter to his senior librettist:

> Ever since I've been running this business I've not been discouraged by failures, and I don't intend to blame anyone else; but it is my duty, which I cannot go on neglecting as I have done up to now, to keep a close eye on the poems which are to be set to music. I am charged by my associates and by the public with laziness in not paying attention to the choice of subjects on which you base your libretti: and now that after *Vascello de Gama* and *Alzira* they hear of *Orazi*, God alone knows what they'll be saying.

The interesting feature of this letter is not so much Flauto's evident dissatisfaction with the choice of *Vascello* or *Alzira*, both of which had resulted in failure, but the mention of *Orazi e Curiazi*. This libretto, with music by Mercadante, eventually appeared in November 1846, but it is not

Mercadante's setting that Flauto was referring to, but Pacini's.

Pacini was under contract to write an opera for the S. Carlo, and on 25 August 1845 Cammarano wrote to him, 'I hope you have received the letter I sent you yesterday with the second piece of *Orazi*. Let me know if you're pleased with it, for my piece of mind and so that I may press on more boldly with work on it'. However, Pacini seems to have been less than pleased with Cammarano's progress on *Orazi*, and complained about it to Flauto. On 5 September Cammarano sent the composer a long letter, (published by Schlitzer in a pamphlet on Mercadante!) which is so full of interest that it is worth quoting in full:

> Without any doubt, the fact that the three pieces from *Orazi e Curiazi* reached you much later than they should (and that because our friend Mira was not aware that you had left Lucca) prompted you to make an unjust complaint against me in the last letter which you sent to Sig. Flauto: I never neglect the composers who work with me and if I could differentiate between them I should certainly have done so in favour of the one who clothed with notes *Saffo*, *Fidanzata corsa*, *Bondelmonte*. But all that on one side: the reason why I'm writing to you is something else: I have made haste to send you Curiazi's cavatina, so as to have a speedy reply from you, in which I hoped to learn that all your unfortunate prejudice against the plot had vanished, but your silence has led me to suspect the opposite, and has thrown me into a depression such as I've never experienced before now. If I am not mistaken in my supposition, if dislike of this subject is growing stronger in you, or if it hardens against the verses I've sent you, we will see if with one bold stroke we can put everything to rights. *Stella di Napoli*, which so much appealed to you, serves as my excuse: when you regretted having left me to choose between *Stella* and *Orazi*, you wanted to return to *Stella*, but I could not, because I had not yet then overcome the obstacles which the role of the father put before me. Afterwards, while versifying *Orazi*, my thoughts turned every now and again to the beloved *Stella*, and these obstacles fell away, and now I could undertake the poetry. It is late, you'll tell me; no, it is not late when two men fervently desire something, one of them daring to want a great success, the other being Pacini, strong in the inexhaustible power of his genius. I can delay the production of your

opera, just as I did with *Fidanzata corsa,* and there can then be more than two months for your work: more than two months is enough for you to gather a new laurel, a laurel which you would not disdain to interleave with those of *Saffo.* I'm waiting, full of anxiety, for your reply: either tell me that I am to send you *Orazi,* or to set aside the poetry and then . . . *Stella*! Reply to me by the steamer, while I will not waste a single moment, and in the time I will write verses for *Orazi* and be ready with the other plot. I hope that this offer on my part will serve as proof of my zeal for Art, and of being

Your true friend
Salvadore Cammarano

Naples 5 September 1845.

Here was Cammarano, writing in early September about an opera needed for production in December; obviously the text of *Orazi e Curiazi* had not been completed, and Pacini had every right to complain to the management of the dilatoriness of the librettist assigned to the project. Even at this late stage, Cammarano was prepared to embark on a new subject, if Pacini felt himself unable to continue with *Orazi.* Pacini was in fact well advised to change horses in mid-stream; *Orazi e Curiazi* was undoubtedly a fine subject for an opera, and it had often been used before, but it suited the slow-moving, statuesque treatment that Mercadante was to bring to it a year later, rather than the more quicksilver treatment Pacini could offer. It is easy to see why Cammarano had difficulty with the hopelessly involved story of *Stella,* but to reverse the original choice, even at such a late stage, was probably the only way out. It is not clear if in offering to delay the production of the new opera, as he had done on an earlier occasion, Cammarano meant that he would be willing to intercede with the management to have the production rescheduled for a later date, or that he would contrive to drag out the preparations by subterfuge.

There is no more correspondence between Pacini and Cammarano on the subject of this project, but on 25 September the impresario wrote to the Superintendent of Theatres seeking permission for a change of subject. Pacini evidently accepted Cammarano's offer to work up *Stella* in the short time available, and the libretto was ready for submission to the censors on 6 November. The opera was produced, with the title *Stella di Napoli,* on 11 December 1845, just thirteen weeks after composer and librettist agreed on the subject. *Stella* is one of Cammarano's most confused and confusing texts: the source remains to be identified, but it reads as if it were a long five-act French drama. It is full of mistaken and disguised identities, coincidences and involved intrigue, and the source play probably required a great deal more attention than Cammarano was able to devote to it. Significantly, it is the only one of Cammarano's libretti to be preceded by a long *argomento* outlining the background to the plot, in the manner of older librettists like Rossi or Romani. The historical basis of the plot is to be found in the complicated relations between Naples and Spain in southern Italy at the end of the fifteenth century, but it would take more than a careful reading of the *argomento* to make much sense of the plot at first hearing. *Stella di Napoli* received eight performances at the S. Carlo in December 1845 and thirteen more in 1846, so it cannot altogether be rated as a failure, though it was revived only a few times in the following decade. It had the advantage of a first-rate cast, typical of a S. Carlo production of those years: Tadolini as Stella, Buccini as Olimpia; Fraschini as Armando, Coletti as Gianni di Capua; and such S. Carlo stalwarts as Arati, Benedetti and Salvetti in secondary roles.

After the first performance, the critic in *L'omnibus* gave it a long notice, for the most part elaborating the historical background to the plot (perhaps he felt that intending opera-goers were entitled to all the assistance they could get). He commended the poetry as always flowing and worthy of Cammarano, and went on to object to the development of the plot at two points, where the conduct of the individual characters departed from what was proper in art, or in social convention, as would befit historical personages. He concluded: 'This impartiality on our part should be clear proof of the high esteem in which we hold the fertile and poetic genius of Sig. Cammarano'. It is perhaps an odd notion that a minor point of criticism could be taken to provide proof of a lack of favouritism, but this remark does perhaps confirm the view that Cammarano was on good terms with the management of *L'omnibus.*

The following year – 1846 – was an important one in the annals of opera in Naples, since, as a letter from Flauto to Verdi of 4 July reveals, the management under the leadership of Guillaume (of which Flauto was administrator) was confirmed in office for the period up to Passion Sunday 1852. In fact, the Guillaume-Flauto management did not survive the upheavals of 1848, and so did not run its intended course. The contract with the Government contained a new element: the management had to keep the S.Carlo open only for the *carnevale* and autumn seasons, and were not required to open in the summer. Consequently in 1846, with the sole exception of an isolated performance of *Lucia di Lammermoor* on 10 May, there were no performances at the S.Carlo between 15 April, when Donizetti's *Gemma di Vergy* was given, and 4 October, when the autumn season opened with *Bondelmonte*. Pacini's opera had been performed regularly over the summer at the Fondo theatre, receiving over thirty performances.

However, once installed in 1846, Flauto lost no time in taking up with Verdi the contract he had earlier negotiated for an opera to follow *Alzira*. Flauto was in a position to offer good singers for 1847, or even for 1848, if Verdi preferred to wait till then. Verdi was willing to agree, on the understanding that he would not be required to journey to Naples to oversee the production. He added the usual stipulation that Cammarano's completed libretto should be in his hands four months before the anticipated date of performance, whether this was to be the autumn of 1847 or of 1848. In the event this project came to nothing, being overtaken by the change of management in 1848, but negotiations were resumed thereafter, leading eventually to the composition of *Luisa Miller* in 1849.

It was a full year from the production of *Stella di Napoli* before another Cammarano libretto came before the public, and when it did, it was the same *Orazi e Curiazi*, but this time with music by Mercadante. There is no extant correspondence between Cammarano and Mercadante covering their collaboration in the 1840s, no doubt because Mercadante was resident in Naples from 1840 onwards, as Director of the Conservatorio S.Pietro a

Majella – a post he held, despite his eventual blindness, till his death thirty years later. *Orazi e Curiazi* was first performed on 10 November 1846, although when the text was submitted for approval on 5 May, Guillaume mentioned that he wanted to give it on 4 October. It had been approved subject to corrections on 16 July. It received great applause, and by the end of that year had already been given nineteen times, despite the usual ten-day closure leading up to Christmas day. In January and February 1847 there were thirteen further performances, but on 1 March all the Neapolitan theatres were closed down for a period of three weeks. When they re-opened, *Orazi e Curiazi* was not revived. It received golden opinions when it was first heard: 'sublime' was the word used by Florimo, 'the culmination of an epoch for Mercadante', 'grandiose and solemn', 'spacious, immense' etc., though he was later to modify his opinion, insinuating that the success was due to the singers. It was certainly a first-rate cast, with Frezzolini, Fraschini and Balzar in the main parts, and with Salvetti, Arati and Rossi among the rest of the cast.

It was quickly produced elsewhere, but by the mid-1860s had disappeared; a single revival at the S. Carlo in 1882 was the last. It seems that it was usually given with grand effect, though some critics accused the composer of too much noise, too much sonority. Today, these criticisms certainly appear justified, as the music lacks harmonic mobility and the grandeur seems overblown. Interestingly *Orazi e Curiazi* was caught up in the patriotic and revolutionary fervour of the late 1840s – according to the Roman journal *Pallado*, when produced in Parma in February 1848 the words 'Guriamo per la patria o vincer o morir' emptied the theatre into the streets – the sort of situation we are apt to associate with the patriotic choruses of Verdi's earlier operas. These words are interesting: the Neapolitan libretto prints 'gloria' not 'patria'. As will be seen later, Cammarano's original text probably read 'patria' and the Neapolitan censors changed it to 'gloria'. Other similar expurgations can be found in this libretto.

The Cammarano/Mercadante opera was not the first to be based on this particular incident in the history of ancient Rome. There were several versions in the mid-eighteenth

century, and a libretto by Sografi was set with great success
by Cimarosa in Venice in 1796, and set again later by other
composers. Cammarano's libretto is based specifically on
Corneille's famous *Horace*. The story is taken from Livy's
history of Rome, and dates from around 650 BC. It tells
how the three Orazi brothers met in armed combat the
three Curiazi brothers, to decide the outcome of the
struggle between Rome and Alba. The fulcrum on which
the emotional balance of the story rests is the fact that an
Orazi sister (Camilla) is married to one of the Curiazi
brothers, and the drama is played out in terms of the
conflict of loyalties to which she is subjected. It is certainly
a fine libretto, well constructed and showing signs that
Cammarano had lavished unusual care on it (the vocabulary is richer and more judiciously employed than in many
of his texts), perhaps because with no other libretto being
required of him during the first part of 1846 he was able to
work without a feeling of pressure. There is no doubt it
suited Mercadante's current style, since the composer had
by that time lost sight of the good resolutions he had
adopted at the time of his earlier tragic masterpieces such
as *Il bravo* and *Il giuramento*. His serious operas had become static and grandiose, though his lighter ones, such as
Leonora (Teatro Nuovo, Naples, 1844), remained popular
over many years.

Cammarano was called onto the stage along with everyone else at the first performance, and *L'omnibus* noted
that even having studied the text with icy severity ('con
fredezza e severità'), they found it perfect: beautiful poetry,
sublime thoughts which recalled the austere times of
ancient Rome, the restrained and resolute conduct.

Two months later, another Cammarano libretto came
before the public, but this was short-lived and unsuccess-
ful. *Eleonora Dori*, with music by Vincenzo Battista, was
produced on 4 February 1847. The composer was born in
Naples in 1823, and studied at the Conservatorio there.
Despite his youth, this was his fifth opera; only the first,
Anna la Prie (S. Carlo, 28 March 1843) had had any success.
He devoted his life to composing operas, writing altogether
a dozen or so, notably to librettos by Domenico Bolognese.
Eleonora Dori was the first time he had worked with

Cammarano, but it is clear that all was not plain sailing. The story is taken from Alfred de Vigny's five-act French drama, *La Maréchale d'Ancre*, first produced in Paris in 1831, which had already been used for a libretto by Prati (one of the distinguished poet's two libretti, the other being *La vergine di Kent* for the composer Angelo Villanis (Turin, 1856)). It deals with the events of April 1617 and the fall of Concino Concini, the Marshall of Ancre, and his wife Eleonora Dori Galigai, two Florentines in the unfriendly court of Louis XIII in Paris. Jealousy of foreigners and an intrigue to discredit the Marshall's wife by exploiting the presence in Paris of one of her former Italian lovers lead to a tragic conclusion.

The libretto printed for the production of this opera contained a most unusual – possibly unique – three-page Preface signed by the Police Censor. It began:

> It is permissible for poets to alter history to make more beautiful poetry. But this facility is not limitless. One restraint is imposed by artistic caution, another by considerations of morality.

The censor went on to point out that people in history are in a dangerous position when their reputation rests more on the wayward imagination of a poet than on the impartial judgement of history. He then outlined the historical facts, and objected strongly to the degradation of such as Concini on the Italian stage – however he might be treated in other countries. In the final paragraph he wrote:

> ... the Censors, who prohibit or modify theatrical works (though not as lightly as some people think) would certainly forbid the performance of *Eleonora Dori*, at least in this form.

He concluded:

> Nevertheless, finding the poetry already clothed with music, the singers accustomed to singing their parts in the form in which they were written, and this new music promised and waited for, and on the other hand, time running out for putting the opera on stage since the contracts of the principal singers destined to sing it are about to expire, the Censors have allowed this unhappy event to take place. But, in yielding to the force of such considerations, the Censorship has required that these words be prefaced to the drama as solemn

witness to its repugnance that, in a public spectacle, igno-
miny should be heaped on men who do not deserve it, and
especially on illustrious Italians.

Something strange seems to have happened to the theatrical administration of Naples. The Censorship appears to
have lost its ability to see and assess the synopsis of works
before they were accepted for performance in the first
place. In this instance, the signs are that it did not wake up
to the nature of the plot until it was too late – the music
was written and the singers had learnt their parts. This
would suggest a couple of weeks, at the very most, before
the intended date of performance. There is, in fact, no
reference to this work in the extant papers of the Superintendency of Theatres. It is a measure of the political
uncertainty already building up in 1847 that the Censors
did not do as their predecessors would almost certainly
have done ten years previously, and just go ahead and
prohibit all performances, or, at least, require such modifications as might be thought necessary, as the price of their
approval. Rather than delay a work already prepared and
awaited, they backed down, merely insisting on a long and
verbose piece of self-exculpation.

Despite a first-class cast – the same singers who had
created *Orazi e Curiazi* a couple of months earlier – the
opera was only given four performances. *L'omnibus* noted
that while the libretto contained some beautiful verses
and ideas, the story was without interest. The haste evidenced from the censor's preface was confirmed by the
reviewer's remark that the old scenery used for the production was hissed, as it had upset the public, though the
costumes had pleased (perhaps they were new). There was
not a word in *L'omnibus* about the Censors' preface,
though the reviewer could not have failed to have read it.

While it is true that there were only four performances of
Eleonora Dori, perhaps because the season only lasted till
the end of February, Regli, in his dictionary, stated that it
had a splendid success, and that the principal pieces in it
became popular. For all that, it was never revived in Naples,
and was only very rarely given elsewhere.

CHAPTER SEVEN

1847–1849

Merope — The S. Carlo balance sheet — The events of 1848 —
Poliuto — *La battaglia di Legnano* — *Luisa Miller* — *Re Lear*

For his next libretto, Cammarano returned to collaboration with Pacini. His experience of working with this
composer had for the most part been very happy. They had
come together in 1840 with *Saffo*, which had already established itself as a major triumph, both in Italy and abroad.
La fidanzata corsa of 1842 had also done well, if by no
means as well as *Saffo*. *Bondelmonte* (1845) seemed to be
launched on a highly successful career. Only *Stella di
Napoli*, the result of a late change of heart and a quick
gestation, seemed to have fallen by the wayside. For their
next venture, Pacini and Cammarano took up an old and
well-tried subject, *Merope*. By the end of April 1847 they
were discussing it together; Pacini wrote to his librettist,
'The reasons you put forward for not proceeding with a
prologue to *Merope* have entirely convinced me, so that I
have nothing to add to the proposal'. He found the Introduction magnificent, and urged him to continue work on
the text. No doubt like all composers in their dealings with
their librettists he had at the back of his mind the fear that
it would come late.

In the event, the opera did not reach the stage of the
S. Carlo until seven months later, on 25 November 1847,
having been submitted for approval on 24 August. Why it
did not appear sooner is not now known – presumably it
was not ready, because when the theatres re-opened after
the usual September closure there were complaints in the
press that the management had not given the public a new
opera such as it had a right to expect. The first new production was Donizetti's *Gemma di Vergy*, and the S. Carlo
struggled on through October and November with a
scratch repertoire until the appearance of the new *Merope*.
The management was by this time in financial difficulties

and there is evidence in the Press of growing public dis-satisfaction. Added to this, there was much correspond-ence about the suitability of lighting the S.Carlo by gas, so it may well be that on top of their financial difficulties the management were faced with some intractable problems associated with the introduction of new technology.

The roster of singers had by this time changed. Barbieri-Nini was creating in *Merope* her first new role at the S.Carlo, as was the baritone Gionfrida. Egisto was sung by Fraschini, and the rest of the cast included Arati in the bass role of Polidoro, and Salvetti, as usual in the role of the heroine's confidant. The review in *L'omnibus* described the libretto as worthy of the author of *Saffo*, for verses that were smoothly-flowing, clear and, above all, restrained.

Merope is one of Cammarano's most straightforward libretti. He prefaced it – as he so often did – with a short announcement to the reader:

> Merope! After the unsurpassed tragedies (by Maffei, Voltaire and Alfieri) which carry at their heads this name, it would be more than boldness, it would be madness to return to the subject: but the action calls out for music, if not for poetry; therefore having been asked to collaborate for such a purpose, I decided on the present work, such as it is; and put in the position of having to award the golden apple to the most beautiful, I chose as my guide the *Merope* of Alfieri. If by chance I have sometimes departed too far from it, I hope I would have the indulgence of those who would give a thought to the severe laws of melodrama, and to the many constraints, the most inflexible laws.

Cammarano did not rely entirely on Alfieri's tragedy, and his libretto is far from being a condensation of it. He turned to Maffei, too, for instance for the role and name of Ismene, Merope's confidant – it would have been almost inconceivable that a heroine such as Merope could find her way through a libretto without a friend to lean on and to confide in. In most other respects he followed the outlines, and, as far as he was able within the compass of a libretto, the nobility of Alfieri's work.

Merope was, of course, a much used subject for operas in Italy, but nearly all previous settings used a libretto by Zeno, which was set more than twenty times between

1711 and 1776. Another text by Butturini, with music by Nasolini, appeared in Venice in 1796 – so that half a century had elapsed by the time Cammarano produced his version. This was a much more human treatment, concentrating on the agony suffered by Merope, given the choice by the tyrant who had murdered her husband and had usurped the throne, of either marrying him or seeing her only surviving son put to death before her eyes. The final scene is magnificently put together. In Alfieri's drama, Egisto (Merope's son) seizes the sacred axe from the priests and strikes the tyrant Polifonte down with one blow, in full view of the audience. (In Maffei and in Voltaire Polifonte's death and the manner of it are reported, not seen.) Cammarano has all his characters, except the populace, enter the temple for the wedding ceremony. The priests in the temple, unseen, begin to sing the nuptial hymn. Suddenly, in the middle of a line, they break off, and the people nearest to the threshold of the temple exclaim 'Oh Gods!' 'What is going on?' ask the ones further away. Those who can see into the temple reply, 'The Prince has brought the double-headed axe of the priests down on the head of Polifonte' and so on – a highly effective treatment of an incident that Cammarano would not perhaps have wished to put on the stage.

Violent death is not in fact all that common on the stage in Cammarano's libretti – many of his characters die, some commit suicide but really violent murder in full view of the audience is rare, and no doubt frowned on by the censors. There are, of course, exceptions – the final curtain of *La fidanzata corsa*, the closing scenes of *Orazi e Curiazi* and *Virginia*, for instance. The way in which Cammarano avoided the difficulty was masterly, and is reminiscent of some of his most skilful scenes such as the opening of *Saffo*.

Before the end of the year, *Merope* had been given twelve times: a further twelve performances followed in the first six weeks of 1848, after which it was dropped from the repertore. When Pacini came to write his memoirs, years later, he obviously confused the date of *Merope* (he was notoriously inaccurate on such matters) placing it in the same year as *Orazi e Curazi* (1846) and the year after *Stella*

di Napoli (1845). In setting about the composition of
Merope, he added, he had decided to move away from
accepted practice and write music in different styles to suit
the particular characters of the personalities – passionate
for Merope, energetic and agitated for Egisto, controlled
and disguised for Polifonte. He flattered himself that he
would be praised for this, but the results did not live up to
his hopes and the opera was never revived. It was perhaps a
pity that Pacini used this particular libretto as a vehicle for
experimentation, for it is certainly a good one, even if
Cammarano sometimes found it hard to get away from
some of the sentiments of the old opera seria for which the
subject was so obviously suited.

This was not the end of the libretto, however, since in
1871 it was set again, this time by Zandomeneghi, and
given in Pesaro. The production provoked the comment '. .
. on the stage, alas . . . Greeks of ancient Messene dressed
like present-day Albanians in white kilts [*gonellino*] and
with red *fez* on their heads.' This setting was a little more
successful, the opera being repeated in Turin four years
later.

1848 was, of course, a year of widespread political upheaval all over Europe, not least in Italy. Naples was no
exception, but before the armed uprising in the middle of
May the administration of the Royal Theatres was already
in grave financial difficulties. On Wednesday 26 April,
L'omnibus carried a long article about it by the owner-
editor, Vincenzo Torelli, himself, headed 'Our Royal
Theatres', demanding a new administration. He put forward three reasons for this: 1, The old management had
served the public badly. Everybody was complaining, and
everybody could not be wrong; 2, Funds had been em-
bezzled, so that the subscribers declared themselves
swindled, and demanded their money back; and 3, The
artists had been cheated, and hadn't been paid. Many had
been imprisoned for debt, others had been eaten away by
money lenders, some had died in desperation, and many
were unwilling sing in the theatres of Naples, or asked
double fees to come at all. Torelli then went on to draw up
a dummy balance sheet for the Royal Theatres, to show
that they could be run properly without making a loss – a

document of the greatest interest since it goes into details under each head of the expenditure. It may be argued that Torelli was not on the staff of the theatres and did not have access to the books, but he was a lawyer and journalist of great experience and standing in the artistic world of Naples and the centre of a group of poets and musicians. There is no reason to suggest that the figures he quoted in his budget were not accurate – or at least representative – and he certainly had people in his circle who were 'in the know'. His purpose may have been to bring about change, but the individual figures inserted are likely to be broadly accurate, at least as far as salaries etc. were concerned. The budget he drew up is so revealing, and gives such a good picture of the organization of an opera house, that it is worth quoting in some detail.

He begins with the cost of hiring singers. The three main 'stars', the soprano, tenor and bass (the term was then used to cover what we would now call baritone and bass) were to be under contract for nine months of the year only, from the opening of the S. Carlo at the end of May; singers of lesser status would have to be available for the whole year, and would be required to sing at the Fondo. The cost of employing singers, with monthly salaries shown in ducats, was broken down like this:

One prima donna, of special distinction	1,200
Another prima donna, of high repute	300
Another prima donna, of less repute, for *opere buffe*	150
Another prima donna, contralto	150
One primo tenor, of special distinction	900
Another primo tenor	150
Another primo tenor, for average roles	100
One primo bass of special distinction	800
Another primo bass	120
Two second tenors	60
Two second women	50
One primo Buffo of merit, for the Fondo	70
Other Buffos for the Fondo	50
Two third singers	30
50 choristers of both sexes	500
Total	4,630

The total makes it clear that 'two tenors . . . 60 ducats' means that they were paid 30 ducats each. When Torelli came to draw up his annual totals, he multiplied the principal singers' salaries by nine and the rest by twelve, so that the figures above represent the true monthly cost, not a figure adjusted to take into account the different periods of contract.

The difference in earning potential is, as expected, enormous, from the star soprano at 1,200 ducats a month to a chorister at 10. (In 1964, Weinstock in his book on Donizetti calculated the ducat as equivalent to just over two dollars then. A very rough approximation of one ducat to the pound sterling gives an idea of the order of remuneration.)

Torelli's next table gave a similar breakdown for the ballet company. The next covered the monthly production costs, in ducats, including the following details:

80 orchestral musicians (including one Violinist-Director)	1,060
Wardrobe	700
Scenery	750
Machinery (for both theatres)	400
Lighting	550
Properties	170

Obviously the orchestral players averaged about half as much again as the choristers, though evidence from other theatres shows that players were often paid at different rates in accordance with their position in the orchestra. Then came another fascinating table (monthly salary shown in ducats):

One poet, responsible for putting operas on the stage	50
Chorus-master	20
Deputy to Chorus-master	12
Director of Music	50
Composer of Ballet music	50
Maestro at the cembalo	15

Torelli then tabulated the cost of commissioning a range of operas and gave a detailed breakdown of the costs of administration. The total annual cost of running the two theatres came to 136,000 ducats, and he showed how this could be met from the Government grant (60,000 ducats), subscriptions to boxes (32,000 ducats), box office and miscellaneous receipts. He also urged the administration to engage a Director of Music 'in fact and not in name' and a Director of Productions with appropriate overall responsibilities.

From these tables of salaries, Cammarano's position stands out clearly. The salary quoted corresponds to that mentioned in the draft contract of several years previously (40 ducats monthly in one year, 70 in others), but it seems he was paid at the same rate as the director of music and the composer of ballet music; two-and-a-half times as much as the Chorus-master, five times as much as a member of the chorus, and three times as much as the average orchestral player.

At the end of the article Torelli added a paragraph dealing with the uproar that had broken out at a performance at the Fondo the previous Sunday. The same production had been repeated there on the Monday when, for the first time ever, the curtain had to be rung down in the face of the hostile reaction of the public. The next day, the theatres were closed down by ministerial order. (Torelli does not identify the opera at the Fondo which caused so much trouble; it was in fact Count Poniatowski's very popular *Don Desiderio.*)

The difficulties of the Royal Theatres were, of course, submerged in the wider problems of the times. Over the early months of 1848 political agitation had been on the increase; there were heated dscussions leading to the adoption of a constitution and, as elsewhere, revolutionary sentiments were in the air. Feelings reached bursting point in May and barricades were thrown up in the city. On 15 May the King ordered the Swiss Guard to open fire on those offering armed resistance, and this led to great slaughter, though order was quickly restored thereafter. Cammarano himself does not seem to have been politically minded, as his son bore witness, but one of the biggest barricades was in the Strada S.Brigida, where he lived (or, at least, had been living several years previously). His brother Luigi, who was one year younger than himself, was, however, an active revolutionary. He was arrested for his part in the uprising and hauled off to the ditches of the Castel Nuovo for execution by firing squad. The story goes that he was recognized by one of the Bourbon officers and set free.

For some three weeks following the closure of the Royal Theatres, there were no performances; on 14 May – on the eve of the uprising – there was an isolated performance at the Fondo of Verdi's *I due Foscari*, but for the next three days all theatres were closed as a result of 'the sad events of the 15th'. A further performance of *I due Foscari* was announced for 21 May, but it was cancelled. Prose drama at the Fiorentini theatre began again on 19 May, at the Sebeto and other 'prose' theatres soon afterwards, but no opera was given till the end of June. The Fondo opened first, on 25 June, with *I due Foscari*, and *L'elisir d'amore* on 29 June. The S. Carlo re-opened on 1 July, also with *I due Foscari* and the Nuovo on 15 July with Gravillier's *Il castello degl' invalidi*. Other operas were gradually introduced into the repertoire – at the S. Carlo, Verdi's *Ernani* and the always reliable *Parisina*.

As the correspondence between Verdi and Flauto reveals, the Government had revoked the licence held by the previous management, headed by Guillaume – according to Flauto, because of the many errors into which it had fallen after his own dismissal. It was replaced by a new management, headed by the tenor Berado Winter, with Achille Smitti and Flauto himself as his associates. By the end of August they were busy bringing order into the confused affairs of the Royal Theatres. They tried to persuade the sopranos Frezzolini and Tadolini to join the company, but they expressed themselves as having faith neither in the Impresario, in the Superintendent of Theatres nor in the Government. By the autumn season, however, the theatres were back in full swing, with a repertoire which included, as well as *Ernani*, Verdi's *I Lombardi*, *Attila* and *Nabucco* – a sign of the times, indeed, that Verdi had come so to dominate the operatic life of Naples.

On a more personal level, Verdi was also to dominate the rest of Cammarano's life, as they were rarely to be without a collaborative venture over the four years that remained to him. Following the performance of *Alzira*, Verdi had agreed to write an opera for the S. Carlo for the autumn of

1847 or 1848. In August 1848, as he had not received the libretto four months ahead of production as stipulated in his agreement, he wrote to Guillaume from Paris, formally but unilaterally cancelling his contract. Flauto wrote back, explaining the change in management. As Verdi had based his action on their failure to supply a libretto by the promised date, Flauto turned on Cammarano, who was already threatened with being sued for reimbursement of salary and possible imprisonment for his failure to deliver the libretto of a work called *Cora*; Cammarano did not know himself who was to write the music, and nothing more is ever heard of this project. Then, on 11 September, Cammarano wrote to Verdi in most anguished terms: he was desperate, and implored Verdi to help him, the father of six children, who had already received no salary for seven months (presumably since the failure of the Guillaume management in February) – would not Verdi save him from the precipice? On 24 September Verdi wrote back from Paris, agreeing to write an opera for the coming season, but for Cammarano's sake only. For his pains Verdi received a very smooth letter from Flauto, thanking him for the generous way he had got Cammarano out of trouble. Replying to Verdi, Cammarano added a footnote, saying that in case he was ever again put in a position of having to write something against his will, letters truly his own would begin 'Amico sempre a me caro'.

On 30 November came the long-awaited premiere of Donizetti's *Poliuto*, almost exactly ten years from when it should first have been staged, at the S. Carlo. Clearly the Neapolitan censorship was anxious to be seen in a more liberal light – the previous February had also seen the first performance in Naples of Donizetti's long-prohibited *Lucrezia Borgia*.

L'omnibus gave Cammarano its usual praise for the libretto of *Poliuto* – a beautiful, clear and sublime story, worked up with care and much warmth of feeling – 'we put it amongst the happiest of Cammarano's creations' – and considered that by it he showed himself worthy of filling the vacuum left by the silence of Romani. *Poliuto*, with Tadolini as Paolina (she had evidently overcome her doubts about appearing in Naples), Bouccardè as Poliuto

and Colini as Severo (and with Arati adding yet another
High Priest to his repertoire), was highly successful, running on for well over twenty performances over the following eighteen months.

During this time, Cammarano was also engaged in preparing a production of Verdi's *Macbeth* at the S.Carlo.
Verdi mentioned in a letter to Flauto that he wanted the
opera to be properly rehearsed; it was more difficult to do
than his others, and the *mise-en-scène* was important. He
confessed to a preference for this work of his, and would
not like to see it go wrong. The letter he wrote to Cammarano (also on 23 November) has been widely quoted, as
in it he complained that Tadolini was too good-looking,
and sang too well, for the part of Lady Macbeth (Mercadante would understand what he meant, wrote Verdi – a
rare compliment to another composer). He added some
instructions on how the apparition of the kings was to be
staged. Some sketches that Cammarano made for *Macbeth*
were published sixty years later by di Giacomo, and give
ample testimony to his artistic ability. *Macbeth* eventually reached the Neapolitan stage in January 1849.

In order to unravel the origins of Cammarano's next
major literary task it is necessary to go back to May 1847,
when Verdi suggested to his publisher, Ricordi, that he
should write an opera, which Ricordi should have produced at one of the major Italian opera houses (except La
Scala, Milan). This was, of course, flying in the face of
convention, since operas were normally still commissioned directly from the composer by the impresario.

By April 1848 Verdi and Cammarano were in correspondence about a subject for this projected opera. The
librettist turned down the idea of basing an opera on
Rienzi, although he had spent a lot of time, fruitlessly, on
it, because it didn't seem to him a dramatic subject – not
because there was no love interest in it – how could he
argue so, Cammarano went on, he who had given to the
Italian operatic stage *Belisario*, *L'assedio di Calais* and
Merope? He suggested instead *Congiura di Fieschi*, *Vespri
siciliani* or *Virginia* (the last being a long-standing interest
of Mercadante, and one which Cammarano was to prepare
for him a couple of years later). Or, better still, *La battaglia*

di Tolosa. This was a three-act play by Méry, first given in Paris in 1828, and regularly in the repertoire of the Fiorentini theatre in Naples, right through the 1830s and into the 1840s. 'If there burns in you as in me,' wrote Cammarano 'the desire to treat the most glorious epoch in Italian history, that of the Lombard League, nothing could be easier than to construct around the Battle of Legnano the same dramatic framework as is offered by Méry's drama, *La battaglia di Tolosa.*'

The suggestion must have found favour with Verdi and Ricordi, because by the middle of June Cammarano was writing to the publisher thanking him for offering to pay for the libretto which he was writing for Verdi, but refusing to accept any payment from him at that stage, firstly because he had scarcely begun work on it and secondly because the Naples management had asked him to do it. His understanding with Verdi was that if Naples did not wish to produce this opera, or was not in a position to do so, then payment for the libretto would become Ricordi's responsibility. Then and only then would he turn to Ricordi for payment. Considering that at that time Cammarano had already been without salary for some four months, his scruples on this occasion do him no little credit.

Méry's play is a domestic drama rather than an exercise in patriotic fervour: the battle and the associated events form the framework for, rather than the mainspring of, the action. It deals with a woman who, believing her lover dead, marries, at her dying father's request, an old friend of her lover. The lover is not dead, but has been away fighting in the army; he returns, but wishes to respect the marriage. On the evening before the battle, in which both men are to fight, the wife visits her old lover to explain her conduct and to say farewell. They are betrayed and discovered. The husband turns on them and locks them both in an upstairs room, in order to prevent his wife's lover fighting in the battle, this being the greatest punishment he could inflict. The lover leaps from the window and dies as the curtain falls.

Clearly, for the operatic stage the patriotic sentiments had to be treated explicitly rather than implicitly, and scenes of pageantry and glory grafted on. Consequently Cammarano had to embroider round the simple story an entirely new dimension, with grand choruses, swearings of oaths, and a full-scale patriotic finale in which the lover, having survived the leap from the window, saves the battle and returns to die a hero. If this is reminiscent of Meyerbeer and the Paris Opera, this is not altogether surprising, since Verdi was living in Paris for most of 1848, and his influence on the libretto was important – it was Verdi, for instance, who wanted Federico Barbarossa on the stage. But the most important influence on the opera was the events of 1848 and Verdi's desire to contribute to the future of Italy.

Correspondence between composer and librettist continued. On 11 July Cammarano wrote that he had added an act but was unwilling to further lengthen the work – but Verdi's idea of introducing Barbarossa had set him thinking. By September, Verdi was complaining that two months had elapsed without his receiving any of the text, and making some suggestions for the last act. Although Cammarano sent Verdi the third act on 9 October, Verdi does not seem to have received it by 21 October, when he addressed a furious letter to his librettist from Paris 'If you are unable to write it, tell me so frankly, but don't leave me in utter confusion'. With the third act Cammarano included, half apologetically, a number of practical details about how the text should be set to music. Three weeks later he despatched the fourth act, again with details of how he envisaged the text being set, how the stage band was to be deployed, etc. The words – dangerous words indeed in 1848 –

Chi muore per la patria
Alma si rea non ha!

were to be sung by all three voices together. The dying Arrigo was to raise himself up to sing 'È salva Italia' with enthusiasm, and was to complete the line with a failing voice, broken by his dying sobs. The Te Deum was to continue till the curtain was right down. And so on.

Although by the end of October Verdi had received all the libretto, this was not the end of the matter. The opera had been set down for performance in Rome at the end of January, but as late as 23 November Verdi asked for an additional scene for the prima donna and four new lines for the end of Act II. He also asked if Cammarano could see any objection to introducing a new part – perhaps a henchman for Arrigo – as he needed an additional tenor line in the Introduction. Within the last few weeks before performance he wanted some changes made in the text – and at the same time asked Cammarano if he had been paid by the Naples management or whether he would ask Ricordi to settle with him.

La battaglia di Legnano was produced on 27 January 1849 at the Argentina Theatre in Rome, with immediate success, the cast including de Giuli Borsi as Lida, Colini as her husband Rolando and Fraschini as Arrigo. For all its appeal to the spirit of the times – or perhaps because of it, as conditions of order were re-established – it was not widely revived during the ten years that followed. On 28 December 1848 – even before the first performance – Ricordi was in touch with Cammarano about an alternative version, with the action removed to the Flemish-Spanish wars, under the title, *L'assedio di Arlem;* Federico Barbarossa was to be replaced by the Duke of Alba, etc. These changes presented the librettist with major difficulties; he proposed to send the text act by act, as it was ready. Anxious to do his best for Ricordi, he had enrolled another poet to help him with the work. On 3 February, Cammarano formally renounced any rights he had in the libretto, adding a refusal to allow his name to appear on any libretto of the new version printed by Ricordi or by anyone acting for him.

Once *La battaglia di Legnano* had been launched, there still remained the opera Verdi had promised to write for Flauto, in order to help Cammarano out of trouble – a project which he remained very unhappy about. Before the first performance of *La battaglia di Legnano* Verdi wrote to Cammarano: 'If before I leave Rome you could send me the synopsis for the opera I shall be writing for Naples, I would be pleased. You will well remember that I am under no obligation to write this opera with you: consequently I will not write it if you do not tell me to do so.' On 14 February 1849 he wrote to Cammarano about the subject, *L'assedio di Firenze* (a subject Verdi had suggested to Piave six months previously). This would have been another highly patriotic opera, based on a romance by Guerrazzi dealing with the fall of the Florentine republic in the early sixteenth century. On 23 March he wrote again, setting out points of importance and enclosing a detailed synopsis of the layout of the last act, as he visualized it, even to the extent of drafting some snatches of dialogue. He concluded with his familiar call for verses.

A few weeks later Cammarano had to break the bad news to him that the project had been turned down by the censors, who had asked to see the synopsis of the proposed opera. Cammarano had submitted it for safety's sake under the title *Maria de' Ricci*, but it was returned as being 'inopportune in view of prevailing circumstances'. 'Placed in such a difficult position' continued Cammarano, 'I don't know what better to do than to return to a plot which you yourself once suggested, *Amore e raggiro* by Schiller, and while waiting for your reply I will draft a synopsis, so as to save time'. Warning Verdi not to overstep the mark, lest he encountered further obstacles, he suggested as an alternative *Cleopatra*, using Gerardini's play, which provided a great spectacle. Verdi replied on 26 April accepting the idea of *Amore e raggiro*, and on 3 May Cammarano sent him the synopsis, to which he had given the title *Eloisa Miller*. It is typical of Cammarano's synopses, a detailed prose description of the action, with the outline of certain stretches of dialogue.

Schiller's play *Kabale und Liebe* (1783) is a searing condemnation of the absolute corruption of absolute power, and is laid in one of the petty German states in the eighteenth century. The political ideas are worked out through the personal tragedy of a music master's daughter, who is in love with the son of the President of the Council, and he with her. His father, however, seeks to see him married to the Prince's mistress, and the consequent intrigues take their course until the lovers die by self-inflicted poison. Twenty years previously, Bellini had had in mind an opera on this subject, but had not been enthusiastic about it, hoping that Romani might have some other good subjects in his head.

Cammarano's synopsis emasculates the whole ideological content of Schiller's play, reducing it to a personal tragedy along the lines of true love never running smooth. It is hard to see what else he could have done, bearing in mind the constraints set upon him by the rejection of *L'assedio di Firenze* and his own strictures to Verdi. The whole ethos of the Schiller play was jettisoned – for instance the deeply interesting figure of Lady Milford, the Prince's mistress, disappears, her place being taken by a young widowed Countess. He also moved the action to Tyrol. Flauto and Cammarano followed up the synopsis two weeks later with a tabulated distribution of the arias, concerted pieces and the like, drawing attention to the problem of how to cast the second soprano part, since it could not be made dramatically important and might be best allocated to a *comprimaria* singer.

Verdi's response to the synopsis was characteristic and detailed. He would have preferred two prima donna parts, and would have wished the second to have been the prince's mistress, just as in Schiller, but he didn't wish to press the point. The intrigue between Count Walter (as the President was to be called) and his steward Wurm seemed colourless besides Schiller's. He did not want a stretta or a cabaletta in the first act finale. He detailed the way he wanted that act to end, paraphrasing the end of Schiller's (second) act. Verdi was also unhappy with the layout of the second act of the opera: he wanted to expand the duet between Eloisa and Wurm, and to have an unaccompanied quartet after the duet between Wurm and Walter. The second part of the act, in his view, ended coldly – after having had a full-scale ensemble to end the first act, would it really do to end the second with just two people on the stage? The third act was most beautiful. He finished 'a tutta voce' by demanding verses.

Cammarano sent Verdi the first act finale on 4 June. Verdi's reaction to the synopsis had just come, he added, but he would reply in detail later. Meanwhile he sent the verses, noting that Verdi's idea that Eloisa's father could have been a soldier wasn't bad; also – a practical touch – the archers would be the basses of the chorus while the tenors and the women would make up the peasants.

Cammarano's response to Verdi's letter provides a most

interesting insight into how he saw his role as a librettist:

> If I were not afraid of being branded as Utopian, I would be
> tempted to say that to obtain the greatest possible perfection
> in an opera, one single mind should be author of both words
> and music: from this notion it follows that my view is that
> where two authors are involved they must at least identify
> with each other, and that even if the words should not be the
> servant of the music, they should not dominate it. Convinced
> of this maxim, I have always worked in conformity with it,
> and the composers with whom I have shared my work were
> always consulted by me on the subject matter.

Having thus established his position, he replied point by
point to Verdi's letter. Schiller's concept of the Prince's
mistress was sublime and he found it difficult to defend
the way he had suppressed the role – but necessity forced
him to do so. To augment the part would destroy the
dramatic balance, and even so no prima donna would agree
to sing the part of a Prince's mistress. The intrigue had
been diluted, yes, but augmenting some of the bass parts to
increase its significance would cause difficulties over casting (though not at the S. Carlo, where they had three basses,
de Bassini, Selva and Arati, available – but what about
other theatres?). As to the layout of the second act, anything added after the end of what he had proposed would be
superfluous; it would be possible to change the order of the
pieces so as to end with the quartet, but this would mean
two arias immediately following each other. Why not bring
on the chorus and otherwise end the act as in his synopsis?

A fortnight later, Cammarano wrote that he had been
thinking about the end of the second act, and still thought
his original idea (of a tenor aria) would be best – particularly if set to music by Verdi and sung by an artist of the
first rank – and if the tempo could be quickened towards
the end of the piece. The curtain could then be brought
down amidst tumultuous applause. In this way the act
would not end with an anticlimax. The quartet was an
essential link in the dramatic chain but to move it would
put it in the wrong place – anyway he had done a similar
scene in *Elena da Feltre*.

At the end of July Flauto wrote to Verdi and enclosed
some more verses from Cammarano, who himself wrote

on 13 August with the rest of the libretto. He had moved Count Walter's cantabile from Act II to Act I, so as to avoid too long a string of pieces in Act II, and to give Count Walter something to sing in Act I. There is thereafter no further correspondence about the libretto which was submitted for approval on 17 September and allowed on 24 September, though in October Cammarano thought it wise to warn Verdi that the finances of the management were in a bad way. Verdi, who by this time had arrived in Naples, responded by reminding Flauto that he had written this opera only to render a small service to Cammarano and asked to be paid in advance.

Luisa Miller was produced at the S. Carlo on 8 December 1849, and remained in the repertoire for several years. The original cast included Gazzaniga as Luisa and Malvezzi as Rodolfo. The three bass parts were allocated to de Bassini (Miller), Selva (Count Walter) and Arati (Wurm). Another S. Carlo stalwart, Salvetti, appeared in her familiar role of heroine's friend.

The libretto – duly praised in *L'omnibus* – is of great interest; apart from anything else, it is one of Cammarano's longest, as if he had learnt from experience that Verdi's style of setting words to music led to excessive brevity and condensation when applied to a libretto of conventional dimensions. It is also free from confusions and loose ends (though the second prima donna role is certainly unsatisfactory), and even though much of Schiller has gone, the story is credible and professionally assembled. The device of throwing the concerted finale forward from its pivotal place at the end of the second act to the end of the first was not new, and in *Luisa Miller* gives more time for the resolution of the plot. At the same time, it raised the problem of how to end the second act (the third can be expected to end itself) and this, as we have noted, caused composer and librettist no little trouble. Cammarano's solution was bold – the gradual piling up of tempo and intensity produces an exciting climax. As he had foreseen, to have ended with a quartet would have evoked comparison with the full-scale finale of Act I. The libretto as a whole gives the impression that Cammarano lavished a great deal of care on it – whether this was from working with a composer who really was interested in what his librettist was doing, or the inherent dramatic possibilities that Schiller had presented to him, or the fact that it was this opera which had saved him from prison, is now impossible to say; but the correspondence suggests the first of these.

There was, in fact, more than the threat of prison to worry Cammarano over these months. Whether as a result of the deteriorating financial situation of the management or because of a personal vendetta against him (which the evidence suggests to be more likely), Flauto had not been paying Cammarano his wages. On 1 September 1849 Cammarano wrote to Flauto reminding him that he had not yet received his July salary; since he had not wanted to interrupt the work he was doing for Mercadente (in fact, on the libretto of *Virginia*) he had not come in person about it. He wrote again a week later, still not having received his salary for July, and in despair since he could not meet his urgent domestic bills. On 11 September he wrote to Flauto yet again. He had sent round to the Administration, only to find that nothing had been provided for him, despite Flauto's promises, and he didn't know which way to turn. On 4 October he had to write once again. He really was at the end of his tether; some private lessons had ceased, and he had only his salary from the theatre. This was insufficient for the barest needs of his family, with six children to educate. He used to be able to borrow from his father, but his sister had died, and the poor old man had accepted responsibility for her children. He was, by his contract, paid for his work after it had been completed; he could afford to wait till the end of the month, but after that everything would go to rack and ruin. He could manage by pawning, as he had done between 1 and 19 September, but this had affected his health and he had been unable to work. He hadn't wanted to refer to this, as it would appear to be a threat – 'pay or I won't work' – and this was not his attitude. He wasn't asking for his September salary, but he had to have August's. Ten days later, at Flauto's suggestion, he sent someone round to the Administration again. The cashier had some money, and was paying out, but had no instructions about *his* salary. He was in despair.

It seems from these letters that he had finally obtained his July salary on 19 September, but since it is not known if the correspondence was continued, we shall never know if his letters had the desired effect. (These letters were found in the Lucchesi-Palli library by Frank Walker, and published by the Institute of Verdi Studies, Bulletin 8.)

As if Flauto's failure to pay his salary was not enough, Cammarano was also in dispute with his landlord, the Duke of Friso. Repairs recently made had been skimped, and there wasn't a room where the rain wasn't coming in. The sitting room was bad enough, but the kitchen ceiling was in such a state, with all the mortar washed away, that it was in danger of collapsing. Poor Cammarano!

Despite all his difficulties with the Neapolitan management, Verdi reached agreement with Flauto for another opera, to be given 'the day after Easter 1850'. As Easter day in 1850 fell on 31 March, he had some six months to choose a subject, receive the libretto, write the opera and see it on the stage. He told Flauto he would need to have the synopsis and the first verses from Cammarano by October (when he was expecting to be leaving Naples following the production of *Luisa Miller*). He also told Flauto to suggest to Cammarano that they might do *Le Roi s'amuse* by Victor Hugo – it was a splendid drama with stupendous situations, with two magnificent parts for Frezzolini and de Bassini.

After this, matters became rather complicated. When he had returned home from Naples, Verdi wrote to a friend that he was glad to know that Cammarano had finished work on *Virginia*, for he could then get down to work on the opera they were going to do together. He hoped that Cammarano would produce something worthy of himself and of the subject – something with good sense in it, however rare that might be in the theatre, but worth the efforts of artists of conscience such as Cammarano and himself: but no word of the identity of the actual subject.

Writing to Ricordi on 31 January 1850, Verdi expressed himself as disgusted by the behaviour of the Neapolitan authorities. He had broken off negotiations for an opera, but as the subject was already settled with Cammarano he proposed to write the opera all the same. He offered the opera to Ricordi to place in an appropriate theatre; it would be ready in four or five months. In the event, things did not work out quite as planned. Verdi had two commitments, both involving Piave as librettist – the 'Ricordi' opera (*Stiffelio*, eventually allocated to Trieste) and one for Venice, which turned out to be *Rigoletto*, taking up the suggestion of *Le Roi s'amuse* which he had made earlier to Cammarano. What then was the subject 'fixed' with Cammarano referred to in the letter of 31 January? If it was *Le Roi s'amuse*, it obviously fell through, but later correspondence suggests that composer and librettist had already set their sights on *King Lear*, a subject which had been in Verdi's mind as early as 1843. On 28 February, Verdi sent Cammarano an outline; the subject was vast and complicated, he wrote, and would have to be treated in a completely new way, without any regard to any theatrical convention whatsoever. At the foot of the outline Verdi added some observations, in pencil, and these were printed by di Giacomo in 1904, from a document now in the Lucchesi-Palli library in Naples. They appear to be points he noticed about the Shakespeare play, rather than the projected opera: 'Many characters, amongst whom 11 principals'; '26 changes of scene, needing 18 or 19 sets'; 'The fool is mad, Lear becomes mad, Edgardo pretends to be mad'. He then lists sixteen instances of violence, either on the stage or reported, and finishes 'But, dear friend, this is not an opera, but a veritable bloodbath. These are all obstacles . . . for the censor!'

Verdi was clearly under no illusions as to what he had taken on, and it is not perhaps surprising that a few months later he had to admit to a friend 'Inevitably these huge plots require too much time, and for the moment I have had to abandon also *Re Lear*, leaving Cammarano the task of adapting the drama at some more opportune moment'.

When Cammarano died, one of Verdi's first thoughts was to retrieve from his papers this synopsis of *Re Lear*. The libretto was completed in the end by Somma, but it was never set to music.

CHAPTER EIGHT

1850–1852

Virginia — Non v'è fumo senza fuoco — Folco d'Arles —
Medea — Malvina di Scozia — Il trovatore

It is now necessary to turn back to the autumn of 1849. Cammarano had completed work on *Luisa Miller* by the middle of August. On 5 November, the Superintendent of Theatres wrote to Mercadante – who had evidently complained of Cammarano's delay in providing a text – that he had given the librettist till 15 November to produce it, otherwise he would face the full rigours of the law. Writing to the composer again on 19 November he said he was unwilling to move against Cammarano while he was producing another opera on the stage (*Luisa Miller*) but he was sure Cammarano would get to work with his customary diligence. By the end of December, Verdi could write that Cammarano had finished *Virginia*, and could return to their joint project; *Virginia* had been submitted for approval on 17 December.

It may thus be inferred that the autumn and early winter were devoted to *Virginia*, which was written for Mercadante. It was the third Roman subject of their collaboration (the others being *La vestale* (1840) and *Orazi e Curiazi* (1846)), and was taken directly from Alfieri's tragedy of the same name, written in 1777/8 when the poet was twenty-eight years old. It was a subject which Cammarano had previously suggested to Verdi, but one which Mercadante had had his eye on for a long time – in December 1839 he had written to the authorities of the Fenice theatre in Venice suggesting it as a suitable subject for an opera he was to write for them (in the same letter he suggested *Nabucco*). Although production of the Mercadante-Cammarano opera was set down for 1851, it was prohibited by the censors, and did not appear till 1866. This prohibition is not altogether surprising, as the story of *Virginia* deals with a direct challenge to established authority. It tells of Virginia, who is sought after by Appio, the leader of the Decemvirs. He is rejected by her in favour of Icilio, a distinguished plebeian. To possess her, Appio arranges for his associate Marco to claim her as a slave born in his house and therefore belonging to him – a claim which is fiercely resisted by her parents. When the courts find in favour of Marco, Virginia's father stabs her rather than see her handed over. It is a noble subject (coming originally from Book III of Livy, though believed not to have any historical foundation) and one which had been the basis for a number of operas, those most recent having been by Nini (with libretto by Bancalari; Genoa 1843) and by Vaccai (libretto by Giuliani; Rome 1845). In the interval between 1851 when Mercadante's opera was written and 1866 when it was produced, Petrella's *Virginia*, with libretto by Bolognese, was given at the S. Carlo, in 1861. All these libretti are notably inferior to Cammarano's, and in no way catch the grandeur and nobility of the subject as his does. It is a libretto full of fine feeling and language, clearly written with Alfieri's drama open on the writing desk, and the reduction of the drama to the confines of a libretto was done with dexterity and an eye to situations of operatic effectiveness, while remaining fully within established conventions.

Mercadante retained a fondness for this opera, and although often asked for it, declined to release it. 'She is sleeping well, closed up in a folder, and therefore does not need to eat . . . let her sleep, for it certainly isn't an everlasting sleep. When times are better she will wake up, and the public will then see if she deserves to be forgotten'. In 1866 he agreed to its performance at the S. Carlo, accepting the – by that time – modest payment of 15,000 lire. It was performed on 7 April by a cast which included Lotti della Santa as Virginia, Pandolfini as her father, Mirate as Appio – and Arati, still singing with the company, as he was for a further twelve years, as Marco. The composer, by then blind, received a tremendous ovation for what was considered to be his swan-song.

The next Cammarano text to reach the stage was one of his very few comic works, *Non v'è fumo senza fuoco*, with music by his brother Luigi, whose career seems not to have been sufficiently affected by his part in the 1848 uprisings to prevent him being allowed to present an opera on the stage of the Royal Theatres. It was produced at the Fondo on 3 August 1850, where it received four performances; two more at the S. Carlo followed, and the following year it was transferred to the Nuovo theatre, where it ran successfully for several years. The libretto was based on a *comédie-proverbe* in one act by Bayard, *Pas de fumé sans feu*, first given in Paris in September 1849, and soon thereafter at the Fiorentini theatre in Naples, where it was announced as 'a comic burlesque' (*una burla comica*). It concerns a husband who suspects that his wife has a lover, since he smells tobacco smoke in the house when he returns home for lunch. He finds out in time that his wife has a secret vice – she smokes! It is a plot subsequently made familiar to opera-lovers through a much later setting, Wolf-Ferrari's *Susanna's Secret* (*Susannens Geheimnis*, Munich 1909).

The opera by the brothers Cammarano is a trivial piece, and when it was revived at the Nuovo in 1852, a few weeks before the death of the librettist, *L'omnibus* wrote 'In the farce *Non v'è fumo senza fuoco* Cammarano has abandoned his pure and dignified style, and he shouldn't have bothered with it'. His task had been a light one, as the libretto is a straightforward condensation of Bayard's little piece. It was later taken up by the Neapolitan composer Lauro Rossi and set to music again, under the title *Lo zigaro rivale*, and given in Milan in 1867. The title is sometimes wrongly given in books of reference as *Lo zingaro rivale*, but only in total ignorance of the title page or the subject. Its late date has also confused cataloguers, and its authorship ascribed to Cammarano's son Goffredo.

The only other record of Cammarano's activities in 1850 concerns an event which must have been a very happy one for him: at their meeting in June, the Accademia delle Belle Arti proposed that he should be elected to membership in the class of writers. The King gave his assent on 22 September and the diploma was duly signed and sealed on 12 October.

At this time Cammarano was working on a libretto for Nicola de Giosa. In August *L'omnibus* had announced that this composer was to write three operas: a *semi-seria* for the Nuovo, with a libretto by de Lauzières, one for the S. Carlo, with a libretto by Cammarano, and a 'brilliant' one for the Pergola theatre in Florence, with a libretto by Tarantini, but of these three only that for the S. Carlo actually reached the stage. De Giosa, who was born in Bari in 1820, wrote a number of successful operas. He is perhaps best remembered as the resident musical director in Cairo at the time of the projected production of Verdi's *Aida*, whom Verdi sought to supplant. (When the post of conductor in the present sense was instituted at the S. Carlo in the 1860/61 season, he and Guiseppe Puzone took turns at the rostrum.)

The subject which Cammarano prepared for the S. Carlo opera for de Giosa was the one he had worked up for Donizetti in 1842, Victor Hugo's *Ruy Blas*. That project had come to nothing. Cammarano resurrected the synopsis and rewrote it with a new title, *Folco d'Arles*, laying out the action into acts and scenes. These two synopses, and many sheets of his rough drafts, covering in all about two-thirds of the final text, mostly in pencil on odd pieces of paper, have been preserved and give a fascinating glimpse at his working methods (to be discussed later). In the process of adaptation to the operatic stage, all the 'bite' of Hugo's play had to go. The action was transferred to fifteenth-century Provence, and became a typical story of rejected love and revenge. Arturo has been spurned by the Countess of Provence; intent on revenge he dresses up his servant Folco as a knight long believed to be dead, and introduces him to her court. When she falls in love with Folco, Arturo insists that he rejects her offer of marriage and reveals his servile position. Folco takes poison, seeking the Countess' forgiveness and her recognition of his true feelings towards her. If the action is at times rather condensed and thus contrived, the story is straightforward with plenty of dramatic situations.

The opera was given at the S. Carlo on 22 January 1851 and proved a modest success. De Giosa remained attached to it, and sought to have it revived at the S. Carlo ten years later (he told his publisher that the rights could be brought back from the 'Ex-kingdom of the Sicilies' for three or four hundred ducats). It had in the meantime been produced occasionally elsewhere. The cast at the first performance was first class: Tadolini, Baldanza and de Bassini in the important roles, with Arati as the Grand Chancellor and Salvetti as the Countess' lady-in-waiting. Critical reaction to the libretto was favourable – verses worthy of Cammarano, plot well articulated – but *L'omnibus* attacked the credibility of Folco's 'behaviour in rejecting the Countess after having been ennobled by her, and returning to a life of servitude at the bidding of his master – though this, the critic admitted, could be partially explained by the old feudal laws.

Six weeks after the production of *Folco d'Arles*, another opera bearing Cammarano's name reached the stage of the S. Carlo. This was *Medea*, with music by Mercadante, and it was given on 1 March. The printed libretto carries a note: 'The text is partly by Felice Romani, partly by Salvadore Cammarano'; it was based on an old libretto, *Medea in Corinto*, written by Romani for Mayr as long before as 1813. It dates, in fact, from Romani's first year as a librettist, and must have appeared very old-fashioned and stereotyped in 1851. It was obviously unsatisfactory as it stood for a new Mercadante opera and required a great deal of attention if anything was to be made of it. A comparison between Romani's original *Medea in Corinto* with Cammarano's version shows that Cammarano began by reducing its length from about 750 lines to 550 – there is a general tendency over the nineteenth century to reduce the length of libretti from about 1,000 lines in 1800 to 600 by 1850, though many of Romani's are long even for the time they were written. At the same time, he divided it into three acts instead of Romani's two. Of the 550 lines in the Cammarano version, only 110 are taken from Romani's original. Clearly the extent of rewriting is large enough to justify treating the libretto – with appropriate reservations – as almost an independent work by Cammarano. Many scenes are omitted, all those remaining are rewritten in part, some wholly. The main thrust of the changes is, however, to shed the abstract, stereotyped response of the characters to the circumstances in which they find themselves and to replace it with human emotion. The rejected

Medea becomes a woman very much of flesh and blood – 'Are you offering me only pity? I want your love . . . I want Jason's wedding bed'. In 1813 Romani could end his libretto with thunder and lighting, Medea crossing the stage in a chariot pulled by two dragons, but not Cammarano, whose Medea throws to Jason the bloody dagger with which she has just murdered their children.

Despite the identity of the plot, the characters and the development of the dramatic action, the two libretti inhabit two totally different worlds, Romani's formalized and restrained, Cammarano's full of intense emotion, with rapid interchange of dialogue at highly-charged moments in the drama. Rolandi, in his book on Romani, notes that Cammarano's version was probably made with the permission of the original author. Although the appearance of both librettists' names would tend to suggest this, it still seems to me unlikely. It was an old libretto, and libretti were frequently re-used and adapted (though not perhaps as extensively as here) and permission would not normally have been expected. Besides, there is some evidence that Romani and Cammarano were not on the best of terms.

When staged at the S. Carlo, *Medea* had the benefit of a fine cast – de Bassini (Jason), his wife Rita Gabussi (Medea); the main tenor role (Timante) is of less importance but was sung by Baldanza. Arati sang Creonte, and Salvetti, Medea's attendant. It was not very well received, although one critic compared it not too unfavourably to *La vestale*. It ran to double figures in Naples, but does not seem to have been performed elsewhere.

At the very end of the same year (1851) came Cammarano's last collaboration with Pacini. On 1 October, *L'omnibus* announced: 'The celebrated Maestro Commendatore Giovanni Pacini is amongst us. He is to write a new opera for the S. Carlo to a new libretto by our beloved Cammarano'. Three weeks later the title was announced, *Malvina di Scozia*. On 8 November came another bulletin, 'The new opera by Pacini for the S. Carlo is finished. It is called *Malvina di Scozia*. It will be performed after the 15th of the month'. Then a silence: on 3 December, 'Maestro Pacini has handed over his new opera, all finished'. It was finally produced at the S. Carlo on 27 December.

In his Memoirs, Pacini tells how the opera came to be written in the form it was – that de Bassini was angry with him as his music never seemed to suit his voice. Meeting by chance in the street, they made it up, and Pacini decided then and there to entrust de Bassini with the major role in his new opera.

The libretto *Malvina de Scozia* has nothing to do with Ossian, however likely that might appear at first sight. As Pacini was well aware himself, it is a re-working of Cammarano's early *Ines de Castro*, long since prohibited. In the event, much of the libretto was completely rewritten, though by no means as much as in *Medea*; about half of it was new. Faced with the censor's prohibition, Cammarano took his usual escape route and moved the action to Scotland, this time to the tenth century. For the King of Portugal, he substituted a King of Scotland; his son Don Pedro becomes Arturo; Ines became Malvina; her rival becomes Morna, daughter of the King of Ireland; the villainous Gonzales becomes Wortimer (a villainous-sounding name, indeed – perhaps a corruption of Mortimer?). Pacini's Memoirs continued: with the trio of singers mentioned – Cortesi (Malvina), Borghi-Mamo (Morna), de Bassini (Arturo), and with the addition of Arati (the King of Scotland), he was consoled by a happy outcome. The distribution of singers in *Malvina di Scozia* is extremely interesting: Cortesi and Borghi-Mamo were sopranos, but de Bassini was a primo baritone; Arati was a bass. In his desire to write a good part for de Bassini, Pacini gave him the equivalent role to that which the famous tenor Duprez had created at the first performance of *Ines de Castro* fifteen years previously. The other two small male parts in *Malvina* are Wortimer, sung by Laudani, a *comprimario* tenor, and the chief of the royal archers, sung by Benedetti, who was often called upon for such roles; he was a *secondo* bass – that is, he was a bass of second rank, not a *basso profondo*. The only other member of the cast was the ever-present Salvetti, singing the role – what else? – of Malvina's attendant. What Pacini did was to write an opera without a part for a primo tenor.

In many ways, *Malvina* is a clearer plot to follow than is *Ines de Castro*, which is long and confused – though it should be recalled that Cammarano was only responsible for the versification of Bidera's synopsis of that libretto. Although there is no record of a production of *Malvina* outside Naples, the copy of the Neapolitan libretto in the British Library has the first scene of Act III removed, the subsequent pages being renumbered in what looks like a contemporary hand. While this would shorten a not-overlong libretto, it would make nonsense of the story, though not perhaps in ways which would have created difficulties for the audience.

Whatever Pacini may have said in his memoirs about the success of *Malvina di Scozia*, it did not remain long in the repertoire. As for Cammarano, it was the last of his works that he was to see launched on the stage. He was already ill, and the last few works he produced – with the notable exception of *Il trovatore* – were all in one way or another 'second time round'. *Folco d'Arles* used a synopsis he had had up his sleeve for some years, waiting for an opportunity to be worked up; *Medea* was an almost rewritten version of an old libretto, *Malvina di Scozia* was an adaptation of *Ines de Castro*. Possibly with his health failing, Cammarano found it desirable, if not actually necessary, to husband his creative writing as far as he could.

Throughout the whole of 1851, and until his death in July 1852, Cammarano was deeply involved in his last collaboration with Verdi, over the libretto of *Il trovatore*. When the suggestion of an opera on the subject of *King Lear* had fallen through – and Verdi admitted as much in the middle of June 1850 – the search for another suitable subject continued unabated. 'I once wrote for Paris a libretto which Mercadante was going to set to music', wrote Cammarano. 'His contract fell through, but the libretto remains the property of the Maestro, because he paid for it. I haven't had time to see Mercadante, but I am almost certain that he would cede it back to me, and I would write him another, later, at a more suitable time'. He went on to identify it as *Caterina Medici di Brono*, to outline the distribution of roles and to conclude: 'the libretto was worked up by me, if I may say so, with all my usual conscientiousness, and if it did not please, it was not my fault'.

If Cammarano ever did approach Mercadante with this

proposition, he was unsuccessful. Mercadante held on to this libretto and returned to it late in life, by which time he was completely blind.

In March 1851, Verdi went to Venice to oversee the first performance of *Rigoletto*. As soon as he had returned home to Busseto, he wrote to the impresario Lanari about a contract for an opera for Bologna. 'The libretto will be at my cost, and I hope it will be by Cammarano'. The contract fell through, but the correspondence between composer and librettist led to the production of *Il trovatore* nearly two years later. Some letters must have passed between them before March 1851, since on 29 March Verdi wrote to his Neapolitan friend de Sanctis; he had turned down the offer of a contract from Colombo (then the impresario of the Royal Theatres). He went on:

> I am absolutely furious with Cammarano. He gives no thought at all to time, which for me is an extremely precious commodity. He has not sent me a word about this *Trovatore*: does he like it or not? I don't know what you mean about the difficulties either of good sense or of theatre!! After all, the more Cammarano gives me novelty, freedom of form, the better I shall do. However, let him do as he wants: the bolder he is the happier I'll be. Just let him bear in mind that the public demands brevity. You are a friend of his, so beg him not to lose another minute. Even though I'm furious with Cammarano, give him a kiss from me.

Verdi's anger with Cammarano was perhaps a little premature, for a letter from the librettist dated 27 March was already in the post. From Verdi's reply to it, it is clear that he had found a number of difficulties in the idea of converting García Gutiérrez' sprawling five-act *El Trovador* into an opera. This Spanish drama, first seen in Madrid in 1836, is an extraordinary work, excessively romantic and highflown in every sense, with a number of highly-coloured threads woven through a background of civil war, love and vengeance. Behind the incidents portrayed on the stage lie Spanish concepts of honour and duty. The events which provided a springboard for the action of the play took place a long time before the action opens – the old Count of Luna (adopting the names of the characters which Verdi and Cammarano eventually settled upon) had burned an old

gypsy woman at the stake, thinking she had turned the evil
eye on his baby son. Her daughter, Azucena, heard her
dying mother call for her to revenge her death, and snatched
up the Count's son, meaning to throw him, too, on a
funeral pyre. Being carried away by emotion she consigned
her own son to the flames by mistake. (Just the sort of
situation which caught the withering eye of W. S. Gilbert.)
When the action begins, the old Count is dead, and his
surviving son rules in his place. Spain is in the grip of a civil
war. Manrico, brought up by Azucena in ignorance of his
origin, falls in love with Leonora, whom the new Count
wants for himself. She takes the veil to escape from an
impossible situation, believing Manrico killed in a duel
with the Count. The Count plans to abduct her, but Manrico bears her away. When Manrico is captured by the
Count, she offers herself for his life, but commits suicide.
As Manrico is sent to the scaffold, Azucena tells the Count
that he has killed his own brother – 'you are revenged, oh
mother!'

Verdi's reply to Cammarano's objections was dated 4
April. In it he makes a number of points: if Cammarano
didn't like the idea of *Il trovatore* why didn't he come up
with something better? The scene where Leonora took the
veil would have to be included – it was very original and
should be played for all it was worth. If the new nun
(Leonora) could not be allowed to flee with Manrico of her
own free will (presumably Cammarano had anticipated
objections from the censors), she could always be carried
away by him in a fainting condition. Azucena had not
saved herself and her son (at the end of the play) because
she was charged with avenging her mother; the last words
of the play are 'You are avenged'. Part of Verdi's letter is
worth quoting *in extenso*:

> With regard to the distribution of pieces, let me tell you that
> when I come to set words to music, all forms and distribu-
> tions are good, and the newer and more original they are the
> better I am pleased. If in operas there were to be no cavatinas,
> no duets, no terzets, no choruses, no finales etc, and the
> whole opera were to consist, so to speak, of one single piece, I
> would find it more rational and right. So I will tell you it
> would be better if you can avoid beginning the opera with a

chorus (all operas open with a chorus) and a cavatina for
Leonora, but begin directly with the troubadour's song and
make one act out of the first two (of the play). These isolated
pieces with scene changes between them seem to me to be
more appropriate for concerts rather than operas. If you *can*
do it. However, I'm not too pleased about Manrico being
wounded in a duel. For the rest, do as you think best.

It is clear from this letter that Verdi's musico-dramatic
development had taken him far beyond the conventional
concepts of operatic organization of the times. The idea of
the 'continuously-composed' opera is, as Julian Budden
has pointed out, that of a Berlioz or a Wagner. It was too
much to expect of Cammarano, who was incapable of
anything quite so revolutionary – though he was by no
means averse to innovation. The detailed synopsis Cammarano sent to Verdi (it is not dated but must have been
sent very soon, since Verdi replied to it on 9 April) consists
of four very closely written sheets, with fifty lines on each
– some 2,500 words in all. It differs from other synopses of
his only in being more detailed and in having an indication
in the left-hand margin of the placing of arias, finales, etc.
It is laid out conventionally in acts and scenes, and certainly includes the scene where Leonora is to take the veil
(it ends 'Di Luna is driven back and Manrico drags Leonora
away with him').

When Verdi saw the synopsis, he was dejected: not surprisingly since although many of his objections at individual points had been taken care of, his ideas on a seamless
form for the opera had been totally ignored. Cammarano
would not mind if he said quite plainly that if the plot
could not retain the originality and the novelty of the
Spanish original, it would be better for them to drop it. He
felt in particular that the vital role of Azucena had lost its
novelty and strangeness. He went on to make a number of
detailed points. He didn't like the Troubadour being
wounded in a duel – he had little enough manhood to lose,
anyway. In the ensemble in the third act, Azucena should
not say that 'the son of the count was burned alive – but I
was not there' (here Verdi quoted directly from the synopsis). Azucena should not be mad during the last scene
(Cammarano had described her as 'affatto demente' – 'right

out of her mind'). He complained that Leonora had no part
in what we now know as the Miserere scene, though this
was the best place for an aria: if the part was then too long,
omit the cavatina (in Act I). He then sketched out a much
abbreviated synopsis himself: this follows Cammarano's
closely, but introduces certain modifications, particularly
in the way he wanted the role of Azucena to be developed.
He ended his own outline with the words 'Yes – he was
your brother. Fool! You are revenged, Oh mother!' (Cammarano had ended the final scene, 'What have you done? . . .
He was . . . your brother!) He ended his letter by reiterating
that he suspected that Cammarano didn't really like the
play – if so, there was still time to drop the subject and find
another.

When Cammarano wrote back on 26 April, he began,
'Your suspicion that I don't like *Trovatore* is unfounded,
also unjust – I wouldn't have betrayed both you and myself
by beginning work on it'. The changes Verdi asked Cammarano to make were smaller than would be realized from
the study of Verdi's letter alone and by and large they did
nothing to shake the organization of the subject out of the
entirely conventional mould into which Cammarano had
forced it. Neither the structure nor the outline were
changed – only points of detail which Verdi saw as height-
ening the dramatic treatment of the subject.

On 10 June Cammarano sent Verdi the introductory
scenes of *Il trovatore*. His drafts of Act I scene I are preserved in Naples, and differ only in a few places from the
text as finally printed. Cammarano did not provide an
opening chorus, thus meeting Verdi's wishes, though interestingly the original synopsis he had sent to Verdi gives a
clear indication that an opening chorus had been intended.
This is in fact the first of his libretti that had not begun
with a conventional chorus, if we set aside the inconsequential *Non v'è fumo senza fuoco* which has no part for
the chorus anyway. The opera begins with five lines of
versi sciolti for the Conte di Luna's henchman Ferrando,
by way of introduction to his narrative 'flashback' which
tells the tale of the burning of the old gypsy woman. To
begin a tragic opera with *versi sciolti* was throwing convention to the winds, though it is to be doubted whether

any member of an audience today realizes this – or even recognizes it for what it is.

On 9 August Cammarano sent Verdi Leonora's aria, the romanza and the Miserere scene: he called it the 'Prece mortuaria' and it is a triumph of subtle versification. Cammarano said he had taken particular trouble over these lines, so that they could be chanted rather than sung, as a contrast to the Troubadour's melody. The whole scene was clearly shaping itself in its final form in his mind as well as in that of the composer. In this letter he mentioned having earlier sent the text of the second act and its finale, and in September Verdi could write to a friend that the libretto was almost finished, so that his thoughts were already turning to theatres and singers. He was anxious to obtain the services of Rita Gabussi for the role of Azucena, but if this meant going back to the idea of the S. Carlo it would take all Cammarano's tact to deal with the negotiations, which would be a delicate matter since Verdi had himself broken them off earlier. Cammarano wrote back on 23 September that he had been out to the country to see Gabussi; she wasn't under contract for Naples, but she might agree to sing in Rome, if the management there could meet certain conditions. However, Cammarano went on, Verdi's instructions as to how he was to treat the finale to Act II had caused him serious embarrassment; he was unable to give shape to his own ideas, so he would have to hold this section back till another letter, sending it perhaps with the ensemble passage in Act III. Clearly the libretto was not yet finished.

Following his usual practice, Cammarano had been sending Verdi the libretto bit by bit as it was written. Several sections of it were closely written in very small handwriting on one or two sheets of paper which were then folded, sealed, addressed to Verdi and sent through the post without any form of covering letter or envelope. On 4 November the librettist wrote that Jacovacci, the impresario of the theatre in Rome, was pressing him for the libretto, and he enclosed a letter in which he detailed the changes the Papal censors would require – no mention of a witch: she was to be just a gypsy; no mention of the stake – it would remind people of the Inquisition; Leonora must not be seen to take poison – suicide is not permitted; no mention to be made of Church, Convent or Taking the Veil. Jacovacci concluded his letter 'In these matters as in the others you, who, without currying favour, are the leading librettist of our day, can get these things across without running into opposition from the censors'.

Three weeks later Cammarano wrote again, discussing the pieces which would fall to the baritone, Colini, which Verdi already had in his possession. Some of the last scene was still to come, as was Azucena's scene in Act II and Manrico's aria in Act III. The finale of Act II (the cloister scene with di Luna's attempted abduction) still caused him much trouble: he would like to do it all over again, but not until it had finally been decided where the opera was to be produced – otherwise he would run the risk of having to revise it a third time.

The next group of letters, three months later, take a sombre turn. On 20 February Verdi wrote to his friend de Sanctis in Naples that the news of Cammarano's illness was as unexpected as it was sad. He hoped that some country air would soon restore his health. He wouldn't conceal from de Sanctis that he wasn't happy at this delay in finishing *Il trovatore,* and he returned to the possibility of a Neapolitan premiere. On the same day he wrote to Cammarano, wishing him courage and hope in his return to health. Having had no further news, Verdi wrote to de Sanctis again on 7 March. Three months later, he still had no news, but assumed that this meant that Cammarano was completely restored to health: 'Ask him to send me the rest of the text as soon as possible, and tell him that when this one is finished, I would be delighted (*beato*) if he wants to do another one for me'. Again, in an undated letter, he urged de Sanctis to get Cammarano to send him immediately the outstanding bits of the libretto. Then on 3 July he wrote once more, announcing that production was to be in Rome, if the censors permitted, and requesting the rest of the text 'subito, subito'.

Verdi soon received the rest of it: an alternative finale to the second act and the last half of the third act, in another handwriting, at the end of which Cammarano had managed to add a very shaky signature; and the last scene of the opera, in yet another handwriting, rather hastily written, and unsigned. Cammarano died on 17 July, but he had completed the libretto, even if some of it had to be dictated from his death-bed. De Sanctis was to write later that the last piece which Cammarano wrote, eight days before he died, was the tenor aria, presumably that in Act III scene 6 – 'Ah! sì, ben mio, coll'essere' with its cabaletta 'Di quella pira l'orrendo fuoco'.

News travelled slowly: the post took ten to twelve days to get from Naples to Busseto. On 19 July – two days after Cammarano had died – Verdi wrote to de Sanctis, 'Your news annihilates me! So Cammarano is seriously ill, really seriously? In truth I don't know how to say how greatly this upsets me. Write to me frequently and let me know daily what happens'. Preoccupied as usual with the opera he was engaged on, Verdi added: if the Roman censors needed some changes made, would Cammarano be able to do them for him? It wasn't till later that Verdi read the news of Cammarano's death, and he wrote once more to de Sanctis: 'I am struck down as if by lightning by the sad news of the death of our Cammarano. It is impossible to describe to you my profound grief! I read of his death not in a letter from a friend, but in a stupid theatrical paper!!! You, who loved him as much as I did, you will understand everything I cannot say. Poor Cammarano!!! What a loss!!' Verdi then immediately plunged on with important matters in hand. The libretto of *Il trovatore* seems to be on the long side. If the censors needed any changes – or if he needed any himself – who was he to turn to for them? Note that none of the changes would in the least bit alter the work of our poor friend whose memory he of all people would wish to respect. Did the young poet Bardare have Cammarano's confidence? Was he suited to the task? The Cammarano family should look after the drafts of the libretto and when acknowledging payment they should cede all rights in it to him. In an interesting postscript he added that he would probably go back to Cammarano's original finale for Act II.

Leone Emmanuele Bardare was born in Naples in 1820, and from his youth he had been a passionate lover of the theatre. He had already tried his hand at a libretto (*Le nozze di Pulcinella)* set by a group of composers in 1851. Over the next twenty years he was to provide about a dozen for a number of composers of the second (and third) ranks, all completely forgotten today. He held a variety of educational appointments.

At the end of September Verdi detailed the changes he wanted to have made in the libretto: 1) In Act II he wanted a characteristic piece for Azucena; instead of Cammarano's eight lines, which began

Stride la vampa, il popolo
Urli di gioia innalza

he wanted six longer lines. He suggested something along the lines of

Stride la vampa, la folle indomita
Urli di gioia al cielo innalza

2) In the original finale of Act II, he wished to add an aria for the Conte di Luna, and to take out his Romanza from Act III, as he had agreed with Cammarano should be done. 3) The full-scale aria for Leonora in Act IV lacked the cantabile section.

Bardare did all this, just as he was told. He wrote 'Stride la vampa' in its present form; he wrote an aria for the Count in Act II – 'Il balen del suo sorriso', excising the fourteen-line Romanza 'I miei giorni tu redesti' from Act III, and leaving an awkward join at this point; for Leonora's aria he wrote the cantabile 'D'amor sull'ali rosee' – all in all, some of the best-known passages in the libretto.

Verdi's last letter about this libretto was written on 14 December, just five weeks before the opening night. In it Verdi himself made major changes at two places. The first was in the Act II finale, the section of the text which had given the most difficulty. He reduced four of Cammarano's lines to two and removed a sixteen-line stretta passage at the end. Most important of all, he rewrote totally the last lines of the opera.

Clearly the most difficult part of the libretto to get right had been the finale to Act II. In his synopsis, Cammarano had laid it out in a conventional way. The arrival of Manrico ('a phantom returned from the dead') at the Cloister created universal surprise; everyone present registered appropriate emotion and comment; the arrival of Ruiz with the news that Urgel was alive and that Castellor had fallen projected everybody into the final stretta; finally Manrico swept up the fainting Leonora and rushed off with her as the curtain fell. This was an absolutely typical way of structuring the pivotal finale of an opera, but it did not satisfy Verdi, who was trying to avoid just such conventional structures. Cammarano's first version of the finale had followed the ground plan of his synopsis exactly, even quoting certain phrases. His second version is altogether shorter: as soon as Manrico appears, Leonora faints and is swept away as the curtain falls – no reaction to his appearance, no arrival of Ruiz and no stretta. In fact, it is far too short and swift, and this must have been obvious to both librettist and composer. Consequently Verdi returned to his original version but at the last moment shortened it by removing the stretta. A fuller account of this finale is given in Chapter 12.

Interestingly, although at the beginning of their work on this opera Verdi told Cammarano that he wanted a libretto not divided into arias, choruses, finales etc., the text he eventually set was as conventional as any of the period, with the exception of the second act finale. The changes which Verdi commissioned from Bardare increased rather than decreased this conventionality, adding the very moments of emotional reflection which stood in the way of swift dramatic propulsion. The two places which Verdi himself rewrote – the endings of the second and fourth acts – both emphasized rapid action where Cammarano preferred a more leisurely pace. The end product of all these changes – particularly the new sections provided by Bardare and the augmentation of the role of Leonora – increased rather than decreased conventional features and resulted in an old-fashioned libretto quite out of keeping with the way in which Verdi's own development was taking him.

The production of *Il trovatore* in Rome on 19 January 1853 was a triumphant success. The cast included Penco as Leonora (she had sung Azucena in Cortesi's *Il trovatore* at Trieste the previous year), Goggi as Azucena and Bouccardé as Manrico. Many of the changes insisted on by the Roman censors (some of them silly in the extreme) were quietly dropped as the opera swept across the stages of the world's opera houses.

The first written indication of Cammarano's ill health which had been preserved came in Verdi's two letters of February 1852. Cammarano had not referred to being ill in his letters of the previous November, either because he did not wish it to be known or because he was at that time still in reasonable health. Presumably his health gradually deteriorated over the winter months until by February he was unable to work. Certainly Verdi did not take his illness very seriously at first, being inclined to regard it as a personal inconvenience to himself. In April, Cammarano wrote to the critic Anzelmi, thanking him for the generous praise he had lavished on *Malvina di Scozia* (the article had appeared as long before as 31 December) and apologizing for the delay in writing. He concluded: 'I would visit you in person, but a serious (*non liete*) illness which keeps me in bed deprives me of that pleasure'.

On 29 March there was a benefit night at the S. Carlo for Cammarano. The programme consisted of Donizetti's *La figlia del reggimento,* and between the acts of this there was a recital of extemporaneous poetry and a cello concerto. There is no indication of whether Cammarano was able to attend the performance or whether, indeed, it was arranged as a direct result of his illness, to improve his financial position. His position in Naples seems to have been precarious and must have added to the worries attendant on his illness. He approached Verdi on the subject, as can be ascertained from the comment in a letter which Verdi sent to de Sanctis on 24 May 1852:

> As to the matter of Cammarano, I would not know what reply to give you; I would not know whether I should or should not advise him to leave Naples. It's a very delicate matter. What I can say is that few of us composers would be able to find the sum that the management in Naples pay him for each libretto. As far as I'm concerned, can I tell you whether or not I will write many more operas in Italy? As you know, I will write an opera for the Lent season in Venice (probably with a libretto by Piave): I shall write this *Trovatore*, now almost finished, I don't know when or where; perhaps I'll write another opera, the one I have asked Cammarano to do (*Re Lear*): then I don't know what more to

tell you. I should add that as a matter of fact you will probably not see this number of operas exceeded in Italy.

This said (which I beg you not to reveal except to Cammarano), I cannot offer advice on the problems our friend is struggling with.

Poor Cammarano – to the end of his life he seems to have been faced with insecurity and financial troubles. Ill and under pressure to finish *Il trovatore*, his last months cannot have been happy.

CHAPTER NINE

1852 and after

Salvadore Cammarano passed away during the evening of Saturday, 17 July 1852. On the 19th, as the *Giornale delle due Sicilie* reported, a large cortège of literary and artistic figures, including the companies of the Fiorentini and S. Carlo theatres, dressed in mourning, accompanied the bier down from the slopes of Vomero to the church of S. Luca, where the coffin was closed over his mortal remains. He was buried in the Nuovo Camposanto cemetery, in the area reserved for famous people, near the father whom he loved. His sister Rosa had a modest headstone erected over the grave, with the following inscription: SALVATORE CAMMARANO / ON WHOM GOD BESTOWED / A MANY-SIDED, POWERFUL TALENT / A MOST PASSIONATE HEART / FIRST DEPICTED ON CANVAS / MEN AND THEIR DEEDS / THEN WITH GREATER POWER / DISPLAYED HUMAN EMOTIONS / WITH GREAT MASTERY / IN DRAMATIC VERSE / SHARING THE GLORY OF THE COMPOSERS / DONIZETTI, MERCADANTE, VERDI. / HE LIES HERE BESIDE HIS FATHER / ERECTED BY HIS SISTER / BORN ON THE 19th DAY OF MARCH 1801 / DIED ON THE 17th DAY OF JULY 1852.

His body had been consumed, according to the *Giornale*, by a long and serious illness. He had sought the air of the heights (Vomero is in the hills above Naples) to repair his shattered health, but had found there only death, which he had met with profoundly Christian resignation, comforted with the rites of his religion. He left a widow and six children, the report added, in honourable poverty. On the 21st, *L'omnibus* printed a long obituary notice by the owner-editor, Vincenzo Torelli, which, together with the rather verbose three-part article by Carlo Tito Dalbono which appeared in *Poliorama Pittoresco* during 1853, has become the principal source of biographical data.

Over a year later, on 17 November 1853, there was a memorial service in the Church of S. Anna dei Lombardi, for Salvadore and his father, Giuseppe, who had died on 2 October 1850. The Vicar General of Naples addressed the assembled congregation, and the singers and orchestra of the S. Carlo were directed by Luigi Cammarano, who had himself written the music with which to honour the memory of his father and brother. (Luigi was himself to die of cholera in Naples the following year.)

What of the widow and children left in penury at his death? Verdi, on reading the sad news, hastened to send them the money owing for the libretto of *Il trovatore*, adding more than was really due to them. He sent a banker's draft for 400 ducats, and on 12 October 1852 Cammarano's widow and eldest daughter signed a document (obviously drawn up by a lawyer) acknowledging that the full rights in the libretto thereby passed to the composer without any reservation or limitation, in consideration of the sum of 400 ducats.

The beginning of this document, which is still preserved in the Verdi archives at his home, S. Agata, in Busseto, is of much interest. 'The undersigned Angelica Cammarano, widow of Salvadore Cammarano, mother and guardian of those children not yet of age; and Adelaide Cammarano, daughter of the said Cammarano . . .' All we know of Cammarano's wife is her name, Angelica; her maiden surname has not come down to us. As for the children, Donizetti wrote to a friend in 1838 that he 'would not have the heart to take the bread from the mouth of the good Cammarano, father of five children'. Cammarano had indicated to Verdi in 1848 – when he was threatened with imprisonment – that he had six children then. Adelaide, the only one to be of age at his death, was perhaps born between 1830 and 1834, when the librettist was in his early 30s. Three of the other children were boys, and their names are known. Perhaps the missing ones were girls, but we do not know what places they occupied in the family.

Michele was born on 23 February 1835, and became a famous painter. In 1858 and 1859 he seems to have been away from home, since we find Angelica writing to him, thanking him for some money he had sent her, enjoining him to work hard and reminding him of his father. Her letters show her as caring, affectionate and courageous. Michele worked for many years in Rome, but returned eventually to Naples, and died in 1920.

In one of her letters to Michele, Angelica mentioned that Mercadante had advised her to enrol her son Ricciardo at the Conservatorio S. Pietro a Majella to study the cello. No more is heard of him.

The third son, Goffredo, became a librettist, though he did not show any of his father's gifts in that direction. A note on the copy of a comedy (*Un errore di un giovine padre*) mentions that Goffredo was the seventh child of Salvadore (presumably one did not survive) and that he was born in 1842. The three libretti which can be attributed to him are: *Zuma, melodrama* in four acts, music by Fornari, Naples 1881/82 (sometimes wrongly attributed to Salvadore by editors who have not taken the trouble to consult the title-page of the libretto); *Regina e contadina, opera semi-seria* in three acts, music by Sarria, Naples 1882, and *Un baccio alla regina, opera comica* in three acts, music by de Nardis, Naples 1890. He is sometimes given credit for the libretto of *Lo zigaro rivale*, for instance in the catalogue of the Rolandi collection in Venice. Rolandi noted in his manuscript index that Salvadore was dead by the time this opera was produced, but did not realize that it was a second setting of an earlier work.

On 22 July 1861 Angelica wrote to Michele to let him know how overjoyed she was at the result of a benefit night which had been given the previous week at the S. Carlo. The takings had amounted to 774 ducats of which, after deducting expenses of 150 ducats she was to have two-thirds – that is, she received about 425 ducats. She did not know if she was in Heaven or on earth. The performance 'for the benefit of the family of the late Salvadore Cammarano' had been on 16 July, and details can be found in the *Programma giornaliera* for that day: the programme consisted of Acts I and III of Verdi's *Macbeth* (which Cammarano had himself staged when it was first seen in Naples), with de Bassini as Macbeth, Galletti as Lady Macbeth and Arati as Banco; the Overture to William

Tell; then Borghi-Mamo and Negrini in Act II of *Il trova-tore*; finally the sixteen-part ballet *Masaniello*, with music by Giaquinto. After this, there is nothing more to report of Cammarano's widow, but it is clear that his death left her in considerable hardship.

If Salvadore's immediate family reacted honourably to the situation in which they found themselves, it is by no means certain that his brother Luigi did. On 28 September 1853 Verdi wrote to him a polite but stiff note:

> You are right: the esteem which I had, and always will have, for your poor brother can in no way be diminished if I tell you frankly that the subject of *Virginia* does not please me. I was never able to get used to those costumes and those senti-ments: you add that I would perhaps run into difficulty with the censors – take up your suggestion then with some other composer. Let me thank you for the courtesy which you have shown me.

It sounds very much as if Luigi had offered Verdi the libretto of *Virginia*, though he must have known perfectly well that it had been set to music by Mercadante and was only unperformed by virtue of the censors's prohibition.

Amongst other libretti remaining unperformed at the time of Cammarano's death, *Caterina di Brono*, written for Mercadante in the mid-1830s, remained the property of the composer. In 1870, by which time he had become blind, Mercadante returned to this libretto, and dictated the music for the first act to two of his students, V. Mag-nella and F. Guaranta. Their manuscript full score is in the Conservatorio in Naples, but there is no trace of the lib-retto. Later, Maestro Magnatta wrote that Mercadante had only got half-way through the finale of Act I, and was still dictating it to them the day before he was struck down with his final illness.

In his obituary notice, Torelli listed unperformed lib-retti, including *La sposa del bandito*, *Teresa e Foscarini* (*sic*), *Caterina di Brono* (M° Mercadante), *Il trovatore* (for M° Verdi). Of these, the second was written for Persiani in 1837, for performance in Paris, but the first is not now known. The catalogue of the Conservatario S. Pietro a Majella in Naples also lists as by Salvadore Cammarano *Estella*, *melodrama semi-seria* in two acts; *Filippo*, *tragedia lirica* in two acts; *Marco Visconti, melodramma* in two acts (this was also the title of one of his early plays); and *Sofia di Siligni, tragedia lirica* in two acts. Unfortunately the collection of which they are a part has disappeared and they cannot now be traced.

What sort of a man was Salvadore Cammarano? There are not many clues to his personality and temperament to be found in his writings: his choice of subject reflected the needs of the composers and theatrical necessity, his method of treating his subjects was determined by the conventions imposed by the form in which he was working. Some evidence of Cammarano the man is certainly available from the letters which passed between him and the composers and managements he worked with, and some more from contemporary records.

On the whole his obituaries do not give much insight into his personality or into the circumstances in which he lived and worked. The account of his funeral in the *Giornale delle due Sicilie* merely said that he was steadfast in his work, desirous of impartial criticism, silent in the face of superficial or senseless comment: praising all those gifts, save for the many which shone in himself, not condemning others or their faults, even when taking them to task with the most reasonable and honest remonstrations; he was dear to all, held in sincere esteem by all, and mourned by those many people who had had the chance to get to know him.

Torelli's obituary notice in the issue of *L'omnibus* which came out a few days after the funeral is the most disappointing of contemporary records from this point of view, since Torelli had obviously known him well, only referring to him as a greatly loved and eminent man. Dalbono, in the second part of his article in *Poliorama Pittoresco* of 1853, had rather more to say, and it is from this article that most of our knowledge of his early life is derived. He wrote that Cammarano was by temperament calm, not very demonstrative, restrained in word; hardworking; it was not arrogance that led him to withdraw himself from the crowd or to live within his poetry, but it was more as if he felt a resentment of the outside world. With this restrained and naturally melancholy tempera-

ment Salvadore Cammarano lived wth his verses, which
he used to put together, indeed to complete, within
his head, putting them down on paper only once he had
returned home. He was to have been seen strolling slowly
among the colonnades of S. Francesco, opposite the Palace,
without the company of friend or relative, pondering his
quartets, his closing arias or his romances. From column to
column he would go, weaving the dramatic canvas or contemplating within himself the adagio of a prayer or the
suppleness of a largo maestoso. Sometimes when ex-
hausted by this mental activity, he would seek support
from the columns, and it once happened that well into the
night he was found asleep there. (It will be recalled that
Donizetti made a similar remark on one occasion, that
while he was waiting for his libretto, Cammarano was
pacing up and down among the columns of S. Francesco in
search of inspiration.)

Di Giacomo, who became a friend of the Cammarano
family later in the century, described him in an article
published in 1903 as an excellent person, calm, restrained,
sober, very hard working, continually pursuing his dreams
and fantasies, both at home and in the street. He was tall,
thin and fair, and on the bridge of his nose were his glasses,
which he never took off. He also repeats the story of the
colonnades of S. Francesco. There, leaning back against
one of the marble columns, he wrote in his notebook the
lines for Verdi, Pacini, Donizetti or Lillo (an interesting
selection of composers, this; what about poor Mercadante?). Sometimes, tired out, he would drop off to sleep.
At the beginning of his article, di Giacomo referred to
Dalbono's appreciation, but whatever he learnt from the
family about the librettist, he obviously relied heavily on
what he had read there. However, he did add one isolated
and rather perplexing comment: 'He was in short a mis-
anthropist', though it is hard to find any evidence for this
other than the need for a measure of solitude for creative
writing.

In his book on the history of the Theatre in Naples,
Viviani points out that it took no little courage in the
mid-1840s to put into the mouth of a singer on the stage of
a Royal Theatre in Bourbon Naples such patriotic senti-

ments as:

La mia patria, sciagurato,	[My native land, O wicked man,
Come questa è sacra piaggia;	Is like this a sacred place
In Italia anch'io son nato . . .	In Italy I too was born
Maledetto chi l'oltraggia!	Cursed be he who insults her]

(from *La fidanzata corsa*, Act I scene 7). Similarly, *L'assedio di Calais* is shot through with deeply-felt patriotic sentiments, and works such as *La battaglia di Legnano* were clearly written against a background of political sympathy – indeed Cammarano said as much to Verdi when he suggested the subject in the first place.

Viviani also tells an anecdote which gives a fascinating glance at Cammarano's family life. It comes from a letter from Michele, and deals with a performance at the S. Carlo of Verdi's *Attila*, at the time of the agitation leading up to the granting of a constitution, when performances of Verdi's operas, in particular, were awaited with eager anticipation and excitement. On 29 January 1848, when Michele was not quite thirteen years old – 'that evening my father took me to the S. Carlo theatre where, as I said, he was stage director (*Direttore del palcoscenico*). I frequently went with him, and my place was in the prompter's box, with Don Salvatore Amato the prompter. There was plenty of room for a comfortable armchair for him. I stood behind his shoulder and enjoyed the performance.' It is a pretty thought – at the height of the political agitation early in 1848, Cammarano taking his little boy to hear *Attila*, with its famous lines 'Avrai tu l'universo/Resti L'Italia a me' (You will have the universe but leave Italy for me'), leaving him in the care of the prompter (where he would get an excellent view of what was going on on the stage) until he could collect him after the performance.

From his letters and those of his friends it seems that Cammarano was able to reach terms of sincere friendship with the composers with whom he worked. Donizetti clearly reached an intimate joking relationship with him, as the postcard Cammarano wrote to him at the time of *Poliuto* reveals, when Donizetti had failed to turn up at the Café of the Two Sicilies to keep an appointment with him – a card in which he poked fun at his own glasses. With Mercadante and Pacini he seems to have been on more professional terms, though the correspondence is too scanty to form the basis of a firm judgement. It is true that the degree of formality varies from letter to letter, but this need not be interpreted as the waxing and waning of their mutual affection; it could be simply the reflection of the business to be conducted. He was on sufficiently close terms with Mercadante to be asked to drop round for Sunday lunch for a chat with some other librettists. It is abundantly clear that Verdi was genuinely attached to Cammarano, as well as having great respect for his work: he was unusually (for him) careful in the way he put his criticisms to him, and was obviously greatly moved by his illness and death, even if his first reaction was concern for how he was going to get the libretto of *Il trovatore* finished.

All the composers Cammarano worked with, and for whom there exists enough correspondence, have one thing in common: they all complained of his delays in furnishing them with the texts which they were to set to music, Verdi, in particular, with anger and bitterness. It was, of course, a typical complaint of all composers against all librettists, but Cammarano seems to have been at least as bad as all the others. It is hard to know now whether this dilatoriness on his part was caused by overwork, high standards or just plain laziness. Unlike, say, Romani or Rossi, who often wrote six or more libretti in a single year, Cammarano does not seem to have taken on more work than he could reasonably have been expected to complete. When he was unable to finish the libretto of *Cristina di Svezia* for its production in Genoa, it was completed (presumably with his agreement, though there is no evidence either way) from his synopsis by Saccherò; similarly when he was in difficulty over the rewriting of *La battaglia di Legnano* as *L'assedio di Firenze* he did not hesitate to bring in another poet, and would accept neither credit nor payment as a result. The dates of performance give only a rough guide as to when he actually wrote the libretti, and there is only occasionally confirmatory evidence in his correspondence, but it seems unlikely that he was ever called upon to write more than three or at the most four, in any one year, and frequently only one or two. Even given his duties as stage manager this does not seem an unreasonable number.

There can be no doubt that Cammarano took his work very seriously and, as will be seen in Chapter 13, laboured long and hard to polish his verses till they reached an acceptable level of versification and style. He certainly does not give the appearance of having been incorrigibly lazy, but we must not underestimate the sheer hard slog of having to write out several copies of a long libretto by hand. Cammarano was very proud of his elegant penmanship, as many examples of calligraphy on the margins of his papers show. His writing, even when hurried, or in his rough drafts, is always clear and easy to read, and his text most beautifully laid out on the page – no doubt a legacy of his early training in the visual arts. It seems to me that the accusations levelled against him that he did not have his texts ready at the right time – which are too many and too convincing to be set aside – probably arose from a combination of a determination not to be hurried into offering work which did not reach the high standards he had set himself and the physical difficulties of getting it down on paper. His life cannot have been conducive to creative work: he seems to have been often short of money. Since he was dependent on the stability of the various managements for whom he worked, he was liable to periods of unemployment and went without salary on at least one occasion for as long as seven months. Even at the end of his life, when he was widely accepted as the leading librettist of the day, a worthy successor to Romani, his sense of security of employment was so poor that he was prepared to consider launching himself as a freelance in what was a notoriously uncertain profession rather than to continue with the Royal Theatres in Naples.

His own letters show him as conscientious: he obviously resented unjust criticism. To Barbaja's complaints over the late delivery of the libretto of *Poliuto* he returned a dignified answer, pointing out that Barbaja himself had contributed to the delay by requiring a change of subject when he had found it possible to engage a first-class tenor who had to have something to sing, 'and if I don't hurry my work it is because I have too much pride in it, too much zeal for your management, and immense respect for the public'. 'As you know, I decline tempting offers so as not to betray my principles'. Later, when Pacini had gone behind his back to complain to Flauto about delays, he reminded him that he had never betrayed the composers with whom he worked. He was obviously willing to put himself out to facilitate even a late change of subject – as when Pacini dropped the idea of *Orazi e Curiazi*, offering to delay the performance beyond the date to find him a little more time.

The most interesting statement of artistic principle remains the letter to Verdi at the time of *Luisa Miller*, when he gave it as his opinion that to obtain the greatest perfection in an opera, one single mind should be responsible for both words and music: that to obtain the right balance, the composer and librettist, if not the same person, had to be of one mind. This was not the view of a mere hack, as which librettists seem frequently to be regarded, and, indeed, as many of them undoubtedly were, but of someone who had thought long and hard about what he was doing. It is not easy today to assess the value of the work a librettist produced. Read in the cold light of dawn, a libretto is a pretty poor specimen of literature – but it was never designed to be read, other than as an aid in the theatre. It is only to be judged in so far as it was able to stimulate a composer to write memorable and effective music for it. Many good libretti have disappeared through being harnessed to unsuccessful music, and even poor ones have been redeemed by the music which has clothed them.

Cammarano's conception of his task seems to have been very much that of a partner who should have a share in the genesis and development of a work of art. In this role he expected to be consulted, and was in his turn willing to revise his synopses and even his texts, right up to the last minute, if this was required of him. He did not do this slavishly, and retained the right to discuss it with the composer. The picture which comes across is not unlike Delfico's caricature which forms the Frontispiece – absent-minded, worried and even harassed; insecure and easily taken advantage of; but a man of sincerity and principle who gained and retained the respect and affection of some of Italy's greatest composers.

CHAPTER TEN

Sources and Choice of Subjects

The choice of a subject for an opera was constantly in the minds of both composer and librettist. The correspondence of composers such as Donizetti and Verdi betray an intense interest in the theatrical scene and a watchful eye for subjects which would make good libretti. Once the composer became emancipated from the system whereby on arrival at an opera house he was handed a libretto by the impresario and was expected to get on with setting it to music, he and the librettist were committed to finding a subject which would meet a number of requirements, not always easily satisfied in the same work. It had to meet the financial and practical demands of the impresario, in particular to be suitable for the singers available for the production; the moral and political sensitivities of the censors; and last but by no means least, the expectations of the public, and thus the intellectual and emotional climate of the times. To the extent that the growing nationalism of Italy in the 1830s and 1840s was incompatible with what the censors considered suitable, a great deal of caution was necessary. The increasing violence and moral waywardness emanating from France and exported through French theatre all over Italy created a climate of public opinion deeply distrusted by the guardians of morality in Bourbon Naples. Nevertheless the older tradition of operas whch avoided tragic conclusions by unexpected twists introducing reconciliation and magnaminous forgiveness was no longer appropriate. Tragic conclusions and the death of the protagonist on stage became generally acceptable in Naples in the early 1830s and by the middle of the decade had become the norm of the serious opera, save on royal occasions where court etiquette still required a happy ending. Death in heroic circumstances, such as in battle, or in stories from classical mythology, was one thing, and had long been accepted: death in tragic circumstances, in which the virtuous could suffer and the villanous prosper, was something new, despite occasional instances during the previous twenty years. Repentance and retribution might or might not be the lot of the villain, but what mattered was the fate of the innocent victim dragged down by inexorable fate. Through all these considerations librettist and composer had to tread a wary path.

The first practical consideration was the need to find a subject appropriate to the company of singers which was being assembled for the season for which the contract had been drawn up. This is well exemplified in a letter from Donizetti to the impressario Lanari of 31 May 1836 – 'He [Cammarano] suggests for you *Pia*, a subject very suitable for your company'. This project soon ran into difficulties with the Superintendent of the theatre (the Fenice in Venice) because it failed to provide a large enough part for a young mezzo-soprano in whom he seems to have had a particular interest. As we have seen, the part of Rodrigo (Pia's brother) had to be expanded to provide for this, out of all proportion to that which the original synopsis suggested. The reconstruction of the finale of the first act after the opera failed when first produced went some way to redressing the balance. The year after *Pia de' Tolomei*, Lanari asked Cammarano to provide two versions of his next project, one with three and the other with four main roles; this must have been a very difficult requirement for him to meet.

Then there was all the trouble over *Poliuto* in Naples. The impresario Barbaja had asked for an opera which would include only a small part for a tenor, since he had had difficulty in finding a first-class singer for the forthcoming season. He then found himself in a position to engage the famous tenor Adolphe Nourrit, just arrived from Paris, and he altered his instructions. Cammarano, as he himself reminded Barbaja, had had to look for a new subject.

By and large, the Neapolitan impresarios did not seem to concern themselves overmuch with the subject, leaving the librettist to negotiate with the censors. It is clear from Cammarano's letter about *Poliuto* that Barbaja did not know what subject he was working on for Nourrit. Some years later his successor Flauto wrote to Cammarano that his associates were accusing him of neglecting his duty to keep an eye on the poems which were to be set to music. It is not clear just what he was complaining about: he cited *Alzira* and *Il vascello de Gama* – both operas were failures but while the latter was a poor subject for an opera there was nothing wrong with the choice of the former. There is little evidence that Flauto mended his ways – at least, Cammarano's choice of subjects did not change.

The availability of singers was always an important consideration in the choice of a subject, as in the run-up to *Poliuto*. When a fine mezzo-soprano such as Buccini was avalable at the S. Carlo, Cammarano produced a number of libretti with important (and sometimes equal) parts for soprano and mezzo, such as *Saffo* (Saffo and Climene), *La vestale* (Emilia and Giunia), *Il proscritto* (Malvina and Odoardo). The end of this period at the S. Carlo overlapped with one in which two top-flight tenors, Basadonna and Fraschini, were available, and at least two of Cammarano's libretti were written in such a way as to take advantage of this – *Il proscritto*, in addition to soprano and mezzo roles has two important and approximately equal tenor roles, Arturo and Giorgio, but as there is no major baritone part, it is possible that Cammarano had originally intended one to be a baritone role. *La fidanzata corsa* similarly has two important tenor roles, Alberto and Piero, but here there is an important baritone part, though not one for a mezzo. *Il proscritto* is also interesting in that, despite two important tenor roles, the part of the young brother Odoardo was taken by Buccini (who had also sung Rodrigo when *Pia de' Tolomei* reached Naples), since this, too, might have been a tenor role. Another *musico* role was that of Eustachio's son Aurelio in *L'assedio di Calais*, an opera in which there is no main role for a tenor, so that one wonders if there was at that time an acceptable tenor in the roster (despite the presence of works like *Norma* in the current repertoire). Clearly, subjects had to be chosen which lent themselves to being treated in such a way as to exploit the strengths and minimize the weaknesses of the company available.

The subjects chosen by librettists to form the basis of an

opera were rarely if ever original, and in this respect Cammarano was no exception. Most subjects were taken from a play, a ballet or a work of literature. Cammarano's were frequently well known (both to him and to the audience) from representations at the Fiorentini theatre (if prose plays) or at the S. Carlo (if ballets or other operas). More than half his subjects came into this category, and it was inevitable that someone of his background and interests should be well acquainted with the past and present repertoires of the Neapolitan theatres. For instance, the following of his subjects were all performed at the Fiorentini theatre in the 1830s and 1840s, and for the most part the plays served directly as his source: *Ines de Castro, Un matrimonio per ragione, Lucia di Lammermoor, Belisario, L'assedio di Calais, Pia de' Tolomei, I ciarlatani, Il conte di Chalais, La vestale, Saffo, Luigi Rolla, Il proscritto, La fidanzata corsa, Ester d'Engaddi, Il ravvedimento, Buondelmonte, La battaglia di Legnano, Luisa Miller, Folco d'Arles, Non v'è fumo senza fuoco*. Ballets on the following subjects were similarly performed at the S. Carlo during the same period: *Ines de Castro, L'assedio di Calais, I ciarlatani, La vestale, Cristina di Svezia, Ester d'Engaddi, Buondelmonte, Merope, Virginia*. It is no accident that some titles occur in both lists, for choreographers were as assiduous as librettists in their search for subjects. Sometimes they based their ballet scenarios on successful operas in the same way that librettists 'borrowed' subjects from their ballets. Cammarano only had to keep his eyes and ears open, and a constant stream of suitable subjects for his libretti presented itself on the stages of the Neapolitan theatres, while literary and theatrical gossip backstage and in the cafés would keep him in touch with a wide range of other subjects. Many of the subjects he treated had been used for operas before (some, like *Merope*, many times over) but would have had to be reworked to make them suitable for the times: this is most clearly seen in his revision of Romani's libretto for Mayr's opera *Medea in Corinto*, originally written for the S. Carlo in 1813, where a comparison of the two texts, nearly forty years apart, shows how far Neapolitan taste and the intellectual climate of the city had changed.

Amongst the papers bound up in the Lucchesi-Palli library in Naples are a number of lists in Cammarano's handwriting. Some of these lists are of plays, others include novels and other non-theatrical works. It is not always clear why these lists were drawn up, but one of them is annotated in such a way as to make it obvious that it was a list of subjects considered for use as libretti. It covers such a wide range of possibilities that it is worth examining in detail, since it throws a clear light on the topics thought suitable for treatment. First, the list, with Cammarano's annotations, then some comments on each of the subjects.

> *Bianca Capello* – Chronicle of the seventeenth century
> Difficulties for the censors – one woman
> *I martiri delle fede*
> Forbidden by the censors
> *Buondelmonte*
> Given with music by Donizetti
> *La fidanzata corsa*
> Plot too savage
> *Tommasso Moor*
> Not dramatic enough
> *Enrichetta d' Inghilterra*
> *I Ghibellini di Pisa* – Rosini
> *Giulia Gonzaga* – historical story
> *Isnardo ossia il milite romano* – Colleoni's romance
> *Foscarini, o il bojo* – romance
> *La rosa bianca e la rossa*
> To be considered – one woman
> *Marco Visconti*
> Without the mother
> *Maria Tudor*
> Already set
> *Ettore Fieramosca*
> Too often seen as a ballet
> *Il solitario e l'incognita*
> Doesn't convince me
> *I cavalieri delle Ebridi*
> *Woodstock ossia i Cavalieri*
> Not the plot for a serious drama.

Taking the list one by one:

> *Bianca Capello* – This Venetian lady (born 1548, *pace* Cammarano's dating), in the course of a stormy life, married

Francesco de' Medici, Grand Duke of Florence, first in secret in 1578, two months after the death of his first wife, then publicly the following year. They both died nine years later. The story of her life might well have made the censors think, though a play on the subject by Giovine was printed in Naples in 1838.

I martiri delle fede – Almost certainly *Poliuto*, prohibited in 1838.

Buondelmonte – The familiar story from the Florentine chronicles had been drawn on for an emergency libretto when Donizetti's *Maria Stuarda* had been forbidden in 1834. Campagna's poem on the subject had been printed in Naples in 1827, and Marenco's play had been in the repertoire of the Fiorentini in the mid-1830s.

La fidanzata corsa – Ducange's play *La vendetta* (1831) was frequently given at the Fiorentini. Despite Cammarano's comment – fully justified – he did eventually use it for a libretto.

Tommasso Moor – Possibly Pellico's five-act tragedy of 1833.

Enrichetta d'Inghilterra – No Italian treatment of Queen Henrietta is known to me, but there was a play *Henrietta von England* (Munich 1826) by the Bavarian government official, Eduard von Schenk, the author of *Belisar*. If one of his works was known in Naples, it is possible that others were, too.

I Ghibellini di Pisa – Giovanni Rosini's historical romance *Il conte Ugolino della Gherardesca e i Ghibellini di Pisa* appeared in 1843.

Giulia Gonzaga – Presumably the Countess of Fondi, who was active in the women's religious movement of the sixteenth century and who was born in 1513.

Isnardo ossia il milite romano – Colleoni's *Racconto italico* deals with the internecine strife in thirteenth-century Italy. It had been published in Naples, but no play or ballet on the subject is known to me.

Foscarini, o il bojo – As Cammarano specified a romance, he could not have been thinking of the plays by Niccolini, and others. An edition of I. Pindemonte's verse novella *Antonio Foscarini e Teresa Foscarini* had been published in Naples in 1792 and may well have been known to Cammarano, who had been engaged in 1837 on an abortive project for an opera for Persiani, on the subject of Teresa Foscarini.

La rosa bianca e la rossa – Mayr's successful opera of 1813 had a libretto by Romani, based on a play by Pixérécourt

(Paris 1809), and had been performed at the S.Carlo in 1819 under the title *Il trionfo dell' amizia.*

Marco Visconti – Grossi's famous poem (1834) had been the basis of a play by Cosenza (Fiorentini theatre 1837). A libretto on the subject, now lost, is catalogued as by Cammarano in the library of the Conservatorio S. Pietro a Majella in Naples.

Maria Tudor – Victor Hugo's drama came out in 1833; Cammarano's remark 'already set' may perhaps refer to Tarantini's libretto for Pacini (Palermo 1843). In April 1834 there were rumours in Naples that Donizetti was to write a *Maria Tudor* for the S.Carlo, but he did not do so.

Ettore Fieramosca – D'Azeglio's famous book appeared in 1833. Cosenza's play on the same subject had been produced in 1831. A ballet by Taglioni was frequently performed at the S.Carlo, in and after 1837.

Il solitario – Possibly Cammarano had in mind D'Arlincourt's *Le solitaire,* which had been performed, in an Italian version by Cosenza, in Naples in 1825.

I cavalieri delle Ebridi – This sounds like Scott, and I owe to Jerome Mitchell, who has studied 'Scott' operas, the suggestion that this subject might have been taken from *The Lord of the Isles* (1815). Bassi's Italian translation of 1827 was reprinted in Naples in 1841.

Woodstock – Almost certainly Scott's novel, first published in 1826. By the mid 1830s, four different Italian translations had appeared.

If these attributions are broadly correct, Cammarano's list probably dates from around 1843, when Rosini's *Ghibellini di Pisa* came out. This leaves out the difficulty of *La fidanzata corsa,* which Cammarano had suggested in 1840 and which he used as a text for Pacini, the opera being performed in December 1842. The later date is suggested by the comment on *Maria Tudor;* the earliest is set by the prohibition of *Poliuto* in 1838.

The other lists in this collection cannot be so clearly identified as having been drawn up for operatic purposes, and they are not annotated, except by marginal signs, now impossible to decipher. The lists include such well-known dramatic subjects as *Il Cid, Ginevra degl' Almieri, Il beretto nero, Margherita di Yorck, Lara, Lord Surrey, Niccolò de' Lapi, Amleto, Macbet* (sic), *Il corsaro, Latude, Luisa Strozzi, Margherita Pusterlà, Gaspara Stampa,* and at least four others which Cammarano did use as the basis of libretti: *Virginia, Luisa Miller, Stella di Napoli* and *Ruy Blas*.

It was not only the librettist who had ideas about subjects, but composers too. Sometimes they returned to a subject several times, perhaps at intervals of some years, before circumstances were propitious. For instance, Donizetti and Cammarano struggled with Lockroy and Badon's *Un duel sous le Cardinal de Richelieu* in 1837, only to give it up when the librettist was unable to get the first act right. He eventually finished the text for Lillo, and the opera was given as *Il conte di Chalais* in 1839. The following year, Donizetti took up the subject again, and again laid it on one side: two years later he remembered it again, this time completing it, to a slightly modified version of Cammarano's text which Lillo had already set, as *Maria di Rohan*. Similarly, Mercadante was toying with the idea of an opera based on Alfieri's *Virginia* in 1839, eventually setting a text by Cammarano ten years later. Just as they had subjects to which they were attracted, composers sometimes found it impossible to work on a subject to which they were not attracted, and the librettist would put the idea on one side, to be offered to another composer when an opportunity arose. Mercadante rejected *Cristina di Svezia*, later to be prepared for Nini; Pacini rejected *Alzira* and *Orazi e Curiazi*, operas taken up almost immediately by Verdi and Mercadante respectively. *Folco d'Arles* was intended originally for Donizetti but put on one side for ten years before being taken down, dusted off and worked up for de Giosa.

The reasons Mercadante gave for rejecting *Cristina di Svezia* are the most interesting, as they show him to have been sensitive to the moral tone of the subject: he was unwilling to accept a text in which he found the principal characters to be loathsome, hypocritical, hateful or vengeful. 'The same plot' (he wrote to Cammarano) 'was suggested to me by Romani and by Rossi and I rejected it, just as Bellini had rejected it – and for the same reasons.' He went on 'In *Elena da Feltre*' (which they had already done) 'the only loathsome, shocking part is Boemondo, but he is a second tenor, who hasn't much to sing and is therefore not wearisome'. Thus in addition to the matter of the principle of morality which was involved, there was the practical problem of the boredom induced by unrelieved evil.

The many references to suitable subjects in composers' letters show that there was a common body of material to which they looked for subjects, many of which recur time and time again. Even a subject like *Nabucco*, which we think of today as typically Verdian, had been considered by Mercadante a few years previously. The extent to which the same subject was taken up by different librettists for different composers demonstrates their dependence on a common stock of ideas. At least two-thirds of all the subjects treated by Cammarano were used by other Italian librettists, and popular subjects were used time and time again. Even such a highly individual choice as *Il trovatore* had been used the year before Verdi's by another librettist and composer. Since the majority of operas did not survive their first season, there was no reason why the subjects could not be recycled – but it was rare for a subject to be taken up again if it had been the basis of an opera which had become well established in the standard repertoire. No one challenged *Lucia di Lammermoor, La vestale* or *Saffo*.

As the appendix to this chapter there is a detailed list of the sources for all Cammarano's libretti. The identifications are as accurate as can be managed, and are based on a textual comparison of play (or whatever source might have been used) and libretto. There may of course be unidentified 'missing links', but this is inevitable. A note on the time and place of the action is also given, as this gives an indication of what was considered to be of popular appeal. The dependence on the source naturally varied greatly; sometimes it was merely a matter of condensation, with stretches of existing dialogue turned into operatic verse: at other times Cammarano had to blend elements from several sources or to work up ideas into a larger scale.

The detailed listing of the sources drawn on does not however give an adequate understanding of the type of subject which was being searched for, nor why from the long list of plays and ballets in the current theatrical repertoire these and not others were selected. Do they have some element or elements in common, some central theme whch attracted him, or which was particularly in keeping with the spirit of the times? Was there, perhaps, some attribute which reflected current ideas on the nature of opera and which were therefore more suited to operatic treatment from the point of view of composer and singer?

The list of sources shows that most of them would have been familiar to Cammarano from performances at the theatres of Naples, in some form or other. Twenty of Cammarano's libretti draw directly or indirectly on French sources, most of them from the years after 1820. Another ten go back to Italian sources: two from German (*Belisario* and *Luisa Miller*), one from Spanish (*Il trovatore*) and one from Scotland (*Lucia di Lammermoor*). Of the four which are not positively identified, *La sposa* and *Stella di Napoli* seem likely to be drawn from French sources, *Elena da Feltre* from Italian sources. Several of his libretti draw on more than one source – for instance, *Pia de' Tolomei* which, while going back to Sestini, also used Bianco's play. I am fairly sure that the reduction of *The Bride of Lammermoor* into an opera libretto was beyond Cammarano's capabilities, and that he used an intermediary play or ballet, as yet unidentified (I do not think it was Ducange's play of 1828). It is very interesting to look at Cammarano's list of subjects for operatic treatment and to note the ones he did *not* set – for instance, he never used any of the 'romances', the historical novels that were so popular in Italy in the 1830s and 1840s, for their recreation of a glorious Italian past (and their scarcely concealed patriotic and nationalistic undertones). He may have avoided these subjects for several reasons: the greater difficulties of adapting a novel rather than a play, an unwillingness to approach the censors with material of this nature, or just plain lack of opportunity. The only subject of this type which he took was *Pia de' Tolomei*, and this was both innocent of subversion and already adapted for theatrical purposes. The importance of an uncontroversial subject cannot be exaggerated: when Verdi and Cammarano suggested an opera based on just one such patriotic historical novel – Guerrazzi's *L'assedio di Firenze* – it was promptly forbidden by the Neapolitan censors. I believe that Cammarano's caution was greater than his patriotism (despite his protestations to Verdi in 1848 – 'if there burns in you, as in me, the desire to treat the most glorious epoch in Italian history') and the pressure of work to which he seems always to have been subjected probably led him to favour works which could easily be adapted for operatic purposes.

A search for the common elements in Cammarano's subjects must begin by eliminating from his list of works a few which are, for one reason or another, atypical. To begin with, two early and rather slight pieces, with happy endings, of a conventional, bourgeois character, *La sposa* and *Un matrimonio per ragione*. Second, two short comedies, both written for his brother Luigi, *I ciarlatani* and *Non v'è fumo senza fuoco*. Two large-scale works finish with a happy ending, *Il ravvedimento* and *Il vascello de Gama*: to this group must be added *L'assedio di Calais*, a work in more than one way *sui generis*. Unique in a different way is *La battaglia di Legnano*, with its underlying patriotic action. This leaves some twenty-eight libretti, all deeply tragic in outlook, all ending with one or more deaths, though not necessarily of the eponymous character. The subjects of these tragic works vary widely in space and time, from the ancient world (*Saffo, Medea, La vestale, Virginia* etc.) through mediaeval Europe (*Ines de Castro, Pia de' Tolomei, Elena da Feltre, Bondelmonte,* etc.) to comparatively recent times, with a concentration in the sixteenth and seventeenth centuries (*Lucia di Lammermoor, Robert Devereux, Maria de Rudenz, Cristina di Svezia, Luigi Rolla, Il proscritto, Alzira, Luisa Miller*). Only *Il reggente* is set in the eighteenth century. Many of the subjects find themselves in strange company, since the setting was often moved to more suitable places (often Scotland where, presumably, anything could happen, it being too far away for the ripples to reach the Bourbon administration in Naples) and times – the long arm of the censorship was never far away.

The most noteworthy aspect of the subjects Cammarano chose for his libretti is the almost complete absence of any heroic quality. Some individual characters do display some such quality, for instance, Arrigo in *La battaglia di Legnano*, though this was an avowedly patriotic opera, and Manrico in *Il trovatore* – significantly, both operas written for Verdi. Some characters, under the pressure of events, respond positively and bravely, as does Decio in *La vestale*, leading an armed uprising to attempt a rescue for the woman condemned to death is a result of his own rashness. Absence of heroic qualities need not involve absence of nobility: Eustachio in *L'assedio di Calais* is, of course, nobleness personified, and in the tragic subjects, Poliuto and Paolina (*Poliuto*) go to their deaths with courage and nobility, Pia (*Pia de' Tolemei*) and Count Murray (*Il reggente*) and Monaldeschi (*Cristina di Svezia*) offering forgiveness to those who had wronged them. Dignity and resignation in the face of death (although a fine way of bringing down the final curtain) is one thing; heroic action, even an heroic search for death, is another.

Cammarano seems to have avoided all those subjects where the protagonist – usually a man – strives to bend circumstances to his will, only to be crushed in the process (assuming that those in which the protagonist succeeded are not likely to make good vehicles for a tragic opera). Whether he avoided them by temperament, or with circumspection or for other reasons is not easy to assess: probably a mixture of all three. Most of his protagonists are women, and they go under not as a result of their own actions, but as a result of the actions of other people. They are pawns, caught up in a complex of circumstances over which they have no control, or have lost any control they might ever have been able to achieve. They are essentially passive, not active characters: action conspires against them. They may not be guiltless, and they may be naive or trusting to a fault, but they definitely are not Men (or Women) of Action. There are signs in some libretti (e.g. *Maria de Rudenz*) that Cammarano was moving towards more active protagonists, though this marks a later stage in the development of the romantic libretto.

It is worth looking further at Cammarano's protagonists. Ines (*Ines de Castro*) dies as a result of personal and political intrigue, betrayed by a rejected suitor. Lucia and Edgardo (*Lucia di Lammermoor*) both die entrapped in the web of political advantage spun by Enrico; Belisario, blinded and betrayed by a faithless wife; Pia (*Pia de' Tolomei*), the innocent victim of civil strife and the jealousy of a rejected suitor – though in engineering her brother's escape from prison she contributed to her own downfall; Roberto Devereux, trapped by his own amours and by the insatiable jealousy of his Queen; Maria (*Maria de Rudenz*) betrayed by the evil genius of a former lover; Elena (*Elena da Feltre*) caught up in political intrigue and surrounded by men whose word was anything but their bond. Maria (*Il conte di Chalais*), in the centre of an eternal triangle, watches her world collapsing around her in a tightening noose of circumstance and misunderstanding. Emilia (*La vestale*) is buried alive, at the end of a chain of events beginning with a mistaken report of her lover's death in battle. Monaldeschi (*Cristina di Svezia*) is out-manoeuvred in the heady atmosphere of the court. Saffo is brought to despair and suicide by a faithless lover. Luigi Rolla yearns for the unattainable, not knowing as he dies that his dreams are about to come true. Malvina (*Il proscritto*) is caught between her husband and her lover, again in circumstances beginning with a false report of her husband's death. Rosa (*La fidanzata corsa*) is engulfed in a family feud and a fierce code of honour. Count Murray (*Il reggente*) is assassinated in a political intrigue by the husband of the woman he loved, and to whom he had once been betrothed. Ester (*Ester d'Engaddi*), the innocent victim of a jealous, rejected lover, is framed in a rigged ordeal. Bondelmonte is murdered in a family feud started when he jilted the girl he was engaged to – though the tragedy is as much hers as his. Stella (*Stella di Napoli*), caught between warring armies, sacrifices herself for a worthless lover. Camilla (*Orazi e Curiazi*) is caught in an impossible position, between love of her husband and her brothers; Eleonora (*Eleonora Dori*) destroyed by a political intrigue in a foreign court, an old lover the unwitting cause; Luisa and Rodolfo (*Luisa Miller*), helpless in the intrigues of a petty tyranny; Folco (*Folco d'Arles*) manipulated by an unscrupulous employer, not man enough to declare his origins and unable to face the future; Virginia, the victim of a tyrant's lust.

All these are characters dragged down by circumstances

over which they have no control, however much they may initially have contributed to them. They are overwhelmed by the lusts and jealousies of others, and are unwilling or unable to fight against their fate. Some of them are neutral in this respect – *Alzira* is a tragedy of chance and circumstance; Poliuto's death has an inevitability once his conversion to Christianity becomes known and he shows himself unwilling to compromise, but in this libretto, as in *La vestale* and *Ester d'Engaddi*, Cammarano displays a hatred of the ecclesiastical establishment and an attitude to the conflict between ecclesiastical and civil authority which is surprising in its vehemence. *Medea* and *Merope*, both old stories of a mythological nature, stand outside this analysis, being studies in revenge.

If there is any one theme running through the corpus of Cammarano's tragic libretti it is that of the individual broken by the inexorable pressures of externally generated circumstances, the helplessness of the individual struggling with forces which are not understood, let alone under control. They are for the most part apolitical, as befitted a writer in Bourbon Naples: where political circumstances exist, they are typically the background to domestic events, and not the *raison d'être* of the story. Those which are grounded on a hatred of tyranny – *Virginia* and *Merope* for instance – are safely located in remote circumstances. His tragedies are tragedies of people, not of ideas, people brought down by an unjust fate.

Although we are accustomed to think of Italian romantic opera as being built round love and passion, this is not an essential element and Cammarano was the first to draw attention to the absence of a love motive in a number of his works. Jealousy arising out of rejected love, or an old love put on one side, are other motives, but Cammarano was certainly prepared to write libretti that had no passionate love scene. As he wrote to Verdi in April 1848, about a proposed *Rienzi*, 'I haven't said that there is no love in it, on the contrary, in the romance the love is there – nor could I hold that as a general rule love is indispensable in melodrama – I that have given to the operatic stage *Belisario*, *L'assedio di Calais* and *Merope*.'

The subjects around which these libretti were constructed reflect the expectations of audience and singers alike, and the role in which composers saw themselves: indeed they go right to the heart of the justification for opera itself. The purpose of the libretto in the 1830s was to provide opportunities for singers to be heard in a range of emotional situations, to enable them to react in appropriate vocal fashions. Audiences came to the theatre to compare singers and to listen to beautiful voices in full flight. The librettist and the composer had to provide such opportunities, and the subjects they chose had to lend themselves to this treatment. Little wonder that one of the librettist's first concerns was to draft out the 'distribution', the list of arias and other pieces allocated to each singer, and that one of the main topics of a composer's correspondence was the eager theatrical gossip on singers' abilities and state of health, particularly pregnancies. Operas were written for singers, not for the exploration of ideas or dramatic verities. Consequently dramatic thrust and action was not an end in itself, but a means to a quite different end, the opportunity for reaction in song to a series of emotional situations. It was Verdi's domination of the operatic scene that changed all this, since he demanded truth and projection that called into question the 'time stood still' concept of the earlier tradition. The relation between action and reaction changed, becoming tilted towards the former. Hence his continuing fear of the dramatic momentum being allowed to slip away, or the dramatic temperature to fall below boiling point. These unfortunate protagonists of Cammarano's libretti did not depend on positive action, which would requre a certain level of dramatic thrust, but were passive, and plenty of dramatic time was allowed for reflection. This is not to say that dramatic events were not included – indeed one at least was always needed to launch the central finale – but that the nature of the plot did not depend on continuous forward propulsion. In a nutshell, the conventions of opera in the 1830s required protagonists who reacted rather than acted. A subject which was based on a constant struggle to impose on circumstances and bend them to a personal advantage simply did not provide the necessary opportunities for emotional expression.

This is the reason for the absence of the heroic from Cammarano's subjects, and why he avoided the historical romances which sprung up like dragons' teeth in the Italy of the 1830s, with their patriotic heroes and their struggles: at least, it is one reason – the other being the ever-present and ever-watchful censorship. Significantly, when he wanted a patriotic subject for Verdi, he chose as the vehicle for it a trivial French play, and dressed it up in Italian colours.

The nearest Cammarano came to an heroic – if defeated – protagonist was in his last libretto, *Il trovatore*. Under the urgings of Verdi, he wrestled with his libretto, doing his best to mould it into a suitable form. The irony of the situation is that the changes to the libretto which Verdi commissioned after Cammarano's death all move it back towards the older conventions. In this, as in almost every other way, Cammarano never changed. His own particular genius, for the creation of limpid, smoothly flowing verses, supported him in this: at the invention of elegaic verses he had no equal. His subjects were therefore not only those which suited the conventions of the operatic scene at the time he came on to it: they were also ideally suited to his own particular gifts.

Appendix. Cammarano's Sources

1. LA SPOSA – *dramma per musica.* Source unknown, but reads like a Scribe *vaudeville.* It is set by Cammarano in Italy at the end of the sixteenth century.
2. INES DE CASTRO – *tragedia lirica.* Sources: a) de la Motte, *Ines de Castro, tragédie,* five acts, Paris 1723. b) Bertolotti, *Ines de Castro, tragedia,* five acts, Turin 1826. c) Cammarano also mentions Greppi, *Don Pedro di Portogallo, tragedia,* five acts, Venice 1792, but he does not seem to have drawn much from it. d) Cortesi, *Ines de Castro, ballo istorico,* five acts, Milan 1831. This has points in common with Cammarano's libretto, notably the name Bianca for the second woman (Constance in a), Costanza in b) and c)). Set in Portugal in 1349.

3. UN MATRIMONIO PER RAGIONE – *melodramma*. Source, Scribe and Varner, *Le marriage de raison, comédie-vaude-ville*, two acts, Paris 1826. Set in the Lyonnais at an unstated period, apparently the early nineteenth century.

4. LUCIA DI LAMMERMOOR – *dramma tragico*. Source, Scott, *The Bride of Lammermoor*, London and Edinburgh 1819. An Italian translation by G.Barbieri appeared in Milan in 1824. My instinct is that Cammarano used a play or ballet, not yet identified, for his primary source. Set in Scotland at the end of the sixteenth century.

5. BELISARIO – *tragedia lirica*. Source, Schenk, *Belisar, Romantisches Trauerspiel*, five acts, Munich 1826. Adapted for the Italian stage (but attributed to Holbein) by Marchionni. Set in Byzantium in 580 (Cammarano), 880 (Marchionni), mid-sixth century (Schenk).

6. L'ASSEDIO DI CALAIS – *dramma lirico*. Sources: a) du Belloy, *Le siège de Calais, tragédie*, five acts, Paris 1765. b) Henry, *Eduardo III ossia L'assedio di Calais, Azione mimico-istorica*, five acts, Milan 1827. Henry acknowledged his indebtedness to a) but introduced many historical elements copied by Cammarano. Set in Calais in 1347.

7. PIA DE' TOLOMEI – *tragedia lirica*. Sources: a) Sestini, *Pia de' Tolomei, legenda romantica*, 1822. b) Bianco, *Pia de' Tolomei, dramma storico*, five acts, Naples 1836. The story of the unfortunate Pia is to be found in Villani's *Croniche fiorentine*, Book 5. Set in Tuscany in 1260.

8. ROBERTO DEVEREUX – *tragedia lirica*. Source, Ancelot, *Elisabeth d'Angleterre, tragédie*, five acts, Paris 1829. An Italian translation by G.Barbieri, *Elisabetta d'Inghilterra* was published in Milan in 1838, but may have been circulated earlier in theatrical manuscript. Set in London, according to Cammarano at the end of the sixteenth century.

9. MARIA DE RUDENZ – *dramma tragico*. Source, Anicet Bourgeois and Maillan, *La nonne sanglante, drame*, five acts, Paris 1835. The original authors place the action of the later acts in Germany, but do not give a time. Cammarano set the libretto in Elvezia in the fifteenth century.

10. ELENA DA FELTRE – *dramma tragico*. Source unknown. A *tragedia, Elena degl'Uberti*, by E.Franceschi was published in Florence in 1852. But for the late date it could be the source, as it deals with the same events. Possibly there was a common source or, again, Franceschi's play may have been circulating in manuscript. Set in Feltre in 1250.

11. I CIARLATANI – *scherzo melodrammatico*. Source, Scribe and Alexandre, *Les empiriques d'autrefois, comédie-vaudeville*,

one act, Paris 1825. A ballet by Galzerani, *Gli empirici*, was given at the S. Carlo in 1828/9. The play is set in Spain, in 1525. Cammarano retains the Spanish setting but changes the period to the seventeenth century.

12. IL CONTE DI CHALAIS – *melodramma tragico*. Source, Lockroy and Badon, *Un duel sous le Cardinal de Richelieu, drame,* three acts, Paris 1832. Set in Paris in the reign of Louis XIII (around 1630).

13. LA VESTALE – *tragedia lirica*. Sources: a) De Jouy, *La vestale, tragédie lyrique* (music by Spontini), Paris 1807. Italian translation by Giovanni Schmidt, Naples 1811. Performed in Naples up to 1829. b) Marchionni, *La vestale, dramma tragico.* There was also a ballet on the same subject by Viganò, S. Carlo 1834/5. Cammarano followed Marchionni where the latter departed from De Jouy (notably in the ending) and may well not have consulted the earlier work. Marchionni sets the action in Rome, not giving a date. Cammarano gives neither place nor date.

14. CRISTINA DI SVEZIA – *tragedia lirica*. Source, Dumas, *Christine ou Stockholm, Fontainbleu et Rome, trilogie dramatique,* five acts, Paris 1830. A ballet by Taglioni with the same title was given at the S. Carlo in 1832/3. Dumas gives no further mention of time or place; Cammarano mentions Uppsala and Fontainbleu, quoting the middle of the seventeenth century.

15. SAFFO – *tragedia lirica*. Source, possibly Beltrami, *Saffo,* Naples 1838. The story of Saffo and Faone was frequently used as a source for plays, operas and ballets, but the central episode, when Saffo interrupts the wedding of Faone and Climene, appears only – as far as I have been able to ascertain – in Beltrami's *Saffo,* which is known to me only from Anzelmi's critical notice in *Il Lucifero* for 28 September 1838, when it was produced at the Fiorentini theatre. Cammarano sets the action in Greece at the 42nd Olimpiade.

16. LUIGI ROLLA – *melodramma tragico*. Source, Lafont, *Le chef d'oeuvre inconnu, drame,* one act, Paris 1837. An Italian version by Marchionni was given at the Fiorentini theatre later the same year, and became very popular. A visiting French company gave it at the Fondo in 1839/40. The action is set in Florence in the middle of the sixteenth century, both by Lafont and Cammarano.

17. IL PROSCRITTO – *melodramma tragico*. Source, Soulié and Dehay, *Le proscrit, drame,* five acts, Paris 1839. This play soon became very popular in Italy, reaching the Fiorentini theatre in 1840. The action was placed in Grenoble in 1817,

but Cammarano moved it to Scotland in the first part of the seventeenth century.

18. LA FIDANZATA CORSA – *melodramma tragico.* Source, Ducange, *La vendetta ou la fiancée corse, drame,* three acts, Paris 1831. This play reached the Fiorentini theatre in 1833, as *La fidanzata di Corsa.* Ducange places the action in Corsica, under the Directoire. Cammarano naturally repeats Corsica, but puts the epoch back to the fifteenth century, no doubt with one eye on the censors.

19. IL REGGENTE – *tragedia lirica.* Source, Scribe, *Gustave III ou le bal masqué, opéra historique,* five acts, Paris 1833 (music by Auber). Although there is no record of Auber's opera being performed in Italy, the plot had already been used by Rossi as the basis of a libretto for Gabuzzi (*Clemenza di Valois,* Venice 1841). For obvious reasons, Cammarano moved the plot from the historical setting of Stockholm, 1792, to Scotland in 1570.

20. ESTER D'ENGADDI – *dramma tragico.* Source, Pellico, *Ester d'Engaddi, tragedia,* five acts, written in prison in 1821 but not published till 1830. Gioia's ballet on the same subject was performed at the S. Carlo in 1835. The action is set in Engaddi in the second century AD, 'about fifty years after the destruction of Jerusalem'. Cammarano follows Pellico word for word in this.

21. IL RAVVEDIMENTO – *melodramma.* Source, Mélesville and Duveyrier, *Clifford le voleur, comédie-vaudeville,* two acts, Paris 1835. This reached the Fiorentini theatre in 1839, in a translation by Rosa. The action was set in both play and libretto in Scotland in 1746.

22. IL VASCELLO DE GAMA – *melodramma romantico.* Source, Desnoyers, *Le naufrage de la Méduse, drama,* five acts, Paris 1839. Hus' ballet on the same source was given in Milan in 1841, but not as far as I know in Naples. The action takes place in France and on board the ship, in 1799–1816. Cammarano moved it to Portugal, 1565–1580.

23. BONDELMONTE – *tragedia lirica.* Source, Marenco, *Buondelmonte e gli Amedei, tragedia,* five acts, Turin 1827, and probably others. This story from the old chronicles of Florence was often used as the subject of plays and ballets. A *Bondelmonte,* probably Marenco's, was played at the Fiorentini theatre from 1834 onwards, and Galzerani's ballet at the S. Carlo in 1827/8. Cammarano followed history by placing his libretto in Florence in 1215.

24. ALZIRA – *tragedia lirica.* Source, Voltaire, *Alzire ou les americains, tragédie,* five acts, Paris 1736. Manfroce's opera on this

subject had been given in Naples in 1818, but I have not been able to trace any other representation there. *Alzire* was a well-known work, and several translations into Italian were available. The opera was set in Lima. Voltaire, in a footnote, mentions historical events between 1517 and 1535; Cammarano places it 'towards the middle of the sixteenth century'.

25. STELLA DI NAPOLI – *dramma lirica.* Source unidentified, but reads like a five-act French historical drama. It deals with the Neapolitan-Spanish wars at the turn of the fifteenth century, and is set by Cammarano in Reggio Calabria in 1495.

26. ORAZI E CURAZI – *tragedia lirico.* Source, Corneille, *Horace, tragédie,* five acts, Paris 1640. A popular source for operas; Cimarosa's setting had been performed in Naples between 1807 and 1824, but not thereafter. The story itself comes from Livy, and is set in and around Rome. Cammarano places the action there at the end of the first century after the foundation of the city.

27. ELEONORA DORI – *melodramma tragico.* Source, de Vigny, *La maréchale d'Ancre, drame,* five acts, Paris 1831. I have not been able to trace any dramatic treatment of this subject in Naples, but Nini's opera (libretto by Prati, Padua 1839) was popular in the north of Italy. The action is set in Paris in 1617.

28. MEROPE – *tragedia lirica.* Sources: a) Alfieri, *Merope, tragedia,* five acts, 1782. b) Maffei, *Merope, tragedia,* five acts, Modena 1713. c) Voltaire, *Merope, tragédie,* five acts, Paris 1743. Cammarano mentions Maffei and Voltaire (as well as Alfieri) in his foreword, but seems to have taken little from them. Maffei's tragedy was given at the Fiorentini in 1839, not having been heard there for a very long time. Taglioni's ballet on the same subject was performed at the S. Carlo in 1845. Alfieri places his tragedy in Messene, but gives no time. Cammarano copies him in this.

29. POLIUTO – *tragedia lirica.* Source, Corneille, *Polyeucte, tragédie,* five acts, Paris 1643. I know of no dramatic representation in Naples before 1838, when Cammarano originally prepared this libretto for Donizetti. Corneille places the action in Melitene; Cammarano adds 'in the year 257 of our era', following Corneille's remarks in his Examen.

30. LA BATTAGLIA DI LEGANO – *tragedia lirica.* Source, Méry, *La bataille di Toulouse, drame,* three acts, Paris 1836, on to which was grafted the historical events of the Lombard League and the defeat of Barbarossa. Méry's play was given at the Fiorentini theatre in 1837, as *La battaglia di Tolosa* (as by

Dumas!), and was very popular. It was set in Spain during the Napoleonic wars. Cammarano moved the action to Milan and Como, in 1176.

31. LUISA MILLER – *melodramma tragico.* Source, Schiller, *Kabale und Liebe, Schauspiel,* five acts, Mannheim, 1784. It was given in an Italian translation, as *Luisa Miller,* at the Fiorentini theatre in 1840. Schiller's play was set in Germany in the eighteenth century: Cammarano moved it to Tirol, in the first part of the seventeenth century.

32. NON V'È FUMO SENZA FUOCO – *farsa.* Source, Bayard, *Pas de fumée sans feu, comédie-proverbe,* one act, Paris 1849. This slight piece quickly reached Naples, as a *burla comica* with the same title as the libretto. The action was set in Paris, with no time given (though a contemporary setting could be assumed).

33. FOLCO D'ARLES – *melodramma tragico.* Source, Hugo, *Ruy Blas, drame,* five acts, Paris 1838. First seen in Naples in 1839 in a version by Belisario, as *Folco Melian.* Hugo set his play in Madrid in the 1690s. Cammarano moved it to Arles in the fourteenth century.

34. MEDEA – *tragedia lirica.* Source, Romani, *Medea in Corinto, melodramma tragico,* Naples (S. Carlo) 1813, music by Mayr. Cammaranos's libretto was a root-and-branch reworking of Romani's earlier text, and, like his, is set in Corinth a few years before the Trojan wars.

35. IL TROVATORE – *dramma.* Source, Gutiérrez, *El Trovador, dramma caballeresco,* five acts, Madrid 1836. There had been no dramatic representation of this subject in Naples, but the choice of subject was Verdi's. The setting is Aragon in 1409.

36. VIRGINIA – *tragedia lirica.* Source, Alfieri, *Virginia, tragedia,* five acts, Turin 1784. The origin of the story is recounted in Livy, Book 3, and there were several operas on the subject. Galzerani's ballet *Virginia* on the same subject was given at the S. Carlo in 1831/2. The setting is Rome, 440 BC, though this is not stated by either dramatist or librettist.

CHAPTER ELEVEN

The 'Number' and
the Structure of a Libretto

In analysing the structure of an Italian romantic libretto, it must be understood that the musical and dramatic structure is quite independent of what may be called the typographical structure – the division of the text into scenes. Conventionally a new 'scene' begins when anyone enters or leaves. Several such scenes were often contained in a continuous short verse passage, particularly at times of action. (The standard English meaning of 'scene', a section of the work taking place in the same set and without a break in time, will be referred to as a 'change of setting'.)

In terms of the musical structure, the basic unit of a libretto was the 'number'. Although certain conventions were recognised concerning the number, which will be discussed below, it was a very flexible unit which could vary from a simple aria, with a minimum of preliminary text, to a complex pattern of an introductory chorus, a long stretch of dialogue with characters coming and going, a cantabile, a long bridge passage incorporating some significant dramatic event, a cabaletta and perhaps a long closing piece of dialogue.

The task facing the librettist as he began to fashion his material was to assemble a series of numbers in a co-ordinated way, building up the dramatic structure into acts of appropriate length. He had to proceed in such a way as to allow the composer to organise his own material into sections of suitable length, and to balance the opportunities given to the different singers in accordance with their importance and their expectations (as singers, not as characters in the drama!). The object of the whole exercise was not so much dramatic thrust but the provision of suitable opportunities for the singers to be heard in a range of emotional situations. The purpose of the dramatic action was to provide occasions for reflection as much as to tell a story. Although the dramatic integrity of an opera was growing in importance, in Cammarano's work it was still less the central purpose of the opera than was the creation of opportunities for the singers.

The balance of the work between the main characters also posed a problem. There were usually three main singers, soprano, tenor and what we would now call a baritone, and they all expected opportunities for vocal expression and display. If a fourth main character – a bass or a second soprano, for instance – was added, he or she too would require to be given an appropriate opportunity. Less important singers would have to be content with contributions to concerted passages in open-verse sections. There was also the chorus to consider: for the sake of contrast and for the development of the drama, the chorus was brought on at intervals, particularly when it was necessary to heighten the dramatic tension, and would almost invariably open a serious opera, and be on stage at the final curtain.

In the overall organisation of a libretto, the structure of the acts was crucial, since the form resembled an arch, with dramatic tension building up to a climax at its keystone, the 'finale', and then relaxing towards the end of the work. The 'finale' was the standard term, not for the end of the opera (which was more likely to be a pathetic death scene) but for a complex and formalized musical section constructed around an event in which dramatic tension is brought to breaking point. In a two-act opera the finale came at the end of the first act; in a three-act opera at the end of either the first or second.

The librettist had to choose what event to build the finale around, and where to place it in the opera. This led to a second problem: the choice of the point at which to attack the dramatic story, and how to provide an effective opening including necessary antecedent information. He had then to construct a series of numbers in which tension could build up to a climax in the finale, and thereafter to bring the work to a satisfactory conclusion; the last act is often an anticlimax, in dramatic if not in musical terms.

The organisation into acts was principally important in

determining the position of the central finale – whether tension was to build up quickly and relax slowly or vice versa. Which scheme was chosen would depend on the nature of the material being made use of. Similarly, the nature of the story, and in particular its source, would determine whether changes of setting were required within the acts. This varied greatly, though two sets per act would be average, perhaps as many as eight in a three-act opera. Some operas have as few as three. By and large they would be arranged in such a way as to provide as wide a variety as could be managed. Both Cammarano's one-act operas are played in the same set throughout.

The importance of getting the structure of a libretto right is seen in the first requirements which were placed on a librettist as he began to prepare a work. One was that he should prepare a detailed synopsis of the plot, for the benefit of the composer, the management and the censors; the other was to provide a 'distribution', a list of the numbers, the purpose of which was to assess the work of each singer.

A conventional structure for a libretto of this period would be in three acts as follows: Act I would begin with a chorus, and contain three or four numbers, the last a duet or terzet. Act II would contain two or three numbers, ending with the finale. The endings of these two acts might, however, be reversed. Act III would contain three numbers, the last being an aria, duet or terzet. Thus the whole opera would be made up of an average of eight or nine numbers, plus a finale.

There is evidence that Cammarano, in preparing synopses, was conscious of the need to balance the work placed on the individual singers. The draft of the early version of *Folco d'Arles*, when he was preparing *Ruy Blas* for Donizetti under the tentative title of *Ermengalda di Provenza*, contains the following partial 'distribution':

Ermengalda — 3   Duetto E – Duetto F – Pezzo conc =
Elisa — 4   Cavatina – Finale – Duetto E – Pezzo conc =
Eginardo — 2   Finale – Pezzo conc =
Folco — 4   Romanza – Finale – Duetto Er – Pezzo conc =
Ugo — 1   Finale.

(i.e. Ermengalda – three pieces: duet with Elisa, duet with

Folco, concerted piece, etc. The distribution continues ...)

> Atto I
> Atto II
> Cavatina – Elisa
> Romanza – Folco
> Finale – Ugo, Eginardo, Elisa, Folco
> Atto III
> Duetto – Ermengalda, Elisa
> Duetto – Folco, Ermengalda
> Pezzo conc = – Folco, Ermengalda, Elisa, Eginardo

It appears that Cammarano was assessing the workload on the singers as he was drafting the structure of the libretto, since the two lists correspond. Presumably he was anxious to see who should contribute to Act I before planning it. The distribution covers the finale and five other numbers, which is not enough for a whole work, so there can be no doubt that a first act really *was* intended and that this schema does not represent a two-acter wrongly numbered. The implication is that he worked backwards, finishing with the first act, or, as I believe, that he planned the finale first and proceeded forward and backwards from that point. This throws an interesting sidelight on Donizetti's comment, when he and Cammarano were thinking of an opera on *Il duello sotto Richelieu,* that Cammarano was having such trouble with the first act that they were looking for another subject.

The conventions applied to the number, for instance the 'scena and aria', at the time Cammarano began his career as a librettist, may now be summarized. The number typically embodied a double aria of two contrasting units, the first slow and lyrical (the cantabile) and the second fast (the cabaletta). The number itself would begin with a section of dialogue in *versi sciolti* or similar open verse form, which would be set as a series of arioso passages with parts, if appropriate, in a declamatory style. This was referred to as the *scena* and might involve several characters and, if necessary, cover several scenes as the characters entered and left. After the cantabile came a bridge passage, the 'tempo di mezzo', similar in form to the opening dialogue. This would be exploited dramatically in such a way as to provide for a change in the singer's emotional state, for instance by the arrival of a messenger with important news, to justify the transition to the cabaletta.

Many variations of this pattern were possible, and by the 1830s the bridge passage could be expanded and developed to such an extent that the two parts of the aria became separated and almost independent. The whole form of the double aria, too, was changing, and here Donizetti's role was crucial. The slow nature of the first part tended to remain, though it was occasionally replaced by a movement in medium or even moderately fast tempo, but Donizetti's innovation was to write slow cabalettas, often in a much slower pulse than the first section. In this he was greatly assisted by Cammarano's ability to provide appropriate words for these slow, often pathetic pieces. This is not to say that it was under Cammarano's influence that Donizetti developed the slow cabaletta, for there are examples in his tragic operas predating their first collaboration. Although the cabaletta is traditionally associated with a display of vocal pyrotechnics, and has often been criticized (for instance by Verdi) on that account, Donizettis's breakthrough in using the second component of a double aria for quite different dramatic purposes changed its character to such an extent that its essential structural identity is often obscured.

Convention required that the important characters had a number to themselves when they first appeared, and this was often referred to as a *cavatina*. This convention was not always respected, increasing use being made of duets for first appearances. A solo number without a cabaletta was known as a *romanza*; such numbers would still include introductory material. Similarly a double aria at the close of an opera was known as a *rondo-finale*: its cabaletta was found to provide an appropriate conclusion, with attention focussed on the principal singer.

Numbers incorporating duets, terzets, etc., followed a very similar pattern, though the format was generally more flexible. The number of components could vary and the choice of tempi was greater, and they could be single (one section) or double (two). However, triple duets and terzets exist but are rare, and there is actually a trend towards a more frequent use of single form in these numbers towards the end of Cammarano's output.

The central finale also had a basic resemblance to the standard number, though it depended more clearly on dramatic justification for its detailed structure. The essential features of the finale were these: at the beginning, in a passage of dialogue, the dramatic tension inherent in the action was screwed up almost to breaking point: then came an event of overwhelming dramatic significance, usually followed by a moment of horrified silence. This event I shall call the *trigger*. This was followed by the slow section, the *largo concertato*, in which each character, or group of characters, responded to the situation with their own emotional reaction; the range of responses was likely to be very wide. After this came the *bridge passage*, in which some resolution of the situation is engineered; finally, the fast *stretta*, in which all the characters come together again on a note of common purpose. Thus a finale develops centrifugally but closes centripetally.

Lucia di Lammermoor may be used to illustrate the way numbers were used to build up the structure of an opera. It is set out unusually in two parts, of one and two acts respectively, but I shall refer to the three acts as Acts I, II and III as in modern usage. Like all other analyses in this book, it has been made from a study of the libretto, without recourse to the music.

Act I

a) Introductory chorus.

b) Two part cavatina for Enrico. Introductory material includes Normanno's suspicions concerning Edgardo: in the bridge passage the chorus returns to confirm these suspicions.

Change of setting

c) Two part cavatina for Lucia. In the bridge passage, Alisa urges Lucia to give up her ill-starred love, providing an opportunity for a change of mood.

d) Two part duet for Lucia and Edgardo, the exchange of rings forming the bridge.

Act II

e) Three part duet for Lucia and Edgardo. In the first bridge Lucia reads the forged letter, which was referred to in the introduction. She sings of her betrayal in the second section while Enrico rubs salt into her wounds. A further bridge brings the fast section in which Enrico is at his most threatening, Lucia crushed and desperate.

f) Two part aria for Raimondo (often omitted). Lucia's reluctant agreement to marry Arturo forms the very short bridge.

Change of setting

g) Finale. Begins with chorus of welcome to Arturo, continuing with dialogue as Lucia signs contract. Edgardo's arrival forms the 'trigger'. In the largo concertato the characters each respond in their own way. Edgardo rejects Lucia in the bridge passage, then everyone else comes together to denounce Edgardo.

Act III

h) Two part duet for Edgardo and Enrico – the Wolfscrag scene (often omitted).

Change of setting

i) Two part aria for Lucia (the 'mad' scene). The bridge passage here has an external dramatic role, when Enrico is prevented from attacking Lucia.

Change of setting

j) Two part aria finale for Edgardo. News of Lucia's death comes in the bridge passage, which is followed by a slow cabaletta. Edgardo kills himself, and the curtain falls as Raimondo and the chorus express their horror.

A plot which lent itself to being organized into a series of eight or nine numbers and a finale had to be simple and direct in approach. There was little room for sophisticated motivation or sub-plots. There had to be a build-up of tension to the finale, and a suitable resolution thereafter, all developed through a restricted number of these units. It ought to be said here that the composer often split up the work into more numbers than the librettist. I have based all my counts of numbers on Cammarano's practice, even if it does not coincide with the numbering adopted by the composer.

The difficulties inherent in this system of unit construction is nowhere better seen than in *Luisa Miller*, where Cammarano had to condense the large canvas of Schiller's five acts, containing a great deal of dramatic action and ideas, into a standard framework. Leaving on one side the additional problems he encountered as a result of Verdi's desire to retain the essential characteristics of Lady Milford, Cammarano was faced with moulding into the conventional structure an unusual amount of dramatic action. Naturally a great deal of Schiller (notably anything approaching political philosophy) had to be jettisoned. The way he met this problem was to write more numbers than in any other work. To fit these into a work of reasonable compass (and *Luisa Miller* is not a particularly long opera, as a result of the way Verdi set words to music, although the text is half as long again as Cammarano's average) he had to move away from the traditional series of double arias and duets. Accordingly, he simplified the individual numbers, making most of them romanzas or single duets, leading to a greatly increased fluidity of texture. A structural analysis of the libretto of *Luisa Miller* as eventually set by Verdi shows how much the text had evolved from the version which Cammarano had first sent Verdi in May 1849. Cammarano's original version is shown on p. 186 (*left*), where he designates Luisa's first piece as a cavatina: he presumably had in mind a double aria, since if he had intended a romanza he would have used that term. The final form of the libretto is shown on p. 186 (*right*).

What does not appear from this analysis is the extent to which the numbers are reduced to 'single' status. Luisa's first scena in Act I is now a romanza; the two pieces that follow it are also 'single'. The aria for Miller and the duet for Federica and Rodolfo are the only 'doubles' in Act I. In Act II, only Rodolfo's closing aria is double, but it is perhaps a special case, being specifically adapted to Verdi's insistence that the scene must not be allowed to 'go off the boil'. This aria has a remarkably long bridge passage, packed with action: Rodolfo facing Wurm with Luisa's letter, then Wurm discharging the duelling pistol, the arrival of the soldiers, the servants and finally Rodolfo's father, and the argument betwen father and son. All this leads to the cabaletta as Rodolfo gives way to despair. In Act III, Luisa's intended romanza has gone, but both the duets are double, the final terzet single.

Luisa Miller is certainly one of the most interesting libretti of the period, and was a brave (and on the whole successful) attempt at reducing the complexities of Schiller's drama to suitable proportions. Although Verdi had insisted on some unconventional matters, such as the

		I	FINALE	II	III	
Luisa	C	aria terz.		aria quart.	duet rom. duet fin.	7
Duchessa	H		duet	quart.		2
Rodolfo	O	terz.	duet		aria · duet	4
Miller	R	terz. aria			duet	3
Walter	U			quart.	duet fin.	1
Wurm	S			quart.		1

		I	FINALE	II	III	
Luisa	1° soprano	C	rom. terz.		quart.	duet duet terz. fin.	8
Duchessa	contr. compr.	H			quart.	aria	2
Rodolfo	1° tenor	O	terz.	duet		duet terz. fin.	5
Miller	1° baritone	R	terz. aria	duet	rom.	terz. fin.	4
Walter	bass compr.	U			duet quart.	duet	3
Wurm	bass compr.	S		duet	duet quart.		3

absence of a stretta in the finale, the libretto as finally set was more complex than Cammarano had originally intended. As a result there were thirteen numbers, with Luisa singing in eight of them, and even the two *comprimario* basses in three each. To achieve this degree of structural complexity Cammarano had to sacrifice the complexity of the individual units. The result is a libretto which moves much faster, where there is more action than reflection, and which appears more seamless. There is thus achieved a greater sense of movement and continuity than is usual in a libretto of the period. Even though this was perhaps what Verdi wanted, it brought its own problems. There are too many characters in the opera for them all to have proper treatment, as Julian Budden points out, and the roles do not fall easily into the conventional criteria.

Verdi's demands for emancipation from the standard forms of opera were to recur in *Il trovatore* (where he even persuaded Cammarano to forego the opening chorus). Although Cammarano's solution here was to approach the libretto in the same way as he had done with *Luisa Miller*, writing 'single' pieces, but developing more ensembles, the strange feature of this libretto is the way that the changes made to the text at Verdi's detailed request, after Cammarano had died, were in the direction of reversion to the conventional, with two single arias becoming double (both by the addition of a cantabile).

Verdi's own attitude to the form of an opera is well illustrated by a letter published by Busch in his documentary study of *Aida*. He referred dismissively – if not scathingly – to the old conventions of 'cavatina operas', which only needed one or two good singers to make a success of individual numbers, in contrast to his works, where the whole opera, and not the number, was the unit and to which the parts had to be subordinated. On 20 October 1874 he wrote to Ricordi, 'The whole is what matters, even a modest *whole*. In that way, both art and the opera gain. Otherwise, go back to *cavatina* operas. A chorus, a *cavatina* for the soprano, one for the tenor, another for the baritone, a finale with a soprano-tenor *adagio* at the octave, together with violins. . . . A second act with a duet, a chorus, a rondo for the prima donna, and that's that.'

The original 'distribution' of *Il trovatore*, added by Cammarano in the margin of the synopsis, is given below. It is particularly interesting as it shows clear evidence of a movement away from the conventional units of structure. Such expressions as 'Ferrando's narrative' are not unusual, usually indicating an interpolation within a number, but to indicate one piece as 'the death of Leonora' is certainly something new.

> *Il trovatore*
> Part I
> Chorus and Ferrando's narrative
> Cavatina, Leonora
> Terzet – Leonora, Manrico, * Di Luna
>
> Part II
> Chorus of gypsies
> Azucena's narrative
> Duet – Azucena, Manrico
> Finale
>
> Part III
> Chorus, romanza, di Luna
> Concerted piece – Azucena, di Luna, Ferrando, Chorus
> Duet – Leonora, Manrico
>
> Part IV
> Romanza – Manrico
> Duet – Leonora, di Luna
> Scena – Azucena
> Death of Leonora
> Finale

* At this stage in the drafting of the libretto, Cammarano called this character Alfonso. I have substituted the familiar Manrico.

Another unusual feature of the terminology is the use of 'finale' for the end of Part IV. 'Terzetto finale' would have been more usual; also, in Part IV the bald description 'Scena' for Azucena, which I am not aware that he used in this way elsewhere.

Finally it is worth examining the way Cammarano integrated the chorus into his numbers. Naturally the extent to which a chorus was used depends on the plot of the opera; in most the chorus is used in each act. The use of the chorus at the beginning of an opera will be discussed in the next chapter.

In later numbers, the chorus may be involved in several different ways. The first is analogous to its use at the opening – to set a frame for the number, perhaps withdrawing into the background or leaving the stage immediately afterwards, returning at the end of the cabaletta to provide a good 'curtain'. A second use is to provide the 'messenger-equivalent' role in a bridge passage, and a third is to participate directly in the action, other than by contributing as a background to large-scale set pieces. This is less common, and I have the impression that choruses could not always be relied on. Usually the chorus was relegated to a subordinate role.

From a structural point of view, one of the most interesting pieces Cammarano ever wrote is the first section of Act III of *La battaglia di Legnano* (as usual, it was an opera for Verdi which shook him out of the conventional mode). This is the scene in which the Knights of Death are assembling in the vaults of the Basilica in Milan, to renew their oath. It is not a number as usually defined, nor a finale, nor an introduction: Cammarano's distribution probably called it a *pezzo concertato*, or perhaps just a *giuramento*.

The curtain rises as they assemble. There follows a chorus of six lines of uneven length, alternating seven and eleven syllables, rhyming ABABCC (Cammarano only used unequal line lengths in set pieces of unusually dramatic situations – see Chapter 14). Arrigo enters, and, in seven lines of *versi sciolti*, seeks to join them. 'He is a Lombard, and a brave man,' sing the Knights. 'Let him be one of our number, as he has requested.' He is then admitted to their ranks and then all swear to free Italy from the tyrants – a rousing twelve-line chorus. This concludes one of Cammarano's most unconventional set pieces – though its unusual structure usually goes unrecognized.

CHAPTER TWELVE

The Opening Scene, the Central Finale and the Closing Scene

The librettist was faced with two particular problems when setting out to design the opening scene of an opera. The first was how to make a suitable 'frame' for the work, to create the atmosphere against which the rest of the story could unfold. The second, which faced all dramatists, was to manage the exposition in such a way as to ensure that the audience is quickly made aware of those matters of past history or background essential to a proper understanding of the plot. On the second point, the extent to which some sort of 'flashback' was needed depended on the point in the story at which the curtain went up.

The conventional way of beginning an opera, especially a serious one, was with an opening chorus. This had many advantages: it allowed for a colourful scene as the curtain went up, lively or static, cheerful or sombre as may have been appropriate; it enabled the audience to settle down during some music to words which probably did not contribute essentially to the development of the action; it set the mood for the piece; and, above all, it provided a 'buffer-zone' before the principals began singing. All Cammarano's libretti open with a chorus of some sort, with the exception of the two comic works written for his brother (*I ciarlatani* and *Non v'è fumo senza fuoco*) and, at Verdi's request, *Il trovatore*.

Cammarano did, however, vary the use he made of opening choruses, which can be grouped into three main categories. What I term the 'detached' opening chorus is one in which the chorus leave the stage when it is finished, and take no further part in the action that follows. The 'integrated' opening chorus is one in which the chorus remain on stage when it is finished and join in what follows in some way: at the least, by supporting the end of a cabaletta with a couple of lines of text (often repeating the last two lines of the cabaletta, with suitable grammatical variation), or, at the most, by becoming involved in the exposition of the drama. The 'off-stage' opening chorus speaks for itself and is normally detached (an exception being found in *Il reggente*, which merits special discussion). The integrated opening chorus is the most common type in Cammarano's work. The only opening chorus which does not fit easily into one or other of these categories is in *Lucia di Lammermoor*, where the chorus, having established an atmosphere of mystery and bustle, leaves the stage for the ensuing dialogue and cantabile, returning in a messenger role to effect the bridge to the cabaletta. It then remains on stage till the end of the number, supporting the end of the cabaletta.

The opening of *Il conte di Chalais* is an example of a detached chorus, and is one of Cammarano's most accomplished. It quickly creates an atmosphere of rumour and excitement, and an awareness that it is dangerous to get too much caught up in affairs of state. It is all done very economically, and is reminiscent of Romani at his best in, say, the opening of *Parisina*. The ladies and gentlemen of the Royal Court are coming together in groups. The text begins thus:

SOME LADIES
    It is true. This palace
    Which has been languishing
    In gloomy silence, is now lit up,
    Opening to festive rejoicing.
A KNIGHT
    Some great happenings shine
    Ominously through these mysteries!
A SECOND KNIGHT
    The minister's star is declining!
A THIRD KNIGHT
    He is falling from his high office!
THE FIRST KNIGHT
    It's no use pulling aside such veils . . .
ANOTHER KNIGHT
    It's not wise to be too rash.
AN OLD KNIGHT
    Leave the destiny of kingdoms
    And kings to the judgement of heaven.   (They leave.)

Notice that not all the ladies sing (though this would depend on what the composer wanted to do), and only four of the men (though again the composer would feel at liberty to set this for groups of men, and the theatre to double these parts if they could not trust individual choristers to do justice to the parts). The electric and threatening atmosphere of the Court is quickly and skilfully sketched in.

Ines de Castro provides a good example of an integrated opening chorus. Like *Il conte di Chalais*, though in a different palace in a different century, the courtiers are found in anxious groups, eagerly discussing current events. In six lines they establish that the day, which should have been given over to festivity, has become ominously clouded over as a result of the outrageous behaviour of – they do not say of whom, but as Gonzales enters, they turn to him:

CHORUS OF GRANDEES
   Tell us: the prince?
GONZALES   He dares to oppose
   The royal decree.
ONE PART OF THE CHORUS
               How rash!
THE OTHER PART   How ill-advised!
GONZALES
   He has refused Bianca's hand.
THE FIRST PART
   How could he!
GONZALES   He will be punished for it.
CHORUS OF GRANDEES
   This day, intended for festivity
   Is darkened over by clouds.

The chorus is used well beyond the opening framework, and is carried on into, and contributes to, the exposition.

Off-stage choruses are usually hymns, as in *Maria de Rudenz*, *Cristina di Svezia* and *Ester d'Engaddi*, and these do little more than act as moments of repose before the action begins. By far the most interesting use of an off-stage chorus to begin an opera with is *Il reggente*. The curtain goes up to reveal an empty stage, the scene being the great hall of the Regent's palace in Edinburgh, with large windows giving a magnificent view over the city. The sounds of military music and much rejoicing are heard, and an off-stage chorus sing a four-line chorus of welcome for the Regent, returning victorious. At this point the two leaders of the anti-Regent faction enter with a number of their adherents. They go up to the windows, look outside, form into groups and say softly amongst themselves – 'Just listen how the vulgar crowds echo his name! New laurels for him! Fate is still on his side! But watch out, proud Regent, you are rushing from your triumph to your grave! Your laurel will soon make way for funeral cypress!' This is a highly effective opening, a gift to the composer, and a rapid establishment of the ambivalent environment in which the Regent has to live.

There are two openings which need special discussion, *Saffo* and *L'assedio di Calais*. In the first of these, the curtain goes up on an empty stage, revealing the outside of the Circus where the Olympic Games were being held. There is a burst of loud applause, much clapping of hands, and the chorus – from within the Circus – is heard, as in the passage below. Alcandro is the High Priest of Apollo : Ippia, his friend, is the Chief of the Aurispices.

CHORUS
    Divine hymns! How well do they display
    The qualities of the dead prince
(*There is a moment of silence, then a growing uproar,*
finishing up as tumultuous shouting.)
    Out of the circus! Your presence here
    Is too deadly!... – Away... Away... Go!
(*Alcandro comes rushing out of the Circus in total disarray,*
his face livid with scorn. He is met by Ippia, who comes from
the other side.)
IPPIA
    What has happened?

From this point, the narrative takes over – Ippia has provided the very excuse needed for Alcandro to put him– and the audience – in command of the situation. The excitement of this opening precipitates the audience into the action and provides a magnificent opportunity for the composer, though it has to be said that Pacini did not rise to the occasion.

L'assedio di Calais in its opening, as in so many other respects, is *sui generis*, and clearly betrays the influence of its ballet source. The curtain goes up on the advance posts of the English army besieging Calais, at the point where the walls of the city reach the sea. The English army is wrapped in deep sleep (they do not appear to have posted any look-outs!). Aurelio, the son of the gallant Mayor of Calais, lets a rope-ladder down from the city walls and descends, searches until he finds some bread, which he ties on to the end of a rope. It is immediately pulled up. Unfortunately one of the soldiers wakes up and raises the alarm, and the camp is roused by the noise.

At this point the soldiers sing a short chorus, in which they threaten to build a heap of corpses where the walls had stood. While the action of this opening scene closely follows the plot of Henry's ballet, the words are Cammarano's – but the significance of this passage does not lie in the words, but in the fact that Cammarano did not follow convention in writing a more usual opening chorus. It would have been just as easy for him to write a suitable chorus for the English soldiers, perhaps before they went to sleep, bemoaning their long absence from home, but looking to a speedy end to the siege now that famine conditions prevailed within the city. Aurelio could then have descended from the walls, and even sung a romanza about the plight of his beloved Calais before finding the bread and arousing the English soldiery. Perhaps in this opening one can detect the hand of the composer – though Cammarano's synopsis shows the scene just as it appeared in the final libretto.

Another unconventional opening is, of course, in *Il trovatore*. Verdi remarked that 'all operas begin with a chorus', and urged Cammarano to break with tradition. While Verdi would not have had an opportunity to see *L'assedio di Calais*, he would surely have known *Saffo*, and in any case knew from their previous collaboration that Cammarano was not wedded to the conventional. It is abundantly clear from Cammarano's original synopsis of *Il trovatore* that he had intended it begin with a chorus in the usual way, but instead he began with Ferrando rousing the Count's retainers, launching almost at once into his explanatory narrative.

Having provided a suitable framework for the beginning of the opera, the next task facing the librettist was to put the audience in possession of the necessary background information. Operas of this period are notoriously hard to follow, but the essential information is usually there. The difficulty is that it often goes by without listeners being aware of its significance, and they are not always willing to undertake the relatively small amount of homework required for familiarization, now that theatrical conditions do not permit them to follow the text with a libretto as the performance proceeds.

The later the point of attack (that is, the point the story has reached at the time the opera begins) the more difficult is the librettist's task, and the more explanation is needed. On the other hand, in a work like *L'assedio di Calais* there is little the audience needs to know about past events in order to follow the story – only that Calais, after a long siege, is almost starving. By contrast, *Il trovatore* has a very late point of attack, and to understand what is going on on the stage a lot of past history must be made known – hence Ferrando's narrative. Indeed one essential piece of information is kept back for full dramatic effect to the very last line, 'He was your brother!' It is not of course necessary that *all* the relevant information shall be available to the audience, still less to all the characters, or the effect of surprise dénouements will be lost, but a working knowledge of the antecedents is essential. The dramatist/librettist has therefore to decide just how much should be made known to the audience, and how to get it across.

Lucia di Lammermoor, being a well-known and familiar text, will serve as an example. What is it that the audience must know of previous events if they are to understand why the course of true love is not to be allowed to run smoothly? First, that Enrico and Edgardo are from two opposed families; that the former has ousted the latter from his ancestral seat. Second, that Enrico's fortunes are waning, and that Lucia has refused the hand of the one man who could help to restore them. Third, that Lucia had fallen in love with a young man, as yet unidentified, who had saved her from a charging bull.

Once all this is understood, the rest of the story can be unfolded as it proceeds. Cammarano manages the opening by using a chorus in which Enrico's henchmen are despatched to search (we are not told what for, except that it will reveal the ghastly truth), so that the shameful mystery can be cleared up. Thus the initial atmosphere which has been created suggests that something has gone badly wrong. As the chorus depart, Enrico comes forward with his domestic chaplain and his faithful retainer, Normanno. The latter begins 'You are worried!' – a typical opening gambit, and whenever Cammarano uses it you may be sure that a narrative of some sort is about to begin. Enrico replies – 'With good cause! As you know, the star of my fortunes is falling, while Edgardo, the deadly enemy of my family, raises his rash head from his ruined tower, and laughs at me. Only one hand can strengthen my wavering power, and Lucia dares to refuse! Ah! She is no sister of mine!' The chaplain intervenes – 'Can a weeping girl, still mourning at the fresh grave of her mother, turn her eyes towards a wedding bed?' Normanno interjects 'Closed to love? Lucia is burning with love' and proceeds to tell the story of the bull, adding that he suspects the rescuer to be none other than Edgardo. Thus in some twenty-five lines of dialogue the whole background is sketched in.

It ought to be added that Cammarano took great care to ensure that his libretti were self-sufficient, and that information needed was given in the text. In this he was in marked contrast with some of his colleagues, who were nothing like as conscientious and often relied on long prefaces to make the background clear. This was something that Cammarano only did once – in *Stella di Napoli* – and there is evidence that he had to prepare this libretto at short notice (see Chapter 6).

Cammarano's libretti vary greatly in their point of attack. One group has hardly any need for background information, and can be allowed to develop naturally as the action proceeds. A second group – including *Lucia di Lammermoor* – have a medium-late point of attack, and one early piece of narrative can cover the situation. A third group have a very late point of attack, and detailed explanations were required, and at these Cammarano was not usually so successful.

A number of Cammarano's plots depend on the same dramatic cliché, the appearance of a lover long believed to be dead. Since the surviving partner has invariably found someone else, this leads to obvious difficulties. Cammarano's problem was how best to prepare for the situation. For example, in *Poliuto*, Paolina, believing Severo dead in battle, had married Poliuto, only to find that Severo was returning as Pro-consul. The information is given very simply when Nearco tells her that the Christians can expect no mercy under the new representative of Rome, Severo.

La vestale depends, also, on this same situation. Hearing that Decio had been killed in action, Emilia has become a Vestal. At the end of the morning hymn which opens the work, the Grand Vestal announces the return of Decio, the conqueror of Gaul. Like Paolina, Emilia is thunderstruck – was he not reported dead? She receives the same answer: rumour lied, he was wounded, and is still alive. It is not till Emilia steps forward with the laurel leaves, and she can have a whispered conversation with Decio, that he realizes what has happened. *Il proscritto* has the same motive; the whole of the first scene, when Malvina's new husband is welcomed, goes by without any hint of worry. It is not till Odoardo arrives by secret paths to take his sister to the altar that there is any mention of her dead husband Giorgio. Giorgio's return later in the act, when he reveals his presence to Malvina, precipitates the action which ends in her taking poison.

The most economical explanation of a complex situation is probably the opening of *Orazi e Curiazi*. The audience must know that Rome is at war with Alba, and that the two families, the Roman Orazi and the Alban Curiazi are related by marriage. There are three Orazi brothers, and a sister Camilla. There are similarly three Curiazi brothers and a sister, Sabina. One of the Orazi brothers is married to Sabina, while Camilla is about to be married to Sabina's brother Curiazo. There is thus a double bond between the families, with each of the two women having divided loyalties, to her brothers one way and to her husband/fiancé the other way. It is essential to have this situation clearly in mind if the plot is to be properly understood. The opera opens with a chorus of Roman women calling for victory over Alba. Camilla and Sabina, having been immersed in gloomy silence, come forward:

CAMILLA
    As the words freeze on my lips
    So there is terror on yours!
SABINA
    You were born Roman, I became Roman;
    And yet it is not permissible for us
    To pray with them! Amongst the Alban ranks
    My brothers are fighting!
CAMILLA   And amongst the ranks
    Of Rome my brothers are fighting!...
SABINA
    And on this side, my husband!...
CAMILLA
    And on *that* side, my beloved!...

Whether the audience can keep up with the two ladies and work out the family ties as this dialogue proceeds is another matter; but it is all there, in a masterly condensed exposition, and the action can proceed from that point on.

There seems to be no relation between Cammarano's choice of detached or integrated opening chorus and the lateness of the point of attack, and he used both types at all stages in his career. The off-stage choruses, however, are all to be found in libretti written between 1838 (*Maria de Rudenz*) and 1843 (*Ester d'Engaddi*).

One other convention was that the entry of the prima donna should be held back till the second number, or even later. This was clearly to add to the impact of her appearance, at a time when the performance had settled down and late-comers were all in their seats. This convention had never been followed slavishly, and Cammarano broke with it seven times. There is also a general tendency in Cammarano's later operas for the opening number to be a romanza or a single duet (whether or not the prima donna was involved), as if he was becoming increasingly aware of a need to move more quickly into the action.

Two of Cammarano's libretti are laid out in a Prologue and either three acts (*Il vascello de Gama*) or two acts

(*Alzira*). It is not easy to see why this division was accepted – although there is a long time difference between the Prologue and Act I of the former, there is not in the latter. From the structural point of view, however, it is noteworthy that Act I of each of these operas is written as if it were the opening act, with a regular opening chorus and exposition.

The placing of the central finale has already been mentioned. Its importance was such that it dominated the whole structure of an opera, and the opportunity for and the placing of a finale must have been very much in Cammarano's mind both in choosing subjects and in making his synopses. If the libretto was based on an effective play it was likely that a suitable opportunity for a finale was already present.

In most of his three-act libretti, Cammarano places the central finale at the end of the second act. This is perhaps what might be expected: it gives more dramatic time in which to lead up to the complex situation, and less time for the run-down to the final curtain. In his earlier works, however, he seems to have preferred the end of the first act, leaving more time for resolution. Up to 1837 only *Lucia di Lammermoor* and *Roberto Devereux* had their finales placed at the end of Act II, but from that time on Act II was the usual, though by no means the invariable choice. Evidently Cammarano came to see the end of the second of three acts as the most appropriate place for the finale, though there seems to have been a pull to an earlier placement; in the four-act operas, it was the second rather than the third act which carried the main weight of the musico-dramatic structure.

The difficulty with an early climax was that the emotional tension of the opera took a long time to wind down. One example of this is seen in *Il Conte di Chalais*, where the price of accepting the early climax was the loss of variety in Acts II and III. But this problem is not necessarily inherent in every early climax. *Belisario* is a loosely structured work, and while Belisario's downfall following the production of the forged letter is the only possible trigger for a finale, and must come in Act I, much of the dramatic interest of the story, and the development of the father-daughter relationship, only emerges in the last two acts. Nevertheless, the third act is dramatically feeble. *L'assedio di Calais* is in this respect, as in so many others, a fascinating work. The obvious place for a conventional finale might seem to be in Act II, with the choice of the six burghers who were to offer their lives in exchange for the safety of the city. It would be easy to construct a finale based on a moment of silence as the English demand is read out; then an ensemble of response as those present give way to their emotions: then a bridge passage in which the six volunteers step forward and a stretta in which everyone is rallied by patriotic fervour and the six are escorted out as saviours of Calais. Cammarano – maybe at Donizetti's suggestion – avoided this and transferred the finale to Act I, where he manufactured an incident with an English spy to launch it, then wrote a highly dramatic end to the second act, with the six stepping forward one by one, moving straight into a prayer before they leave amidst general lamentation. By avoiding the easy and conventional, Cammarano achieved a scene of great dramatic strength and integrity.

Pia de' Tolomei also presented problems with the finale, though these were not inherent in the subject matter. One of the difficulties was the need to pad out the role of Rodrigo, and as the work was laid out in two acts this retarded the climax unnecessarily – though this is not the reason why the finale failed and had to be rewritten. The obvious 'trigger' for the finale is provided by Pia's husband, Nello, breaking into her room when she was, as he thought, entertaining her lover; her visitor was in fact her brother, his enemy, whose escape Pia had engineered. Nello breaks down her door, but she overturns the lights and her brother disappears through a secret passage. As servants enter with torches, Nello rushes on Pia to kill her, but is restrained. Everyone launches into a concluding stretta as the act ends with Pia fainting and Nello led away. The trouble was that the finale was too much abridged: it has no largo and no resolution, only direct action. Following the first performances, Donizetti touched up the orchestration, but it was still unsuccessful. The impresario Lanari wrote to him a week later, 'the revised stretta of the finale of *Pia* does not produce any effect'. In fact the whole ground plan of the finale was defective: there was no opportunity for the expression of emotional diversity and hence no need for unification in a stretta, which therefore became merely a quick way of bringing down the curtain on some pell-mell action.

The revisions that Cammarano proceeded to make to this finale were therefore fundamental. As well as suppressing much of the role of Pia's brother, he eliminated the earlier scene of Nello's homecoming and his interview with Pia, which is dramatically superfluous, despite its dramatic irony, since all that is required of Nello is that he should arrive in time to break down her door. The end of the act was thus brought forward, and then rewritten. After Nello rushes at Pia to kill her, she falls senseless to the ground. Then comes – in Cammarano's own words – 'un momento di spaventole silenzio' ('a moment of fearful silence') as Pia, white as a corpse, is helped to a chair. He then wrote the words for a conventional largo of response. A bridge passage follows, with Nello's men reporting that the intruder had got away and Pia refusing to name him. Furiously Nello orders her to his castle in the Maremma and the act ends in a tumultuous stretta. In fact Cammarano substituted an entirely conventional finale for one which had broken with convention.

The problem of the central finale of *Il reggente* was of a different nature: it was not where to place the finale but which one to chose, since the obvious way of reducing Scribe's five-act *Gustave III* (written as a libretto for Auber) to a three-act Italian libretto was to choose for the end of the first act the scene where the fortune-teller warned the disguised king that the man who next shook his hand would be his assassin; and for the second, the moment when the kings's friend discovered that the veiled lady he was escorting from a rendezvous with the king was his own wife. (The plot is familiar as that of Verdi's later *Un ballo in maschera*). The first Italian treatment of this subject, Rossi's *Clemenza di Valois* (music by Vincenzo Gabussi, Venice 1840), solved the problem by having two full-scale finales. Cammarano did very much the same two years later. He treated the first-act finale in the same way, making it the major finale. In the second act, the discovery of Amelia's identity is followed by 'Qualche momento di silenzio' and a short ensemble, obviously suitable for a largo, and set, expansively, in this way by Mercadente; a short bridge passage as the meeting with the conspirators is arranged, and a short stretta. This is probably the shortest finale Cammarano ever wrote, but it is absolutely regular and reads very well. By making the two finales of such different weight, he avoided closing the two acts with large-scale finales, and placed the dramatic balance firmly forward.

When Somma and Verdi approached the subject fifteen years later, they, too, placed the main finale at the end of the first act. It was in the second-act finale that *Un ballo in maschera* breaks away from convention: instead of the expected largo, the identification of Amelia releases that magnificent sardonic chorus in which the conspirators poke bitter fun at the man caught with his own wife. Instead of building up into a grand ensemble, the music fades away as the conspirators disappear into the night.

The most difficult problem Cammarano encountered was with *Il trovatore*. It is quite clear from the synopsis that Cammarano intended to write a full scale finale for the end of Act II, the scene in which the Count of Luna planned to abduct Leonora as she was about to take the veil, only to find himself thwarted by the unexpected appearance of his rival Manrico, whom he thought he had killed in a duel. The synopsis of the end of this scene goes as follows:

> The sacred ceremony begins, hymns are heard from the Church, Leonora advances slowly to enter it to take her vows. 'Stop' exclaims the Count 'Not God Himself takes you from me – you are mine!' So saying he rushes towards Leonora to seize her, but between him and his prey appears Manrico, like a phantom arisen from the tomb. Surprise and horror everywhere; but once the first shock is over, and while the fury between the rivals reaches new heights, the place is overrun by a band led by Ruiz. Castello has been taken by Urgel's men. The Count is repulsed and Manrico drags Leonora away.

Here the finale structure is quite clear. The appearance
of Manrico is the event which initiates it. Cammarano's
words 'surprise and horror everywhere' are a typical
description of the awestruck moment before a largo ensemble begins. The Largo itself could easily be written
round the contrasting emotions of those present – Leonora's mystification and hope; Manrico's defiance; the
Count's thwarted fury. The arrival of Ruiz and his men can
form the bridge passage to precipitate a stretta as Manrico
bears the fainting Leonora away and the Count is repulsed.
The first version of the libretto bears this out. The words
for the largo are there, three eight-line stanzas, one each for
Leonora, Manrico and the Count, with some lines for the
chorus. Similarly, at the end of the scene the words for the
stretta are there – four lines each for the various characters
present. In fact, with the exception of the stretta, the text
in the autograph manuscript is very close to that eventually printed.

Nevertheless, this finale did not suit Verdi, and Cammarano wrote another version – very much shorter, lacking any of the components of a conventional finale. As the
Count goes to seize Leonora, Manrico steps forward, and
the light from a lamp shines on him: everybody draws
back horrified, shouting 'Il Trovatore!': as the curtain
falls, Manrico drags Leonora away. No largo, no bridge, no
stretta, just an abrupt piece of action. This ending did not
please Cammarano, who had it in mind to rewrite it, but he
died before he could do so. Verdi returned to the original
finale, but set the concerted passage not as a largo but in
quick tempo, judging it be more effective that way. Consequently he did not need a stretta (perhaps, he said, Cammarano only wrote it because it was customary). He therefore shortened the bridge passage and struck out the whole
of the stretta, after adapting a couple of lines from it for the
last two lines of the act as they are now printed.

The problem here was that Verdi did not want the finale
to go 'off the boil', with the characters just standing still
and singing. The stretta was dramatically unnecessary and
should therefore be jettisoned. It was not a question of
whether a finale was needed or not — Verdi equally
rejected the quick curtain of Cammarano's second version,

which provided an end to the act without an ensemble finale. He accepted the need for such a finale, but required the conventional form to be modified in the interests of dramatic momentum.

The dramatic situations with which Cammarano chose to project these full-scale ensembles were, of course, many and varied, depending on the nature of the dramatic material with which he was wrestling. Certain types recur. Although a few defy categorization, most of Cammarano's finale situations will be found to fit into one of the following types: the sudden appearance of someone believed dead (or far away); the production by one party of another not known to be in their power; the admission of identity; the disclosure of a well-kept secret; accusations (true or false) of treason, infidelity etc.; or recognition of a long-lost relative.

The importance of choosing the right incident to launch the finale is well illustrated by the problems inherent in making an opera out of Scott's *Bride of Lammermoor*. The structural problem again revolves round the choice of an incident for the central finale. The most dramatic moment is Edgardo's arrival at the signing of the contract. If this is used, and particularly if the finale is brought forward to the end of the first act, the rest of the opera has to be padded out, and a way found for disposing of Edgardo, Scott's quicksand being theatrically out of the question. If, however, the contract scene is held back till the third act, a quick end to Lucia and Edgardo has to be found, and the early part of the opera would require padding out, with some suitable incident – preferably one which would not foreshadow the contract scene – found for a central finale. The result does not have to be true to Scott, of course, but it would be a pity to lose Lucia's murder of her bridegroom, and her subsequent madness, and the challenge between the two rivals. In this respect, and bearing in mind the 'arch' structure of an opera, Cammarano's solution was workmanlike and in many ways the best possible. He avoided a first-act finale, for the first time in his career; he laid out the opera so as to use the contract scene as the pivot of the work. Bucklaw's murder and Lucia's death take place off stage, leaving Edgardo to carry off the final scene on his own. The opera is, in fact, well paced – though not if the Wolfscrag scene is omitted, as it usually is today. The best feature of it is the inexorability of the growth of dramatic tension from the very beginning of the work towards the climax in the contract scene, but by and large Cammarano seems to have found the build-up of tension in the first half of an opera easier to handle than its relaxation in the second.

The situations which Cammarano used to project a central finale all embodied that element of surprise needed to evoke a varied emotional response from those present. Given such a trigger – and one usually lay to hand in the source play – it was not difficult for Cammarano to write a large-scale ensemble. Whereas in the spoken play it was likely that this surprising event would quickly be followed by the fall of the curtain, the requirement of a coming-together and a measure of unity at the end of the opera finale made the resolution of the situation harder to work out. Consequently the bridge passages between ensemble and stretta vary greatly in length and complexity.

It is a measure of Cammarano's skill as a librettist that his finales are so well constructed as not to be seen as forced into a conventional mould. They grow naturally out of the dramatic context and develop effortlessly towards the strettas. Only a few of them could come under the heading of 'shoddy *coup-de théâtre*' of which librettists are often accused. After the unsatisfactory attempt in *Pia de' Tolomei*, it was not until Verdi demanded an end to long-drawn-out reflection that this type of finale had to be reconsidered. The history of their collaboration shows how hard it was for him to rethink the central tenets of his operatic design. Verdi required dramatic action, not emotional reflection, and Cammarano's experience was geared to the latter. A survey of his finales shows little development in his style: from time to time he would try something new, as in *Il reggente,* but by and large his technique was established in his earlier works and changed little thereafter.

The traditional way of ending an Italian serious opera had been for the prima donna to be given a rondo-finale with a bravura cabaletta, which, with appropriate support from the rest of the cast and the chorus, could be relied upon to bring the curtain down on a proper note of enthusiasm. This was all very well, but as the old form of serious opera, which usually ended on a situation of reconciliation, triumph or magnanimity, began to give way to more romantic concepts, in which the pathetic death of the protagonist on stage was a more likely conclusion, some escape from this tradition had to be found. The old tradition died hard, and was still strong in the mid-1830s, as Donizetti found when he ran into trouble with the soprano Méric-Lalande over the ending of his opera *Lucrezia Borgia* in 1833. Eventually he had to write a closing aria for her (the story goes that he deliberately wrote one beyond her capabilities in order to take a subtle and damaging revenge). The stumbling-block was really the old convention that operas should end happily, and that even though it was acceptable that characters should die at the end of the work, tragic, particularly violent, deaths on stage were not to be permitted. This was fairly easily accommodated, since where a violent death was essential to the dramatic action, it could take place off-stage and be reported by a suitable eyewitness. For instance, in *Virginia*, the culmination of the whole story comes when Virginia's father stabs her in public rather than see her pass into the hands of the tyrant Appio. The conventions of the *spoken* drama permitted Alfieri's tragedy of 1784 to end in this way, but when Romanelli's libretto was set by Casella in 1811, her death was reported to the mass of the populace on stage. The subject then fell out of use (there had been five settings of various libretti between 1785 and 1800), and when it re-surfaced in the 1840s, when Nini's (1843) and Vaccai's (1845) operas came out, Virginia's death could take place in full view of the audience. Mercadante's opera, to Cammarano's text, was written in 1850, but not allowed by the censor, due, I suspect, to a general distaste for the political undercurrents of demands for freedom from tyranny in the years after 1848 rather than for the spectacle of a violent death. (The comparison of versions of the same story made at different times and for different cities provides a valuable means of assessing trends and tastes.)

The tradition of happy endings or, at least, that which prevented the display of violent death on stage, began to loosen its hold, as far as I can judge, in the mid-1820s, though the various authorities were able to hold back the flood-tide at their own rates. It seems to have been around 1830 that the Neapolitan censors began to yield. Even so, there were limits, and as late as 1837 the libretto of *Maria de Rudenz* was considered by the management of the Fenice theatre in Venice to go too far, and the mayhem of the final act had to be reduced. Many of the libretti of the 1830s are ambivalent as to the precise fate of the protagonist: many heroines were described as *svenuto* as the curtain fell, and this means unconscious or fainting rather than actually dead.

It was not so much the fact of death which worried the censors, but the manner of it, since violence in the theatre was considered to be a corrupting influence on the moral sensibilities of the audience. Death of a politically active figure, as a result of a conspiracy, perhaps at the hands of an assassin, was dangerous, while that of a reigning monarch was out of the question – hence the trouble that Cammarano went to to move sensitive subjects to remote, out-of-the-way places like Scotland and to earlier epochs.

A common way of avoiding the display of violence on the stage was for the murder to be committed off-stage, with witnesses reporting what had been done, before the victim staggered on to the stage, living just long enough to finish the rondo-finale. Another way of avoiding violence on stage was to have the heroine going out of her mind; in this way Anna Bolena (Romani/Donizetti, *Anna Bolena*, Milan 1830) cheats the executioner, dying before she could be taken out to the block. On the other hand, another Queen of England, Leonora di Guienne, wife of Henry II, stabbed her rival, the fair Rosamond, in full view of the audience and the opera ends on a note of exultation (Romani/Coccia, *Rosmunda d'Inghilterra*, Venice 1829). Obviously the old conventions were losing ground.

Consequently by the time that Cammarano began writing tragic, romantic libretti, the old conventions had begun to be disregarded, and the use of death or suicide on the stage had become generally acceptable. The whole development of the Italian romantic opera had become more and more dependent on the use of plots set in the middle ages, or more recent times, with their implied commitment to violent solutions to political and personal problems. Violent death on stage could no longer be avoided, and the librettist faced the problem of handling it. Remembering that the musico-dramatic weight of the opera still rested heavily on the central finale, the overall dramatic structure could not be one which culminated in some climactic event at the final curtain. From the fulcrum of the central finale, the dramatic intensity (if not perhaps the pace) had to slacken, so that there was a presumption against an heroic death at the final curtain. The discussion of Cammarano's choice of subject matter in Chapter 10 has revealed that super-charged, heroic situations were inappropriate to the reflective, time-stands-still, nature of Italian romantic opera, where attention tended to be concentrated on the sufferings of the individual caught in a complex of inimical circumstances out of his or her control. Consequently it was inevitable that most of his protagonists would die in despair rather than in action.

There are, of course, some exceptions, and some libretti do not end in death at all – *I ciarlatani* is a comedy, *Non v'è fumo senza fuoco* a farce; of the serious works, *La sposa*, *Un matrimonio per ragione* and *Il ravvedimento* all end with the sound of approaching wedding-bells. *L'assedio di Calais* ends with a hymn of praise for the magnanimity of the English king (which must have gone down very well on a Royal Occasion). *Il vascello de Gama* (described, uniquely, as a *melodramma romantico*) ends with the survivors of the shipwreck being rescued from their raft after many days at sea, though not before the villainous Bruno is despatched to a watery grave. *Merope* is in this respect an old-fashioned text, in that Polifonte is murdered off-stage in the temple, though there is nothing old-fashioned about the way in which Cammarano treats the description of the scene, as discussed in Chapter 7. The opera ends on a note of deliverance and rejoicing. Apart from this handful of exceptions, all of Cammarano's texts end with at least one death, though in one of them – *Roberto Devereux* – this is reported and not seen; Queen Elizabeth brings down the curtain on a note of fury, in an old-fashioned 'barnstormer'. This uses the device of a 'messenger' bridge in the aria finale, with news of the death ushering in the cabaletto, which Thomas Kaufman, in his notes accompanying the recording of Donizetti's *Gemma di Vergy*, traces back to *Parisina*.

How, though, is a pathetic death scene to be handled, structurally, in a libretto? One way, by far the most common in Cammarano's work, is to end the work with a conventional double aria (the aria finale), with the chorus and other characters joining in at the very end as the protagonist dies. A similar variation, used more frequently as Cammarano's career proceeded, was to substitute a duet for an aria, and three of his last operas, *La battaglia di Legnano, Luisa Miller* and *Virginia,* end with a terzet, in all cases single rather than double.

These double aria finales still had to be constructed within the conventional number. To illustrate this, one example will suffice. In the last act of *Pia de' Tolomei* there is a change of setting about half way through, and the curtain rises on Pia's prison, where she is sitting on a rough stool, ill and shuddering. Ubaldo, her gaoler, brings her in a poisoned drink, which, after a passage of *versi sciolti*, she drinks, not knowing what it is. At this point comes the first part of her double aria, in which she prays for her husband Nello to hurry to her side, while there is still time. The bridge passage sees the return of Nello, now aware of her innocence, but not realizing that he comes too late to countermand his orders for her to be poisoned. He seeks and receives her forgiveness and then, questioning Ubaldo, realizes what has happened. There now enters Pia's brother Rodrigo with a party of Guelphs, to rescue her. He goes to kill Nello, but Pia stops him. She then moves into the cabaletta, not a display of vocal fireworks, but a pathetic slow one, in which she begs them to reconcile their differences and, in the second stanza, welcomes a gentle death. The opera ends with a supporting passage for the chorus.

This is only one example out of the dozen or so which could have been selected to show that the conventional organization of the number could form the basis for a closing death scene. It only needs to be added that most of these are written for the prima donna to have the aria finale, the exceptions being tenors (in *Lucia di Lammermoor*, *Il reggente* and *Luigi Rolla*) and a baritone (Gusmano in *Alzira*).

A second type of ending occurs when the dramatic situation requires some action after the end of the cabaletta. This type is not frequent, but *Lucia di Lammermoor* offers a good example, with Edgardo's suicide and the bystanders' intervention.

The ending of *La vestale* requires separate discussion. It is set in the place where Emilia is to be buried alive. The populace gather, Emilia is brought on in a bier, half crazed, imagining herself with Decio. This is set as the first part of a duet with her friend Giunia, but Giunia finds she cannot get through to her. As the bell ceases its tolling, Emilia faints into her friend's arms. At this point the High Priest urges a swift completion of the ceremony; Rome is in tumult, Decio up in arms. The lictors go to drag Emilia to the tomb, and she and Giunia then sing the cabaletta of the duet finale, four lines each of farewell. At the end of the cabaletta, as the tomb is closed, Decio rushes in with his followers. He demands her back, but his father, the Consul, declares him an enemy of the State, and the High Priest adds, of the Gods also! Decio rushes at the latter with his sword, but his father bars the way, and Decio turns his sword upon himself. Decio then has a four-line stanza, similar in every way to the pathetic, dying cabaletta given to so many of Cammarano's dying protagonists, though shorter. There is thus here a double ending, a regular double duet, for Emilia and Giunia, ending after the cabaletta with the descent of Emilia into the tomb, and a further ending for Decio, with a single, short aria with concluding choral support. In fact a number of performances ended at the entombment, omitting the whole of the last section, with Decio's uprising and death (either because the management wanted the work to end with the prima donna, or because of the sentiments of the last scene). I have examined many copies of the libretto printed for different performances in the 1840s and about one quarter end at the entombment, suppressing Decio's attempt at rescue.

Another ending that calls for special analysis is that of *Poliuto*. This is structured as a double duet finale for Poliuto and Paolina; Poliuto is about to be thrown to the lions and, in the cantabile, his wife begs him to renounce his belief in Christianity while there is still time. Then, in the bridge passage, she experiences an instant conversion herself and resolves to die with him. In the cabaletta they express their joy as they hear all around them the sound of angelic harps. The doors of the prison are thrown open, and a huge crowd is seen in the amphitheatre beyond. Poliuto is given a last chance to renounce his religion but he rejects it, and, to the horror of all present, Paolina announces her intention of going to the lions with him, denouncing the Gods of Rome. This could well mark the end of the work, with the curtain coming down as the martyrs go forward into the arena, but Cammarano keeps the action moving; the position of Severo, Paolina's former betrothed, is still to be resolved. He therefore repeats the words of the cabaletta for Poliuto and Paolina, adding a further eight lines for Severo, lines which match exactly in metre and rhyme. The crowd meanwhile are getting very restive – 'Death, death to the evil-doers! Your God, where is he now?' As Poliuto and Paolina are driven into the arena, Severo tries to kill himself, but is disarmed as the curtain falls.

Thus the conventional structure is stretched to include an effective and dramatic ending, this time by repeating the cabaletta of the duet and converting it to a terzet, making use of an additional bridge passage at the same time. The third section does not really convert the double duet into a triple duet with an added part, since the cabaletta is repeated, and the bridge passage does not lead to a change in the dramatic situation as far as Poliuto and Paolina are concerned. When Donizetti came to set this to music he completely recast Cammarano's text, so that this impressive piece of dramatic craftsmanship goes for nothing.

The most interesting of Cammarano's endings of this second type – though for quite different reasons – is that of *Cristina di Svezia*, since it affords a direct comparison

between his work and another's. It will be remembered
that it was written for Genoa, for the composer Nini, and
that due to unforeseen circumstances the third act was
written by Saccherò. The following year Cammarano himself completed the text and it was given in Naples, with
music by Lillo. There is sufficient evidence of common
wording in the two versions of the third act to make it
quite certain that Saccherò was working from Cammarano's original synopsis, as would indeed have been
expected, so that we are presented with two versions
worked up from the one synopsis by two different librettists. Saccherò was still a beginner, having written only
one libretto previously, but his subsequent output (some
fourteen libretti) is strong on dramatic sense but weak in
poetry. (Cammarano would never have written, nor would
the Neapolitan censors have permitted, such lines as:

> Io vo' miralo, irriderlo
> Nell' agonia mortale;
> Io vo' di lui le viscere
> Squarciar col mio pugnale;

> (I want to watch him, mock him
> In his mortal agony;
> I want to disembowel him
> With my dagger;)

which Saccherò puts into the mouth of Count Sentinelli in
his version of the third act.)

In *Cristina di Svezia*, Cristina is in love with the
Marchese Monaldeschi, but has a rival in Giulia, by whom
Monaldeschi has a son. Monaldeschi has been condemned
to death, and Guilia brings the little boy to Cristina to beg
for mercy. I strongly suspect that the synopsis would have
read at this point 'duet finale, Cristina and Guila', and this
is how Saccherò begins. The cantabile has Guilia's plead-
ing and Cristina's remorse; in the bridge passage Giulia
and her son throw themselves at Cristina's feet; in the
cabaletta comes Cristina's pardon and Giulia's rejoicing.
But it is too late – Monaldeschi is already mortally
wounded, and staggers in to collapse with an eight-line
passage, in which he assures Giulia of his everlasting love,
and dies blessing his son. However, Cristina then launches
into a single aria finale, with concluding choral support, in

which she gives full rein to her rage and hatred, falling back
in a faint into the arms of her ladies. All-in-all, effective
theatre but loosely constructed.

The equivalent section of Cammarano's own version is
laid out initially in the same general way. The cantabile of
the duet is similar, but in the bridge passage there is a long
dialogue, not in *versi sciolti*, but in fourteen lines of highly
expressive, rhyming verse. Cristina then agrees to pardon
Monaldeschi, and the cabaletta expresses their reactions –
Giulia delirious with joy, Cristina with very mixed feelings. At this point Monaldeschi enters, as in Saccherò's
version, and has a brief, pathetic solo, in which he com-
mends his son to God, embraces Giulia for the last time,
and dies. One final line closes the work:

GIULIA, CRISTINA
 Monaldeschi?...
CHORUS   He is in Heaven!

When the two texts are read side by side, the superior
poetic quality of Cammarano shines through, but so too
does the dramatic superiority of the ending. The work was
originally to be called *Monaldeschi* (as we know from
Mercadante's letter when he rejected it), and Cammarano's ending focusses attention, rightly, on him. Saccherò gives the final word to Queen Cristina (perhaps the
management of the Carlo Felice, or the prima donna,
Antoinetta Raineri-Marini, wanted it that way) and her
final outburst is reminiscent of the ending of Cammarano's own *Roberto Devereux* of three years before.
However effective Saccherò's ending may have been in the
theatre, Cammarano's is more genuinely tragic, just as his
use of the bridge passage in the duet is more assured – it is
much more effective to use the pardon of Monaldeschi in
this position rather than put it into the cabaletta as does
Saccherò.

The third way in which an opera could be ended was not
traditional or conventional, but was imported, I suspect,
with a particular type of French play. It is what I will
describe as the 'stagey curtain line', a dramatic statement
forming a strong tableau on which the curtain can descend.
Cammarano used this form of ending in three libretti, *Il
conte di Chalais, Il proscritto* and *Folco d'Arles* – all works

derived from French source plays which end in precisely
the same way, and with the same lines. *Il conte di Chalais*
provides a good example: there is a terzet finale, quite
regular, for Maria, her husband Chevreuse and her lover
Chalais, who has returned secretly to take her away with
him, although the Royal Archers are searching for him.
During the bridge passage, they learn that the Archers are
already in the building. After the cabaletta, Chevreuse
takes Chalais into a side room to fight a duel. As the
Archers break down the door, two shots are heard; Chevreuse appears, dishevelled and pale. The libretto ends thus
(stage directions omitted; Fiesque is the Captain of the
Archers):

FIESQUE
    The Count?
CHEVREUSE   To escape
    The hand of the executioner,
    He killed himself.
MARIA   Ah!...
FIESQUE   Go and see...
CHEVREUSE
    For him, death.
MARIA   Cruel!...
CHEVREUSE
    For you a greater punishment;
    Life, and remorse.
MARIA   Oh heavens!

Il proscritto ends with an even stagier curtain line. Malvina, caught between her husband, Giorgio, and his intended successor, Arturo, takes poison. Again there is a
regular terzet finale, and by the end of the cabaletta she is
dead. Then:

GIORGIO
    Oh Malvina!...Dead!...
ARTURO   Dead!...
GIORGIO
    Dead or alive, she is mine still!

Interestingly, all Cammarano's stagey curtain endings
occur in libretti where there is no chorus on stage at the
end (with the exception of a handful of archers in *Il conte
di Chalais*, but they do not sing). They are, in fact, the only

libretti to end without the chorus, and this technique – a terzet finale and a stagey curtain line – seems to have been Cammarano's solution to the problem of ending without a chorus. It would have been easy enough in, say, *Il conte di Chalais,* to have the chorus come helter-skelter on to the stage at the sound of the shots, in time for a more conventional ending.

Il trovatore is, as often, the odd man out, since in it Cammarano was making a conscious effort to break away from convention. The final section of the opera is placed in the prison, where Azucena dreams of returning to her homeland, with supporting lines from Manrico. Then Leonora enters, dying, and there is a single duet for her and Manrico, followed by a long dialogue in open verse in which she explains to him what she has done. As she dies, the Count di Luna enters. Furious, he orders Manrico to the scaffold. From this point, Cammarano concluded the libretto with eleven lines of verse in which Azucena tells the Count that Manrico was his brother. Verdi found these last eleven lines too slow-moving, and rewrote them himself, into four lines. What Verdi gained in the compression he lost in the theatre, since there is hardly time for Manrico to be rushed out to execution before the Count is telling Azucena that he is dead: if anything, the end of the opera comes too quickly, but it was what Verdi obviously wanted.

One other aspect of Cammarano's final scenes, though not unique to him, are of such regular occurrence in his libretti as to become almost a finger-print for his work. This is the use of broken lines in a death scene. He used them first in the 1832 version of *Belisario,* but the first published occurrence is in *Ines de Castro,* when Ines, her mind wandering, is dying of poison.

INES

   È vero . . . è vero.
Gelo in un tempo . . . ed ardo . . .
Mi strazia . . . il rio . . . velen.

(It's true . . . it's true / At one moment I freeze . . . and burn . . . /
The evil . . . poison . . . tears me apart.)

Then, as she dies:

Ti conforta . . . i miei tormenti
Lascio in terra . . . e un . . . fragil velo . . .
Ma non moro . . . vada in cielo
I miei figli . . . a riveder . . .

(Comfort yourself . . . I leave on earth / My torments . . . and
a . . . fragile body . . . / But I do not die . . . I go to heaven / To see
again . . . my children . . .)

Cammarano did not use this type of broken line in his next tragic opera, *Lucia di Lammermoor,* either in Lucia's 'mad scene', or, where it might have been expected, in Edgardo's final cabaletta. However, when Donizetti came to write the music for the end of the opera, he repeated the slow melody of the cabaletta on the cello, and broke up the vocal pattern as if Cammarano had written

A te vengo . . . o bell ' alma . . .
Ti rivolgi . . . il tuo fedel
Ah! se l'ira . . . dei mortali . . .

and so on. It may well have been Donizetti's use of these lines (though later the tenor Duprez was to claim the credit for having suggested it) that encouraged Cammarano in his subsequent use of them, since he almost invariably used broken lines in death scenes thereafter, from *Pia de' Tolomei* right through to *Folco d'Arles.*

These passages, despite the interruption in the flow of words, always scan perfectly, and often contain some of Cammarano's most well-wrought expressions. This way of writing for a dying – or a mad – person was not, of course, new, but was not nearly so often used by others. Such phrases were sometimes used by other contemporary librettists, as in Rossi's *Giovanna d'Arco* of 1827:

Le nubi m'innalzano
La terra . . . allontanasi
Eterna . . . è . . . la gioia
È bre . . . ve . . . il dolor.

Rossi here actually breaks a word (*breve*) into two, something that Cammarano does not do. Also from 1827 comes this example from Romanelli's libretto *Gli Arabi nelle Gallie;* Romanelli was not a librettist given to experimental writing, and most of his work was rather severe in style, but Agobar dies after six broken lines, ending

Tre ... mu ... la ... luce ... appena ...
Ad ... dio

Both these poems were almost certainly known to Cammarano. More interesting examples come from the work of a Neapolitan librettist, Tottola. First, from the final scene of *Ermione*, a text written for Rossini in 1819:

ERMIONE

Va pur ... sia ... vindice ... quel flutto ... in fido de' ... tuoi ...
delitti ... del mio ... dolor. (*Cade svenuto.*)

Second, from *Imelda de' Lambertazzi*:

IMELDA

Padre! ... son ... rea ... lo vedo!
(*Fra i singulti di morte*)
Ma son tua figlia ancora! ...
Almen ... nell'ultim' ora ...
Non ... mi ... scacciar ... da te!

It is perhaps a fairly obvious form of words to put into the mouth of a dying person, and certainly adds to the realism of a death scene. It required the total abandonment of the old concept of a bravura ending, and the acceptance of a pathetic death scene as the end point of the structure. The use of broken lines gave great dramatic opportunities to composers, whether or not they took advantage of them, and were not, of course, confined necessarily to closing scenes (Ghino, in *Pia de' Tolomei*, dies most impressively to broken phrases early on in the last act). Used in final scenes of a tragic nature, they were able to reconcile the structural need for a cabaletta in the aria (or duet) finale with the requirements of the dramatic situation, which could not admit of a protagonist dying in a bravura passage of pyrotechnic vocalization. It was, in fact, Cammarano's particular – and not atypical – way of finding a structural solution to a dramatic problem which was, none the less, compatible with the spirit (if not the letter) of the conventions of Italian opera.

CHAPTER THIRTEEN

Cammarano's Working Methods

Little is known about the working methods of the librettists of the Italian romantic opera. None of them left an account of their work, or a systematic collection of documents on which proper studies can be based. No doubt for the most part they saw their work as ephemeral, finished when the opera reached the stage. Franco Schlitzer has an interesting chapter in his book *Il Mondo Teatrale dell' Ottocento* on the collaboration of Romani and Bellini in the writing of *Norma*, and the extensive revisions demanded by the composer, who was, as he himself admitted, very sensitive to the words he set to music. Similarly, Romani's widow, Emilia Branca, in her hagiography of 1882, has quite a lot to say about his approach to his work. A study of Cammarano's working methods helps to explain how the operas of his times progressed from the choice of a subject until reaching the stage, and enough scattered documents from different parts of his career have survived for us to piece together an account of how he put his libretti together.

The first step was obviously the choice of subject. Cammarano's sources have been dealt with in detail in Chapter 10, but the suggestion that a certain plot might be used for a particular occasion may have come from a number of people. The lists Cammarano kept indicate that he watched out for suitable plays and other models for elaboration when needed, and then it became a matter of suiting a plot to composers, singers and management. The suggestion for a subject may have come from him: Donizetti wrote to the impresario Lanari (on 31 May 1836) 'Cammarano suggests *Pia*, a subject very well suited to your company'. Sometimes – as, for instance, with *Il trovatore* – the suggestion came from the composer, who was equally engaged in watching the theatrical press for possibilities, as the letters of Bellini, Donizetti and Verdi provide ample evidence. There is a wonderful cartoon of Verdi, standing in his library, with bays of books labelled 'French Drama', 'Spanish Drama', 'English Drama', etc. The suggestion that Corneille's *Polyeucte* should be used for the S. Carlo contract of 1838 seems to have come from the tenor Nourrit, and it is not hard to imagine that when two librettists met, this was a prime subject of their conversation, along with the stinginess of managements and the demands of composers.

By and large, the Naples management does not seem to have involved itself all that deeply in the subjects Cammarano took for his libretti. At the time of *Poliuto*, Barbaja was clearly ignorant of the subject that librettist and composer were working on, for one of Cammarano's letters begins 'The title of the drama I am writing is *Poliuto*' (16 June 1838). Some years later, Flauto made it quite clear to Cammarano that he never interfered in his choice of subject as a matter of policy, even though his lax oversight had brought him into trouble with his associates. The Venetian authorities were, however, more circumspect, and took an early opportunity of expressing their dislike of *Maria de Rudenz*.

Once the subject was agreed, the next important stage was for the librettist to prepare a synopsis (his *programma*), but there is a document which suggests that Cammarano on at least one occasion was prepared to provide an outline of the plot: this was probably for the benefit of the composer and may well have been written for his information in the discussions leading up to the choice of subject. The library of the Conservatorio S. Pietro a Majella in Naples contains a number of Cammarano manuscripts which seem to have been in Donizetti's possession – the synopses of five of his libretti for him, and the same number of libretti, though not always of the same works. Many of these libretti have Donizetti's marginal notes on them, and had obviously been used by him at the time of composition. Amongst them, bound up with the synopsis, is a one-page summary of the plot of *Maria de Rudenz*. It is in Cammarano's handwriting, not in his best copper-plate, but in a fairly hurried script, with a number of corrections. It could be an outline prepared by Cammarano to help him clear his own mind when preparing his synopsis, but if this were the case, it would hardly be expected to have come into a group of papers associated with Donizetti. There is no way to be sure, but I suspect that Cammarano put it down on paper as a guide to Donizetti. However that may be, it clearly antedated the elaboration of the synopsis, and is worth reproducing as, probably, the earliest stage in the librettist's work on a subject. It should be recalled that the French source was a ramshackle five-act drama which required much condensation, including the loss of the whole of the first act, so that the librettist's task was not easy. The outline of the plot of *Maria de Rudenz* goes as follows:

> Maria de Rudenz, under the influence of a guilty passion, was a long way from home when her father died. In his will he had stipulated that if, after one year, his daughter had not re-appeared, his ancestral inheritance was to pass to his own niece, Matilde di Wolf; and this woman was about to give it – along with her own hand in marriage – to Corrado Waldorf. Then Maria, who ardently loved Corrado, turns up unexpectedly and repossesses herself of her rights, taken from her by her cousin, in order to win back her fiancé from her.
> Enrico, Corrado's brother, discloses to Maria that he secretly loves Matilde, and Maria gives him hope that, without violating the ties of blood, he can marry the woman he loves. Corrado arrives: Maria, basing all her hopes on his returning to her earlier feelings for her, is on the point of sacrificing her cousin to her jealous fury, when Corrado, so as to remove Matilde from imminent danger, plunges his dagger into Maria's breast. Everyone thinks that Maria is dead. Enrico, who had received by an unknown hand evidence that he was not Corrado's brother, tries in vain to oppose the wedding of Corrado and Matilde. But she is already in the nuptial chamber when a loud cry is heard: Maria, having survived the wound, has killed her rival.

This outline certainly gives the main points of the plot, necessarily oversimplifying it, highlighting the jealousy between the brothers though underestimating the roles of the two women. The plot became much more elaborate when the synopsis itself was prepared, and there is evidence from the corrections that Cammarano made as he went along that it gave him no little trouble.

This synopsis was the next step which had to be taken. A number of Cammarano's synopses survive, closely written documents of six or more pages, extending to three or four thousand words, and outlining the development of the plot in great detail. Of the libretti set by Donizetti, synopses for *Lucia i Lammermoor*, *L'assedio di Calais*, *Pia de' Tolomei*, *Roberto Devereux* and *Maria de Rudenz* are in the Conservatorio in Naples; two synopses for *Folco d' Arles* (one originally destined for Donizetti and signed as approved by the censor Gaetano Royer in 1842) are in the Cammarano papers in the Lucchesi-Palli library in Naples; Abbiati printed the synopsis of *Luisa Miller* in the second volume of his *Verdi*; the synopsis of *Il trovatore* has been made available to me by the kindness of Signora Carrara-Verdi, from the archives at Busseto.

The synopsis of *Lucia di Lammermoor* is reproduced in translation as an appendix to this chapter, as the story is probably the most familiar. It is a good example of Cammarano's synopsis; the 'numbers' are clearly indicated, though there is no separate distribution list accompanying this synopsis; the plot is rather more elaborate than in the final libretto; the dialogue is quite detailed. There are a few places where the libretto departs from the outline given in the synopsis. For instance, Bucklaw's throwing down his glove in challenge at the end of the finale (the contract scene) was suppressed, with a consequent alteration to the next scene, the duet for Edgardo and Enrico at Wolfcrag. Similarly, in the synopsis Lucia wore Edgardo's ring on a necklace rather than on her finger (a necklace being a more reasonable place in the circumstances, when she had just signed the marriage contract with another man), and in the 'mad scene' her hands wandered to her neck in search of it. Both these details were suppressed in the final libretto, though to its disadvantage. The only structural change of any significance concerns Enrico's entry in the 'mad scene': in the synopsis he joins Bidebent and the assembled company during Bidebent's narration, and is prevented from rushing into Lucia's room to find out what is happening. At this point, Lucia enters, so that Enrico is on stage throughout the whole of her double aria, which would be a difficult situation to handle on the stage.

In the libretto, his entry is held back, and he comes on during the bridge passage, providing a dramatic justification for the cabaletta and easing his own position vis-à-vis Lucia.

Much of the wording of the synopsis found its way into the final text in the libretto, though less, perhaps, than in other libretti. Stage directions were often transferred almost word for word, as, for instance, in the description of Edgardo's room in the ruined castle of Wolfcrag. This is how the synopsis describes it:

> Salone nella Torre di Wolfcrag – una tavola spoglia d'ogni ornamento, ed una vecchia sedia ne formano tutto il córredo. Vi è nel fondo una porta fiancheggiata da due finestroni, che avendo infrante le invetriate, lasciano vedere le rovine di detta Torre. Il luogo è fiocamente illuminato da una tetra lampada.

The libretto, though rather more detailed, repeats so many of the same words that it is obvious that Cammarano had the synopsis in front of him as he wrote.

> *Salone* terreno *nella torre di Wolfcrag,* adiacente al vestibulo. *Una tavola spoglia d'ogni ornamento, ed un vecchio* seggiolone *ne formano tutto* l'arredo. *Vi è nel fondo una porta* che mette all' esterno: essa è *fiancheggiata da due finestroni, che avendo infrante le invetriate, lasciano* scorgere gran parte delle *rovine di detta torre,* ed un lato della medesima sporgente sul mare. È notte: *il luogo* vien debolmente *illuminato da una* smorta *lampada.* Il cielo è orrendamente nero; lampeggia, tuona, ed i sibili del vento si mescono coi scrosci della pioggia. [Words common to synopsis and libretto are in italic.]

Similarly, dialogue is frequently carried over, with the minimal changes required for versification. A couple of examples will suffice to illustrate Cammarano's working methods. In the Wolfcrag scene, the synopsis reads:

> (EDGARDO) 'E vero: ed io sacrai la mia spada alla vendetta del padre mio. Quando?' – 'Al primo sorgere del nuovo giorno' – 'Dove?' – 'Presso i sepolcri di Ravenswood' ...

The libretto at this point reads:

EDGARDO
> So che al paterno cenere
> Giurai strapparti il core.

ENRICO
  Tu!...
EDGARDO Quando? (con nobile disdegno)
ENRICO   Al primo sorgere
  Del mattutino albore.
EDGARDO
  Ove?
ENRICO Fra l'urne gelide
  Dei Ravenswood.

Again, when Bidebent enters in the bridge passage of Enrico's aria finale, with the news that Lucia is dead, the synopsis reads: 'Dove corri infelice? Ella non è piu in terra'. The libretto has: 'Ove corri sventurato?/Ella in terra più non è'.

Cammarano's usual practice was to use the synopsis as a basis for 'working up' the final text. One example out of many can be taken: the moment when Lucia, having been told that she is to marry Bucklaw, turns to Bidebent for consolation. In the synopsis this passage reads:

'Voi siete l'ultimo raggio della mia speranza (ella gli dice)
Che mi recate?' – 'Figlia mia, la vostra speranza è tramontata
per sempre. Io volli prestar fede a vostri sospetti, che Milord
vostro fratello arrestasse le vostre lettere: io stesso tolsi
l'impegno di far giungere un vostro foglio al Sere di Ravenswood: sia adempito alla mia promessa, e son certo che il
vostro scritto giunse nelle mani di lui; intanto nessuna
risposta'.

The text of this section, turned into standard *versi sciolti*, reads:

LUCIA
  Ebben?
RAIMONDO
          Di tua speranza
  L'ultimo raggio tramontò! Credei
  Al' tuo sospetto, che il fratel chiudesse
  Tutte le strade, onde sul Franco suolo,
  All' uom che amar giurasti
  Non giungesser tue nuove: io stesso un foglio
  Da te vergato, per secura mano
  Recar gli feci ... invano!
  Tace mai sempre ...

Incidentally, in the synopsis Cammarano always calls the domestic chaplain 'Bidebent'. In the libretto it is always 'Raimondo', though the cast list describes him as 'Raimondo Bidebent, tutor and confident of Lucia'. His religious status is clearly downgraded, even though he is allowed to quote the scriptures in the finale. In fact the only place in which he is referred to as 'a man of God' does not appear in the printed libretto, though it is found in Donizetti's original manuscript, suggesting that the text was changed – almost certainly at the instance of the censor, since Raimondo's behaviour is not always compatible with his calling – after Donizetti had set the original text he received from his librettist. There is clear evidence of the same thing in other operas, where 'sensitive' words are changed between the draft stage and the final printed text, but remain unchanged in the text accompanying the music.

This correspondence between synopsis and libretto is often much closer than in *Lucia di Lammermoor*, perhaps because other synopses are more detailed and carefully thought out. Compare, for instance, the opening dialogue of the opening scene of *Maria de Rudenz*, as the two brothers meet after a long period of separation; the synopsis first:

> 'Enrico!' ... – 'Corrado!' – I due fratelli sono già l'uno fra le braccia dell'altro. 'O Corrado, appena ebbi il tuo foglio, volai dal campo per abbracciarti: è più d'un lustro che noi fummo divisi!' – 'Da quante, e quali vicende fu agitato il viver mio' – 'Qui la fama, allo sparire di Maria De Rudenz, ti disse il di lei rapitore' – 'Il vero disse. Io la chiesi al padre: *La darò prima alla morte* grido quel crudele!'

The libretto elaboration of this passage of dialogue goes:

ENRICO
Fratello! ...
CORRADO   Enrico! ... (*Abbracciandosi l'un l'altro con tutta la tenderezza fraterna*)
ENRICO   Appena
Il foglio tuo mi giunse,
Volai dal campo ad abbracciarti ... Un lustro
Volge che più non ti rividi!
CORRADO   Oh quante

Il viver mi turbaro
Procellose vicende!
ENRICO   Qui la fama
Rapitor di Maria ti disse.
CORRADO   Il vero
Disse. La chiesi al padre: ah! pria, l'altero
Conte rispose, pria svenarla.

The rest of the long expository dialogue which follows –
some thirty lines of *versi sciolti* in the libretto – matches
the synopsis as closely as does the opening quoted above.
Many other extended passages of *Maria de Rudenz* show
the same close comparison, and the same is true of the
other synopses. Look at the two versions of Rodrigo's letter
to Pia, intercepted by Ghino in the first act of *Pia de'
Tolomei*: in the synopsis:

> Quando il mondo fia ravvolto nel silenzio e nelle tenebre, per
> la via del parco enterò furtivo nelle tue stanze: l'assenza dell'
> abborito tuo sposo mi procura, forse per l'ultima volta, il
> soave conforto de' tuoi amplessi, e solo questa mercede mi fa
> supportare la vita.

and in the libretto:

GHINO   Quando sepolto
Fia nel silenzio della notte il mondo,
Inosservato per la via del Parco
A te verrò: l'assenza
Del tuo sposo abborrito a me concede
D' abbracciarti la gioia, e tal mercede
Soffrir mi fa la vita.

Clearly all Cammarano had to do was to work up the
synopsis into acceptable form, as far as possible using the
same words, or, if that was not possible for reasons of
metrical necessity, using them as a basis for development.
The more advanced and detailed was the synopsis, the less
work he had to do to provide the finished text, though, as
will be seen, the simplest passage could give him a great
deal of trouble.

Once the synopsis had been accepted by composer and
management, and had been approved by the censor, the
full libretto had to be completed. This involved working
up the dialogue and similar sections, and writing the

verses for arias, duets and similar concerted passages. These solo and other sections were not as a rule described in the synopsis, though an indication of mood and sentiment might be included. After all, they were moments of repose in the drama, with the characters commenting on the dramatic situation, and require no new statement of fact in the synopsis. The synopsis stage was probably the more important in laying out the text: its further elaboration was a matter of writing acceptable *versi sciolti* and verses for arias, etc.: it could, if necessary, be elaborated by another librettist.

The best evidence of the way in which Cammarano shaped his words is found in *Folco d'Arles*, since his papers bound up in the Lucchesi-Palli library in Naples contain a number (many of them mere scraps) which when identified and assembled in proper order provide a sequence of drafts for sections of the final text. I have described and discussed these drafts in detail in an article in *Italian Studies* for 1980, to which anyone who wishes to examine the evidence more closely may refer. These drafts include passages of *versi sciolti* as well as verses for arias and the like; for some sections it is possible to compare a number of passages all the way from synopsis to libretto.

As an example, we may trace the evolution of a few lines which were to take their place in Act 1 scene 4. The relevant section of the synopsis reads: 'Palagio Rivers – Folco ha fra mani un volume di poeti provenzali – Esso è il giovane dei fiori – ha un manoscritto per sormontare i cancelli del Parco – Suo esaltato amore per la Contessa – si addormenta'. ('Rivers' mansion – Folco has in his hands a book of Provençal poetry – he is the young man of the flowers – he has a manuscript in his hand to throw over the park gates – his passionate love for the Countess – he falls asleep'). Cammarano's practice seems to have been to begin by writing down a prose version, elaborating the synopsis, in a form suitable for versification. The prose version for this section, written out like all his drafts without punctuation or attribution to the various characters, begins: 'O dolci versi d'amore o sublimi esempi di prodezza' ('Oh sweet lines of love oh sublime examples of valour'), which was to form the first sentence of the text.

Cammarano's versification was always precise, following convention; in *versi sciolti*, for instance, the syllable count was always accurate (seven- or eleven-syllable lines, *piano*) (see Chapter 14): adjacent lines sometimes rhyming, particularly if of unequal length or at the end of a scene; lines running on, but not awkwardly, with frequent use of internal stops.

Following the fate of the first sentence only of this passage, Cammarano first drafted it thus:

> O gentili d' amore
> Soavissimi carmi! O di valore
> Teneri e dolci carmi

These three lines are metrically regular (seven, eleven and seven syllables respectively); the first two rhyme, but the repetition of 'carmi' is obviously unsatisfactory. The second attempt turned out to be closer to the prose version:

> O soave d' amore
> Versi gentili! O belli di valore
> Sublimi esempi

The repetition of 'carmi' is avoided, by substituting 'versi' in one place and 'esempi' in the other, but line 3 has only five syllables, and would need to be completed by the addition of another two – to make a seven-syllable line – or six – for an eleven-syllable line – with the beginning of the next passage. However, it seems that Cammarano was still not satisfied, for he crossed out all he had written, beginning again:

> O gentili d' amore
> Teneri e dolci carmi O di valore
> Sublimi esempi.

This is, in fact, a combination of elements from the earlier versions, and became the text finally adopted.

A number of similar instances could be quoted either for the same scene or for others, some of which gave Cammarano much more trouble than this one, though a few lines went through untouched into the final text. Not all the ideas he put down in the synopsis or the first prose version were taken up – some were never used, others were tried and rejected. A study of all the passages in these drafts shows that he was anxious to mould his words into as compressed a form as possible, without either wasting or repeating words, while leaving a text which would run as smoothly as possible. At one point he had to begin a scene following one which finished with a seven-syllable line. Consequently he could either begin with a new line (of seven or eleven syllables), or take up the unused four syllables to expand the final line of the preceding scene from seven to eleven syllables, and his drafts show how he tried various ways of proceeding until he found an acceptable solution. The outstanding qualities of his *versi sciolti* are accuracy and economy, and he only achieved this with the most careful redrafting. His meticulous attitude to accuracy is well brought out in a sarcastic comment on some changes made to one of his texts by another hand – 'A recitative which begins with a *quinario*! At least he cannot be denied the merit of novelty!'

It is probable that Cammarano did not always need to write out a prose version of his *versi sciolti* before versifying them. Sometimes – as with the excerpt from *Maria de Rudenz* examined above – the synopsis itself was sufficiently detailed to provide him with the outline he needed. The only other such prose draft to have survived comes from *Il reggente* (the synopsis of which is not available for comparison). A page of the prose version of some dialogue in Act II is bound up in an autograph copy of the libretto of *Poliuto*, at the point where, as we shall see, Cammarano lifted a stanza from the earlier text and incorporated it into the new one. The implication is that he had the sheet containing the prose draft in front of him as he turned to the remembered verses of the old (censored) text, and that it subsequently became gathered up and eventually bound up as part of *Poliuto*, without its identity being recognised.

In this section of prose, Cammarano did for once give some indication of punctuation and speech attributions. It covers what was to become nineteen lines of *versi sciolti*, at the point in the action when Hamilton, the chief minister, comes to the deserted burial ground to warn the Regent that the conspirators are gathering around him, only to find him with a heavily veiled woman – his own wife, did he but know it. It begins:

A. Non odi un calpestio? . . .
R. Alcuno qui giunge precipitoso . . .
H. Amico?
R. Il tuo sposo! . . .
A. Ah!
H. È dunque vero, etc.

(A. Do you not hear hoofbeats? . . . / R. Someone is coming rapidly . . . / H. Friend? / R. Your husband! . . . / A. Ah! / H. Is it true then, etc.)

In the printed text (leaving out the very full stage directions) this becomes:

AMELIA
    Non odi un calpestio?
REGGENTE   Precipitoso
    Alcun qui tragge! . . .
HAMILTON   Amico?
REGGENTE   (Oh Dio! . . .)
AMELIA   (Lo sposo! . . .)
REGGENTE
    (Io tremo! . . .)
HAMILTON   È dunque vero;

Here, the first few lines of Cammarano's prose draft fall almost unchanged into acceptable *versi sciolti*. The second line had to be padded out with an 'Oh Dio' to make up the eleven syllables needed, and the 'Ah' of the next line in the prose version had to be expanded to 'Io tremo' to provide the necessary seven syllables. The most interesting change is however in the attributions, not the verse, with the words 'Il tuo sposo' transferred from the Regent to Amelia herself as 'Lo sposo!', strengthening the dramatic impact of Hamilton's entry.

Another passage from the same draft can be quoted; it comes from the point when Hamilton is trying to ensure that the Regent evades the conspirators:

H. Ma una tuttavia rimane allo scampo . . . È quella . . . tu sei destro al nuoto . . . in brevi momenti giungerai salvo all' altra sponda. (H. But all the same one way of escape remains . . . It is this . . . you are good at swimming . . . in a few moments you will reach safety on the other bank.)

In the printed libretto this becomes:

HAMILTON   Pure
   Uno scampo riman ... Destro qual sei,
   A nuoto varca il fiume, e l'altra sponda
   Salvo t' accolga.

giving two complete lines of eleven syllables, and one of
five, to be completed to seven by the addition of the
Regent's outburst 'Io salvo!'.

Writing verses for solo numbers and the like was a task
of quite a different order than drafting *versi sciolti*. The
requirements were, for a start, different and involved a
choice of line length and rhyming pattern. There were
certain constraints on line length – lines of five and, particularly, six syllables tend to be more often used in comic
works, and as a rule different lengths was chosen for the
first and second parts of a double aria and similar pieces.
The text itself had to be smoothly flowing and fluent to
sing, without internal breaks which could interrupt the
vocal line. There was more choice in rhyming pattern,
particularly in long stanzas, and although Cammarano's
workmanship in this was obviously based on care and
attention to detail, pattern was of less importance than
with line length (which determined the ways in which the
composer could set the piece to music) since rhyming
patterns were lost in performance and usually escape
notice. There is only one instance in his working papers of
the drafting of some verses for an aria, and that comes, too,
from *Folco d'Arles*, and I have analysed it fully in the
article already mentioned. The aria in question is the
Countess' cavatina in the first scene of Act I, which in the
final text consists of eight lines (two *quartine*, each of four
seven-syllable lines). There are two drafts of these lines, as
well as the final printed version. Each of the two drafts use
a different rhyming scheme: the first version is the same as
in the printed text – ABCD, EBFD, a pattern common in
Cammarano's work, as in the work of many others. The
pattern of the second version is less common: ABBC, DEEC.
There was however a more important difference: the first
draft had lines 1, 3, 5 and 7 *sdrucciolo* (see the appendix to
Chapter 14). The second draft adopts a different scheme,
with only lines 1 and 5 (that is, the first lines of the two
quartine) *sdrucciolo*. The closing lines are, as usual,

tronco. The effect of a *sdrucciolo* line is to make the passage move on rapidly and, while the repetition of too many can easily become wearing on the ear and sccm rather cheap, their judicious use certainly has a propulsive effect on the verses.

The second *quartina* of both drafts may be compared with this in mind. The two drafts read:

> (*first*)
> Non mai la cara immagine
> Dimenticar poss' io
> Fuggì dal guardo estatico
> Ma non fuggì dal cor.

> (*second*)
> Non mai la cara immagine
> Dimenticar potrei
> Fuggì dagli occhi miei
> Ma non fuggì dal cor.

When he came to assemble the final version for the libretto, Cammarano took the best line from the two drafts, choosing the metrical and rhyming patterns of the first. In fact, the whole of the second *quartina* came unchanged from the first draft, though in the first *quartina* one line from the second draft had to be changed from *piano* to *sdrucciolo*:

> (*second draft*)
> E l'anima un istante

> (*final text*)
> Ed un istante l'anima

In this rewriting, Cammarano has achieved the change he needed by breaking the *sinalefe* between 'anima' and 'un' by changing the word order, and by avoiding one between 'E' and 'un' by changing 'E' to 'Ed'.

The result is a smoothly flowing text, avoiding awkward expressions such as 'occhi miei' in favour of 'guardo estatico', a more poetical expression. Obviously Cammarano's reputation for writing beautiful verses rested on a great deal of meticulous work.

The correspondence between Cammarano and the composers who set his libretti to music suggests that he was usually late in forwarding his texts to them, despite the

deadlines which were often written into the contract between management and composer. It also looks as if he
was in the habit of sending sections of the text as he
finished them, and that they were not necessarily completed in the proper order. Certainly his correspondence
with Verdi shows that he sent sections out of order
(though Verdi claimed at the time of the revision of *Simon
Boccanegra* that he liked to compose the music in the right
order). However infuriating and frustrating his delays
must have been – (and there is plenty of evidence for that)
– it probably did not matter to most composers that the
numbers arrived out of sequence; they had the detailed
synopsis which would have placed the number securely
within the text as a whole.

The text once complete had still to be submitted to the
censor, although by this time most of it had probably been
set to music, strictly against the regulations (with
Eleonora Dori the work seems to have been already well
advanced in rehearsals before the censors saw the text). As
had already been mentioned, this is what probably happened to the character of Bidebent in *Lucia di Lammermoor*. Similarly, in *Folco d'Arles*, a number of expressions
of a religious nature were removed between Cammarano's
draft and the final printed text – yet the original expressions remained in the words accompanying the music. For
instance, 'magico' substituted for 'angelico', 'Siccome il
ciel' for 'Siccome Iddio', 'Oh caro labbro' for 'Divino
labbro'. A comparision between the printed text and the
words set to music and retained in the printed scores at
places like these often reveals that only the printed libretto
has the 'cleaned-up' version, indicating that the composer
had been working from the unexpurgated text. Where an
autograph libretto has survived, a comparison with the
printed text can reveal directly where changes have been
made. The autograph libretto of *Roberto Devereux* has a
number of changes in the handwriting of the censor (and
authenticated as such by Cammarano's son Goffredo in
1889). This is the final, fair copy that had been submitted
for approval. The censor went so far as to rework the
ending of the central finale, when Roberto is arrested and
led off, removing a rather spiteful outburst from Queen

Elizabeth and the gloating of the courtiers over his fall. The censor himself wrote a new stage direction – 'at a sign from Elizabeth, Roberto is surrounded by guards'. (Cammarano's original stage direction had been: 'Elizabeth glances at Gualtiero (Raleigh) who opens a secret door. A squad of armed men appear, at their head a man of sinister aspect'). Some of the censor's other marks obliterated the original, but where Cammarano's text can be made out it is clear that the intention was to tone down the language. For instance, 'Il patibolo s'appresta'! (the gallows draw nearer') is changed to 'Il supplizio a lui s'appresta'; ('punishment draws nearer to him') 'L'onor mio da voi trafitto' to 'Quest cor da voi trafitto' (a nobleman's heart could be pierced, it would seem, but not his honour). The words set by the composer were Cammarano's, not the censor's, and although the ending of the finale follows the censor's instructions, one line he had crossed out (Elizabeth's 'Ho sul ciglio la benda dell' ira' – 'I am blinded with rage') found its way into the music.

The sequence seems to have been this: Cammarano first produced a synopsis, which he submitted via the management to the censor's office for approval. At the same time he would write out another copy for the composer, since those that were used by Donizetti and Verdi do not have the censor's approval on them. (It is of course possible that Cammarano waited to receive approval before copying out and sending a synopsis to the composer, but it is more likely that he sent both copies at the same time.) He then turned his attention to the text, giving or sending it to the composer in bits and pieces as it was ready. This is not to say that no changes were made to the text after this point; if librettist and composer were in regular contact – as when Donizetti was living in Naples – there was probably a lot of discussion and alteration (as when Cammarano counted up the number of eyes he and Donizetti had between them, which they could bring to bear on a section of text).

Sometimes long passages in the text were struck out and rewritten. The autograph libretto of *L'assedio di Calais*, which was used by Donizetti and has many of his marginalia on it, was clearly at a fairly early state and seems to have been put together from a number of different pieces, lacking pagination or any evidence of continuity of writing. It is indeed bound up in many places in the wrong order. The cabaletta of Edoardo III in the last act was at some stage completely rewritten, with the two *quartine* of *settenari* ('Questo guerriero plauso/Di tue vittoria il suono'), which he addresses to his Queen, replacing a much more warlike section twelve lines long. Similarly, one section of *versi sciolti* at a pivotal point in the opera was rewritten. When the six burghers who were to hand Calais to the English had been selected, Cammarano had written six lines of *versi sciolti* for Eustacchio, the mayor. He later changed these, altering *inter alia* 'Andiam confronte atterra/Al superbo Edoardo' ('We go with lowered brow/to the proud Edward') into 'Andiam sereni in fronte/Al superbo Edoardo' – and giving the last three lines of the passage to another character. The way this manuscript is written, with pages headed 'After the ballet', 'Beginning of the duet' and the like, gives all the evidence needed to show that Cammarano worked up his synopsis into a libretto in random order, subsequently assembling a complete text.

The libretto of *Pia de' Tolomei* also differs at many points from the text finally set (leaving aside the two versions of the central finale). In two places, whole sections were rewritten, the most interesting being the chorus of Rodrigo's soldiers at the beginning of Act II – the splendid chorus 'Cinto de rosse nubi' replacing a violently anti-Ghibelline set piece, full of oaths and fury.

Having put together a text, Cammarano wrote out a fair copy for the management to submit to the censors for approval (up to this time they had seen only the synopsis). If the censor was unhappy about anything, he would make a substitution himself, and the text thus amended would go to the printers for them to set up the libretto in type – this would probably be done at the last minute. In the meantime, the composer had set the unamended text to music, and singers presumably had to be instructed to alter their words, since vocal scores – at least in the examples I have studied – follow the original wordings, being made from the composer's autograph manuscript, or perhaps from the theatre copyist's version of it. For instance, Donizetti's autograph full score of *Lucia di Lammermoor* and such vocal scores as I have examined, have Enrico turning to Raimondo after the 'mad scene' and addressing him as 'Uom del Signor' ('man of God') though the libretto clearly prints 'Pietoso amico' ('compassionate friend'). If my conjecture that the censor wanted to remove all traces of Raimondo's religious profession is correct, the substitution would have been made by him; but Donizetti had already set the words 'Uom del Signor', and performance material and, later, the vocal score to be sold to the public were prepared from his autograph. However, the libretto was printed from the copy altered by the censor to read 'Pietoso amico', and therefore represents a later version of the text.

It must not however be assumed that all discrepancies between the text accompanying the music and the printed libretto are the result of the intervention of the censor. Most arose from the way the composer set the text to music. Indeed, it is difficult to see why a librettist like Cammarano should have taken so much trouble with the words, so little regard did composers have for them. This is particularly true of *versi sciolti*, but it is not confined to them. Apart from everlasting repetitions of odd words or phrases that composers like Donizetti used to extend the music of arias and other formal pieces, they omitted or changed many words, often playing ducks and drakes with metre and syllable count. To take *Lucia di Lammermoor* once again, 117 lines out of the 690 of the printed text differ from the lines as set by Donizetti in small or large degree. While a few of these can be ascribed with varying degrees of certainty to the activities of the censor, most are small and innocuous changes clearly introduced by Donizetti to suit the flow of his music. Since Donizetti was no mean word-smith himself, his changes usually fit the metrical pattern, but not always. A putative censor's change is found in the opening chorus: Donizetti set 'l'esecrabile vero' while the libretto reads 'il teribile vero' (presumably it could never be held that the truth could be execrable: remember that the censor's approach was fundamentally a moral one). The possibility that Donizetti 'sharpened up' the words at this point is, in the context of this chorus, much less likely. When he came to set Normanno's account of the charging bull, and Lucia's first meeting with Edgardo, he shortened Cammarano's text, which, in the printed libretto, reads:

NORMANNO   ... dove la madre
   Giace sepolta: la sua fida Alisa
   Era al suo fianco ... Impetuoso toro
   Ecco su lor si avventa ...
   Privi d'ogni soccorso,
   Pende sovr' esse inevitabil morte! ..
   Quando per l'aere sibilar si sente
   Un colpo ...
(NORMANNO   ... where her mother
   Lies buried: her faithful Alisa
   Was beside her ... A raging bull
   Rushes towards them ...
   Bereft of all help,
   Inevitable death hangs over them! ..
   When through the air is heard to whistle
   A shot ...)

What Donizetti set was this:

NORMANNO   ... dove la madre
   Giace sepolta ... Impetuoso toro
   Ecco su lei si avventa ...
   Quando per l'aura rimbombar si sente
   Un colpo ...

While this abbreviation had the benefit of shortening a passage of expository *versi sciolti* without altering correct line length, two changes have crept in: one in the elimination of Alisa, and the consequent change from 'them' to 'her', and the second the substitution of 'rimbombar' (echoes) for 'sibilar' (whistles), presumably for the sake of euphony.

Line lengths were not always maintained, as when Donizetti changed 'È ver ... quel folle ardia' to 'È vero ... quel folle ardia', thus adding a syllable to the *settenario*. Some changes are quite inexplicable, however trivial. The substitution of 'sconsigliato!' (which we might translate as 'Rash intruder!' in the context, which is immediately after the sextet, in the central finale) for 'Ravenswood!' can be accounted for, though, by the desire to avoid a foreign word which does not go well in Italian.

The point of discussing these changes is not so much to

note the extent to which Cammarano's words were altered in the setting as to draw attention to the lack of control a librettist had over his material. The verses were not changed so much, except for occasional words, but the metrical and rhyming patterns were totally obliterated in the setting, by the break-up of phrases, the endless repetitions and failure of the composer to take any regard for the *sinalafe* on which metrical integrity depended. Unless the listener has a particular interest in such matters, he is unaware of line lengths and metrical patterns in the opera house, and may not even be aware of the transitions to and from *versi sciolti* – and this is entirely as it should be. The wonder is why a librettist should labour so hard to get his words right – it must have taken a very real sense of pride in his craftsmanship to persevere in the face of such provocation.

Although Cammarano had certain stock expressions and sentiments which turn up again and again in his work, he did not as a rule re-use his verses, even if the opera to which his text had been written had been taken off after one or two performances and could safely be considered buried for all time. He might reasonably have concluded that it was safe to recycle verses that he had worked over and polished to an acceptable standard, but he did not do so, with a couple of trivial exceptions and one major one.

The trivial ones first: when *Roberto Devereux* was produced in Paris, a new aria was provided for Sara, in place of 'All' afflitto è dolce il pianto', in Act I. The words of the replacement aria began 'Giovin leggiardra, amabile/Ti vidi è t' adorai'. As Don White has pointed out, in his notes accompanying the Opera Rara recording of Donizetti's *Gabriella di Vergy*, these lines occur in that work too. *Gabriella di Vergy* has a complicated history, but the use of this aria suggests that the original librettist was Cammarano – not conclusively; Donizetti, looking around for an aria for Paris, could easily have lifted one from an unused earlier opera without regard to the authorship of the words. It is possible that *Gabriella di Vergy* was the opera set aside in 1838 when the engagement of Nourrit required a work with a major role for tenor, a change of plan which led to *Poliuto*.

The other instance of the re-use of verses is curious. The opening chorus of *La sposa* contains a second stanza beginning 'O giovinetta sposa/Soave sei, gentile'. It is charming and lyrical, and Cammarano must have been fond of it. The first four lines – completed rather differently to make a set of eight lines – recur in *Maria de Rudenz* (Act III scene 5), *Luigi Rolla* (Act II scene 6) and *La fidanzata corsa* (Act I scene 6). In the last case it is used as a serenade: the other uses are all for women approaching the wedding service. It is rather surprising that Cammarano did not write new verses, however appropriate the old ones may have been to their new setting.

The libretto of *Poliuto* provided the only really important instance of Cammarano's self-borrowing. I have published a full examination of this libretto in the *Journal of the Donizetti Society* for 1980. When *Poliuto* was prohibited in 1838, Cammarano was left with a text which he thought would never see the light of day. Consequently a number of his verses for arias, duets and the like were, he reasonably thought, lost for ever. In the years that followed, therefore, he returned to the text of *Poliuto* from time to time, using it as a quarry. When *Poliuto* finally reached the stage in Naples, in November 1848, he was in a dilemma: in a foreword to the libretto (as described in Chapter 3) he explained what he had done – it was better to own up than to cobble up some new verses to fit Donizetti's music. He had in fact transplanted four of the *Poliuto* verses into *La vestale* (1840); one into *Saffo* (1840); one into *Il proscritto* (1842) and two into *Il reggente* (1843).

The interesting feature of the re-use of the verses is the situations in which they recur. For instance, the stanza beginning 'Perchè di stolto giubbilo', in *Poliuto*, comes when Paolina learns that Severo, with whom she had been in love before she married Poliuto, had not been killed in battle as she had believed and was, moreover, about to put in an appearance. She is predictably confused and anxious. In *La vestale*, it is used in an almost identical situation: Emilia had been in love with Decio, but when he was reported killed in battle she had become a Vestal Virgin. He, too, was alive and duly arrived in Rome. She, like Paolina, was predictably confused and anxious. Similarly, the chorus 'Plausi all' inclito Severo' with which the populace welcome their new pro-consul in *Poliuto* was very easily adapted to become a welcoming chorus for the returning hero in *La vestale*. Poliuto's prayer for divine guidance becomes Giunia's prayer for her friend in *La vestale*. In all the eight instances, the dramatic situation is identical, though the setting and timing of the action may be worlds apart – a magistrate's wife in Mitelene in the third century AD rejects an old suitor with the same words as the chief minister's wife rejects *her* old suitor in sixteenth-century Edinburgh. The human situations are the same, and evoke the same emotional response, so that the words they use are understandably the same. After all, the task of the librettist and composer was to provide suitable opportunities for the singers to portray a range of emotions, and the way Cammarano re-used these verses emphasizes the significance of those parts of the opera when time stood still.

Appendix. Synopsis of *Lucia di Lammermoor*

LUCIA ASTHON
Synopsis for a lyric tragedy

CHARACTERS

Lord Asthon . . . Sigr Coselli
Lucia Asthon . . . Siga Persiani
Sir Edgardo di Ravenswood . . . Sigr Dupre
Lord Bucklaw
Bidebent
Alisa . . . Siga Zappucci

Relatives of Lord Asthon – hunters, attendants,
men-at-arms, peasants.

The action takes place in Scotland in the seventeenth century.

First Part. One Act only

Hall of Ravenswood Castle

Introduction and Asthon's cavatina
A group of hunters is scattered over the stage. They are joined by Normanno, who orders them to cover the surroundings of Wolf-

crag, and to enquire there of the unknown man, and to find out his name. If his suspicions were to be verified, they were to return at once to Ravenswood to let him know. The hunters leave. Lord Asthon followed by Bidebent, comes from Lucia's apartments. The worry which is written on his face provokes Normanno to ask the reason for it. Asthon replies that neither his advice nor the intercession of the Reverend Bidebent have been able to persuade Lucia to accept the distinguished marriage with Lord Bucklaw, a marriage which alone could raise a barrier against the impending fall of his family. Normanno tells him that he thinks he knows the reason for Lucia's refusal: he then tells him how Lucia, while walking across the park which leads to her mother's tomb, was about to be attacked by a bull, a danger from which an unknown man had rescued her and that the gratitude she had shown him was such as to be confused in her mind with love – and that she had seen her rescuer many times since. Asthon shudders at Lucia's behaviour. The hunters return: they have solved the mystery. The unknown man is Edgardo of Ravenswood. When Asthon realizes that his sister is in love with his mortal enemy, none other than that Edgardo who was close to recovering his rights over the Lordship of Ravenswood, he swears that either Lucia will consent to the marriage as he orders, or a horrible vengeance will punish the outrage suffered by his family.

Park – on one side, the side wall of the castle, on the other the fountain of the Siren – it is dark: the moon is shining.

Lucia's Cavatina

Lucia and Alisa come from the castle: the latter reproaches the other for her thoughtless behaviour. Lucia replies that an urgent message from Edgardo had decided her to it, but protests that after this conversation she would not again be so daring as to take further risks. Meanwhile she recounts the start of her love, and forecasts the disastrous consequences of it – a foreboding all the more strengthened by the ill-fated place in which she finds herself: since it was established by tradition that an ancestor of Edgardo had killed his beloved near the fountain of the Siren in a fury of jealousy and that a few drops of her blood had clouded the clear waters of the fountain.

Duet – Edgardo and Lucia

As Edgardo comes on Alisa leaves, to watch that no one can surprise the two lovers. Edgardo tells Lucia that he must cross to the continent on a political mission. He suggests that before he leaves, he should tell Lord Asthon about their love. The idea makes Lucia shudder, and instead she advises him to defer this announcement till his return. Edgardo, seeing into Lucia's heart, and knowing the fear that worries her, reminds her what he has sacrificed for love, and the hatred which he rightly nourishes against her family, and the horrible oaths he has sworn to revenge the death of his own father, who had been hastened to the tomb by the loss of his possessions and titles. 'From that you understand', he adds, 'that my life rests on one love alone, and that if you were unfaithful it would be the last, and the most dreadful, of my misfortunes'. Lucia, deeply impressed by his scruples, offers to pledge her faith. Edgardo, taking his ring, passes it to Lucia, who, following a Scottish custom, reciprocates by giving her own ring to Ravenswood. Someone who takes to his heart the pledge of a sacred love he has received swears to keep it till death. The east brightens with the first signs of dawn, and they break away from each other.

End of the first part

Second Part. First Act

Lord Asthon's Apartments

Scena and duet. Asthon and Lucia
Asthon is sitting at a little table reading a letter: Normanno joins him, and tells him that Lord Bucklaw would arrive at the castle in a few hours. In the conversation which follows it transpires that during the absence Edgardo of Ravenswood they have intercepted his correspondence with Lucia, and that by their machinations they have arranged for Lucia to hear a rumour suggesting that Edgardo has contracted a promise of a splendid marriage on the continent, a rumour which Asthon was ready to authenticate by a letter forged in such a way as to deceive the unfortunate Lucia. Normanno receives from Asthon his orders for meeting Lord Bucklaw, and departs. After some moments, Lucia, called by her brother, comes to him. Her appearance bears witness that the unwonted sufferings have sadly affected her health. At the very sight of her overbearing brother she gives a convulsive shudder: with a most severe expression, he addresses her thus: 'Lucia, your foolish and wicked love allows me all the rights of exercising over you the most severe treatment, to restore the impugned honour of a family of which I am head: but I do not want to forget that I am your brother: so, pitying that weakness which made you consider it treachery to give your hand to another man, without Edgardo absolving you from the vain promise, I allowed you to write to him: the time fixed by you yourself for waiting for his answer

expires today' – 'Allow me at least the whole course of this day' –
'Can you still entertain such a foolish hope? Then I must tear the
veil from your eyes' and so saying he gives his sister the letter,
whose contents are intended to convey the news of Edgardo's
marriage. When Lucia has read the letter she seeks from her
brother the right to end her days in the solitude of a retreat.
Asthon, annoyed by her constancy, is on the point of giving vent
to more violent oaths, but is interrupted by sounds of joy which
announce the arrival of her bridegroom, Lord Bucklaw. 'Lucia!'
(thus Asthon turns on his sister) 'just as your love for Edgardo has
placed a stain of disgrace on our family, so your refusal of Lord
Bucklaw means its loss. Only his influence can save us . . . know
then that in the political vicissitudes in which we find ourselves
my possessions . . . and my life . . . are threatened. Tremble . . . your
obstinacy opens the grave for me; and the shades of our ancestors
would rise from their tombs to curse a brother's murderer'. Thus
saying, he takes himself off rapidly. The unfortunate Lucia is in a
state of great anxiety. Bidebent approaches her. 'You are the last
ray of hope for me' (she says to him) 'where am I to turn?' – 'My
daughter, your hope has disappeared for ever. I had wanted to
believe your suspicions that my Lord your brother was holding
back your letters: I myself took the opportunity of sending
one of your letters to the Knight of Ravenswood, according to my
promise, and I am certain that your letter reached his hands:
meanwhile no-one replies. You are then free of any vows made
with him, and I urge you with fatherly solicitude, with which I
have always looked over your days, as I swore to your dying father,
I urge you to comply with your brother's wishes' – 'You advise me
thus! . . . Well, I am the victim, sacrificed for him'.

*Magnificent room, pompously decorated for
the reception of the bridegroom*

Asthon and his noble relatives receive Lord Bucklaw. He is happy
to be forging an alliance with a family for which he has always
nourished feelings of lively friendship. Asthon warns him that he
will not perhaps find Lucia as he saw her in Edinburgh, since the
loss of both her parents, let alone the other disasters falling on the
house, have produced a noticeable change in her. Lucia comes
forward, supported by Alisa and Bidebent, to meet her bridegroom. Bucklaw puts Lucia's appearance down to that bashful
modesty which girls usually show when proceeding towards marriage. Asthon and Bucklaw sign the marriage contract. Lucia,
beside herself, continually threatened by the fierce look of her
brother, adds her signature to it . . . In the next room is heard a

noise, as of servants trying to prevent someone going through . . .
A door is burst open . . . A man comes in . . . Who is it ? . . . Edgardo
of Ravenswood! General confusion. After a few moments of surprise, Asthon turns on Edgardo, reproaching him for his rashness,
and calling on him to withdraw. With the confidence bred of
despair, he replies to him that life is a burden, but that he would
sell it dearly if he prevented him from receiving from Miss Asthon
a statement such that Scottish custom gave him the right to
demand. Bidebent, to prevent the spilling of blood, interposes
himself between Asthon and Ravenswood. The latter, addressing
Lucia, says to her: 'Do you not know me ? I am that Edgardo who
for love of you had from the bottom of his heart forgiven the
murderer of his father. I am that Edgardo who has kept his faith
with you wholly. Can you say the same ?' All the blood freezes in
the veins of the unfortunate girl and she loses the normal power of
speech. Bidebent, hurrying to her aid, says to him 'My Lord, there
is no use you tearing your heart out further. Heaven does not want
you to be united'. So saying, he shows him the marriage contract.
Edgardo turns to her a second time and pointing out her signature
asks her – 'Is this your handwriting?' A 'yes', scarcely spoken,
more like a groan, comes from Lucia's trembling lips. 'Enough'
says Edgardo 'here is the pledge of your faith: return mine to me',
and lifting from his breast Lucia's ring he throws it at her feet.
Lucia, swooning, and helped by Alisa, takes Edgardo's ring mech-
anically from the necklace from which it was suspended, and
gives it to him. 'May heaven not punish you for your broken
promise' – so saying, Edgardo begins to leave: Bucklaw throws
down his glove before him, telling him that after three days they
would see each other again. Meanwhile Asthon's wrath and
Lucia's terror have reached a climax . . . In this moment, when
everything is in confusion, when love, hatred, scorn and vengeance show themselves in all their might, the curtain falls.

Second Act

*Great Hall in Wolfcrag Tower. A table stripped of all ornaments
and an old chair make up all the furniture. At the back there is
a door flanked by two large windows which, the glass being
broken, afford a view of the ruins of the tower. The room is
weakly illuminated by a dim light.*

Duet – Edgardo and Asthon
Edgardo is deep in melancholy reflections. The sound of a fearful
storm is heard. After several moments Edgardo is roused by the
stamping of a horse. 'Who can come here at this hour, and through

the raging of the storm?' – 'Me' – 'Asthon' – 'Yes: you came to my castle. I come to return your call. Hitherto I have not been able to since I have had to assist with Lucia's wedding banquet'. A flash of lightning which streaks across the window lights up on Asthon's terrible face the much more terrible feelings in his heart. 'You may have accepted Bucklaw's challenge' he continues 'but you cannot deny that my right of blood is much older' – 'That is true: and I have consecrated my sword to avenging my father' – 'When?' – 'At the first signs of the new day' – 'Where?' – 'By the tomb of the Ravenswoods. There one of us will remain, and maybe both of us'. The storm howls horribly and reflects the rage which invests the two cruel enemies.

Room in Lucia's apartments

Lucia's scene and Aria

The stage is crowded with Asthon's relatives. The bewilderment they show is the sign of a terrible event that has happened. They question Bidebent when he joins them. 'The wound is not mortal' (he replies) 'but his life is perhaps in serious danger'. Asthon hurries in. 'Is it then true?' he exclaims. 'Ah, alas' (Bidebent replies) 'She plunged his own sword into her husband's side'. – 'Ah, wicked girl' cries Asthon, rushing towards the room where Lucia is, but Bidebent stops him, saying 'The unfortunate girl is out of her mind, and I fear for her life'. Lucia enters, accompanied by Alisa: her clothes are in disarray, and her face is that of someone who has returned from the grave. The barely connected words she utters demonstrate that her madness is at a peak. She throws a glance at her wedding garments, and believes herself being taken to the altar to marry Edgardo – her eyes light up for a moment of lively joy – she wishes to show Ravenswood the fatal ring as a pledge of her faith, but raising her hands to her neck to find the ribbon on which it was suspended, to recover it, and seeing her right hand wet with blood, she is assailed by a multitude of cruel memories and falls fainting into Alisa's arms. All present give a cry of terror.

Outside a chapel, near which is the tomb of the Ravenswoods

Aria finale of Edgardo

Edgardo, immersed in deep gloom, comes to the site of the duel. He turns from the side of the castle, exclaiming 'Lucia, faithless Lucia, while my heart is cruelly torn, you are happy in your husband's arms!' The sound of sad moaning assails his hearing, and weeping people come from the castle. When he questions them, they tell him of the lamentable state of Lucia, and her approaching end. Edgardo's surprise and his grief are inexpressible. The slow and doleful sound of the passing-bell begins. Edgardo wishes to see Lucia again, for the last time, and makes some rapid steps to enter the castle. He is already on the threshold when Bidebent comes out. 'Where are you rushing to, unhappy man? She is no longer on earth' – 'No longer on earth. . . I am rejoining her'. Pronouncing these words, Edgardo plunges a dagger into his heart.

Language and Versification

Critical opinion throughout Cammarano's lifetime always returned to the quality of his verses, and it was on these, rather than on his dramatic techniques, that his reputation rested. This was as it should have been: if the purpose of opera is to provide opportunities for singers to display their ability to portray a variety of contrasting emotions, the dramatic structure needed to be little more than a suitable framework on which to hang the verses. The purpose of a libretto was to provide words for music: it was never intended to stand on its own feet (still less to be read as literature or poetry), and the test of the librettist was his verses. In terms of dramatic structure, there may have been little to choose between the librettists of the period, though some may have been more tidy and economical than others: the real differentiation came in their ability to write suitable verses. As we saw in Chapter 13, Cammarano went to great pains to polish his, avoiding awkward phrases that might have stood in the way of the music. Smoothly-flowing was the adjective most frequently used to describe his work, and this is how they still read today. Unlike many of his contemporaries' lines, they actually *sound* well, and to this extent are already half-way to musical expression.

No study of the language and verse techniques of an Italian librettist can avoid using a number of technical terms, and it would be understandable if the general reader more interested in the music and drama of the opera decided to skip this chapter. I have tried to present the material in as simple a manner as possible, because it is important to an understanding of what Cammarano was attempting to achieve. Nevertheless, there comes a point where over-simplification leads to statements which are meaningless if not actually misleading, so I would hope that the interested reader will persevere. To this end I have added, as an appendix to this chapter, a short simplified account of Italian versification, which the knowledgeable can ignore, but which can be read at this point by others, and turned to as technical points require elucidation. It is, of course, too simplified to be anything but a few rules of thumb.

It is a common complaint that the language of the Italian romantic libretto is stilted and confused – as indeed it often is. Thirty years ago, in an essay *Donizetti: An Italian Romantic* which first provoked my own interest in the subject, Edward Dent hit the nail on the head: 'Cammarano's literary style is always turgid and involved; he is like his English contemporaries who say "sire" for "father" and "steed" for "horse".' In this last instance, Dent was more accurate than he probably realized. All the many references to horses in Cammarano's libretti use the word 'destriero', the direct equivalent of 'steed', except in two places, one in *I ciarlatani*, a comedy in which the more usual 'cavallo' (= 'horse') might be expected, the other in *Il conte di Chalais* (Act III scene 3) and interestingly, when some other librettist prepared this same libretto for Donizetti as *Maria di Rohan*, 'cavallo' was replaced by 'destriero'. Although he often used 'genitore' for father, he had no compunction about using 'padre', though he usually avoided putting it at the end of the line, since there were few possible rhymes except 'madre'!

It is incontrovertible that his language, like that of his colleagues, is sometimes turgid, involved and stilted, but while he never reaches the elegant simplicity of the classically-inclined Romani at his best, he rarely lapses into incomprehensibility or crudity. Libretti were written in a language of their own, and the conventions of the genre have to be accepted and understood. Cammarano's own poetic – and to some extent, dramatic – usage is largely derived from the works of Alfieri, as Fabrizi has pointed out in an important essay. Both Fabrizi and Arruga (whose essay on the influences operating on the librettists of the period is also essential reading) drew attention to the many points of evidence of the importance of Manzoni, Leopardi and others in moulding the language of Cammarano and his colleagues. This language was highly stylized, and many expressions recur in the work of all librettists, even if, as Fabrizi in particular has emphasized, each has his own formulae which he would use with minor modifications throughout his work. These formulae scarcely attain the status of literary fingerprints to be used for identifying the various librettists: they are too much part of the common stock of expressions drawn upon by all for them to serve any such purpose, and we frequently find Cammarano's most overworked formulations in the writings of others.

Cammarano's vocabulary, for a start, contained a number of words which can be held to be of 'poetical' status. To obtain an estimate of how many of his words come into this category is not easy, since the category is arbitrary and a modern dictionary would be expected to list many words as 'poetical' which have reached this status since Cammarano's time. Consequently his vocabulary was tested against Davenport and Comelati's dictionary of 1854, and their accordance of poetical status taken as the test of Cammarano's usage. This equally depends on the arbitrary decisions made by the compilers, but it certainly confirmed that many words listed as 'poetical' in the Sansoni-Harrap dictionary of 1970 were not accorded that status in 1854. On the 1854 basis, some forty-five words in Cammarano's libretti were of poetical usage. Some of them are obsolete spellings rather than words as such (*spirto* = *spirito*; *foco* = *fuoco*; *odire* = *udire*, for example) but the majority do not fall into this category. Some of them are of universal occurrence in libretti: for instance *acciaro* and *brando* for sword, though Cammarano often uses the more common *spada* and, though once only, the rarer *daga*. Poetical words frequently used by Cammarano, and well known to readers of Italian libretti of the period, include *speme* (hope), *avito* (ancestral), *avello* (tomb), *aura* (breeze), *singulto* (sob), *delubro* (temple, usually in connection with a wedding), *vegliardo* (old man), *prence* (prince), *claustro* (cloister), *crine* (hair). Some words occur less frequently – *tosco* (poison, in place of the more usual *veleno*), *certame* (combat), *speglio* (looking-glass), *margo* (edge), *vorago* (abyss), *fiedere* (to strike), *squadre* (troops), for example. Others are used very rarely, perhaps once only in his writings – *sobuglio* (sedition), *bipenne* (two-headed axe), *vanni* (wings). These words were not used in such a way as to evoke a deliberate sense of archaism, but as part of the regular vocabulary, and occur throughout Cammarano's libretti, from *Belisario* to *Il trovatore,* regardless of the place or time in which the story was set.

Similarly, his vocabulary included a whole range of words which, although not achieving poetical status in contemporary terms, nevertheless are not those which would come most readily to mind. *Pargoletto* or *pargolo* for boy, not *figlio* or *fanciullo; averno* for hell, not *inferno; lumi* or *rai* for eyes, not *occhi; occulto* for hidden, not *nascosto* or *celato; nappo* for cup, not *tazza* or *coppa.* This straining for words of heightened expression is so common, so much part of the regular 'librettists' Italian', that examples are too numerous to warrant quotation. Some of the usage was, of course, concerned with the deliberate avoidance of words with everyday connotations, or to add variety and point to the dramatic events, while the requirements of metre and rhyme made a wide vocabulary essential.

Apart from the use of poetical or out-of-the-way words, the language of these libretti is always inflated and exaggerated, best described perhaps as fustian, in the best 'First Player' style. No one weeps – his cheeks are furrowed by tears, or maybe his heart sends bitter tears to his eyelashes. No one is pale – a deathly pallor is painted on his face. No one is upset – thick clouds cover his face. No one keeps away from his beloved – he distances himself from her side. It is never dark – night has drawn her gloomy veil over the earth. No one marries – he (or more often she) ascends the nuptial bed (*talamo* is a most over-used noun) or they approach the nuptial altar. Cannons are hollow bronzes. And so on – the form is familiar enough, and it is no wonder that librettists have come in for a great deal of criticism for their devaluation of the language.

Fabrizi, in his invaluable essay, lists a number of typical expressions and traces their origins. Some of Cammarano's – not all of them listed by Fabrizi – can be examined. They occur in a number of related forms, slight variations on the same theme. Several of them are used in situations when someone is terrified: 'I gelo' ('I freeze') occur in eight of his libretti, four times in *Luisa Miller* alone. A similar turn of phrase 'Io gelo ed ardo' ('I freeze and burn': as we might say today, 'I am hot and cold all over') occur in nine other libretti. 'Il gelo di morte' ('the chill of death'), or its near relations, occurs in fifteen libretti, while 'Un brivido' (or 'gelo') 'mi corse per le vene' ('a chill runs through my veins'), or its equivalent, is perhaps the most widespread expression he used, turning up in twenty-eight texts. Someone's blood freezes ('Tutto il sangue mi si agghiaccia') in ten libretti. Someone in a state of eager anticipation feels their heart bounding ('Balzar mi sento il cor') in sixteen libretti, and they find their hair standing on end ('Il crin mi drizzera') in ten. A typical expression used of a cruel or implacable enemy, or someone who feels no pity is 'Ha di tigre in petto il cor' ('he has the heart of tiger in his breast'), which occurs in various forms in nine libretti, though once a heart of stone ('Ha di macigno il cor') is substituted for a wild beast's. There are many other such recurrent expressions – 'Giunta è l'ora per me' ('my hour has come'), 'D'amore avvampo' ('I am afire with love'), 'La morte è un ben per me' ('Death is a boon to me'), 'Le mie luci ricopre un vel' ('A veil covers my eyes'). 'Sul capo un fulmin piomba' ('A thunderbolt falls on my head'). The contrast between *sospetto* and *certezza* (suspicion and certainty), between *talamo* and *tomba* (wedding and tomb), etc., occur regularly. Another one – carefully and most strikingly used – is 'La macchia dell' onore/col sangue io laverò' ('I will wash away with blood the stain on my honour') or its equivalents, with tears taking the place of blood. These expressions, in one form or another, are the common coin of 'librettist's' Italian' in the romantic era (though these are amongst Cammarano's most frequently used) and it is easy to find examples in the work of other writers. One striking example will suffice: an expression of terror which Cammarano used several times over, 'Fredda man mi stringe il cor' ('a cold hand grips my heart') (*Ines de Castro*, Act I scene 3), echoes precisely Romani's *Amleto* of 1822 (Act I scene 14) – 'Son di gelo, son di sasso/Fredda man mi stringe il cor'.

The importance of these recurrent expressions in Cam-

marano's work is not so much their picturesqueness, nor
their roots in the dramas of, say, Alfieri, but their per-
vasiveness in his libretti. From the very beginning of his
career to the end, these same turns of phrase are ubiquitous. None of them were taken up early in his work, only
to be dropped as time went by; nor did others appear for the
first time half way through. He seems to have started off
with a ready-made, inherited vocabulary of words and
phrases, and persisted with them to the end of his life. As
in almost all aspects of his work, there is little sign of
evaluation or development. I think this confirms the view
that he was using the language accepted as appropriate to
the romantic libretto.

This is not, of course, to say that all his texts contain the
same number of his most well-used expressions. If we
group together the first eight listed above – from 'Il gelo' to
'Di tigre in petto il cor' – the number of instances in his
libretti varies from one (*Merope*) to ten (*Luisa Miller*),
with an average of four to five in each. I have excluded the
two comedies (*I ciarlatani* and *Non v'è fumo*) from this
analysis, since, as Bentivogli has pointed out, the language
of tragedy and comedy was different. There is no evidence
of any variation in the use of these stock expressions with
either composer or source, and it is interesting that the
libretto with the highest number of them (*Luisa Miller*)
was one on which he devoted a great deal of care. It is hard
to find a reason for their abundance in this libretto, but the
extreme condensation of Schiller's drama, and the many
dramatic incidents crowded into the three acts, may
perhaps have offered more opportunities for deploying
them. The next highest· concentration occurs in *Poliuto*
and *L'assedio di Calais*, and again it is difficult to see why.
It may be equally significant that the two works with
fewest are mythological in origin, *Merope* and *Medea*
(though the latter was not, of course, all original Cammarano). The lesson to be drawn from the use of these
stock phrases is that they were used as appropriate to the
context, and little more.

Another turn of phrase to which Cammarano was ad-
dicted was the repetition of a word within a line, often
separated by an 'ah!'. This seems to have been used

rhetorically, for emphasis, but the suspicion lingers that it was occasionally resorted to to pad out the line to its proper length (as were the ever present interjections such as 'Oh! Dio!'). This type of construction occurs over fifty times in Cammarano's work, and a typical example can be found in the final scene of *L'assedio di Calais,* when Queen Eleanor is beseeching her husband to release the captives:

> Cedi . . . ah! cedi invitto sposo,
> Al mio pianto . . . a' preghi miei . . .
>
> (Yield . . . ah! yield, all-conquering husband . . . /
> To my weeping . . . to my prayers . . .)

About a third to a half of all instances of internal repetitions of this type use the construction with 'ah!'; the others repeat a word, or words:

> Un destin . . . destin tiranno!
> Mi perseque dalla cuna! . . .
>   (*Il vascello de Gama,* Act I scene 3)
>
> (A fate . . . an unjust fate! / Pursues me from the cradle . . .)

A few further examples can be taken from *La battaglia di Legnano,* to show how this form of expression could be used within a single libretto:

LIDA
> Ma son madre! . . . madre io sono! (Act I scene 4)
> (But I am a mother! . . . a mother am I!)

ARRIGO
> T'amai, t'amai qual angelo (Act I scene 8)
> (I loved you, I loved you as I would an angel)

LIDA
> Son rea . . . son rea . . . puniscimi . . . (Act I scene 8)
> (I am guilty . . . I am guilty . . . punish me . . .)

ROLANDO
> Ma trema, ah! trema, coppia esecrata . . . (Act III scene 6)
> (But tremble, ah! tremble, accursed couple!)

This construction also occurred frequently in the work of Cammarano's contemporaries. Romani, in particular, was fond of it – there are, for example, as many as six instances in *Emma d'Antioccha* (written for Mercadante,

Venice 1834), and few of his libretti are without some examples. Again, it was part of a librettist's stock in trade, and was used by Cammarano throughout his career.

Despite Cammarano's addiction to these overblown words and phrases, he could when the need arose write direct, clear and straightforward dialogue. This he did particularly when the dramatic situation necessitated a sharp and quick exchange, as in the central finale of *Lucia di Lammermoor*:

RAIMONDO
    Questo amor per sempre obblia:
    Ella è d' altri!
EDGARDO   D' altri!... ah! no.
RAIMONDO
    Mira. (*gli presenta il contratto nuziale*)
EDGARDO
    (*dopo averlo rapidamente letto, e figgendo gli occhi in Lucia*)
    Tremi!... ti confondi!
    Son tue cifre? (*mostrando la di lei firma*)
           A me rispondi:
    Son tue cifre? (*con più forza*)
LUCIA   Si...

RAIMONDO
    Forget this love for ever:
    She belongs to another!
EDGARDO   To another!... Ah! no.
RAIMONDO
    Look. (*shows him the wedding contract*)
EDGARDO
    (*after having read it rapidly, and fixing his eyes on Lucia*)
    You're trembling!... You're all confused!
    Is this your handwriting? (*showing her the signature*)
           Answer me:
    Is this your handwriting? (*with more force*)
LUCIA   Yes...

Many other such examples of direct exchange can be quoted showing clarity of expression without lapsing into crudity. To give just a few:

ALBERTO
    Qual' osa resistenza opporre
    Fia punito di morte.
      (*La fidanzata corsa*, Act III scene 6)

(Whoever dares to offer resistance / Will be punished with death).

CHALAIS
Maria, se la vicina
Ora squilla, e non vieni, a morir teco
Io riedo.
(*Il conte di Chalais*, Act III scene 3)
(Maria, if the next / Hour sounds, and you do not come,
I will return / To die with you).

DECIO
Ah! l'amor nostro Emilia
Come obbliar potesti?...
EMILIA
Ti piansi estinto...
DECIO   Oh smania!...
EMILIA
E cinsi il vel...
DECIO   Che festi!...
Ma vivo, io vivo...
PUBLIO   Incauto!...
GIUNIA
Calmati.
EMILIA   Ah! l'amo ancor!
GIUNIA
Ahime! che dici!...
(*La vestale*, Act I scene 4: stage directions omitted)
(D. Ah! Emilia, how could you / Forget our love?.../
E. I mourned you dead... D. Oh, madness!.../ E. And
took the veil... D. What have you done!.../ But I'm
alive, alive... P. Take care!.../ G. Calm yourself. E. Ah!
I love him still!/ G. Alas! What are you saying?...)

Similarly, when the need arose, Cammarano could write descriptive passages of some force and expression, without excessive resource to fustian. A passage from *L'assedio di Calais* is often quoted, from the scene where the mayor of the besieged city muses on its plight:

EUSTACCHIO
Qual silenzio funesto! – Un gemer fioco
Sol tratto tratto l'interrompe!... Ahi! pianto
È dell' afflitto, che spirarsi accanto
Mira il padre, o il fratello! È derelitta
Sposa, che plora del compagno estinto

Sulla gelida salma!
È singhiozzo di madre, a cui le fonti
S'inaridir, che vita
Furo al lattante pargolo . . .
    (Act I scene 2)
(What fearful silence! – A weak groan / Breaks it from time to
time! Ah! it is / The lament of the afflicted, who all around
them / Watch father or brother dying! From desolate / Wives,
weeping over the chilly remains / Of their dead partner! /
From sobbing mothers, whose springs / Have dried up, which
gave life to the / Sucking infant . . .)

Or, again, in *Il reggente* when Amelia comes alone to the
graveyard, at midnight:

AMELIA

Giunsi . . . Qui tutto di spavento è pieno! . . .
Tutto! . . . financo il sordo
Mutar de' passi miei! – L'orrendo è quello
Asil di morte! . . . – O Ciel, tu guida il mio
Piè vacillante . . .
    (Act II scene 1)
(I have arrived . . . Everything here is full of terror! . . . /
Everything! . . . Even the silent / Movement of my feet! How
horrible is that / Refuge of death! . . . O Heavens, guide / My
wavering steps . . .)

Or, *Stella di Napoli* – Stella is in prison, and feels her life
ebbing away:

STELLA

La mia giornata dunque, innanzi sera
Tramonta! . . . nè veder mi fia concesso
L'ultima volta il padre! . . . il padre mio,
Che tanto m'ama! e ch' io
Tanto adorava! . . .
    (Act II scene 3)
(The course of my days, then, sets before / Its evening! . . .
If only it were allowed me / To see my father for the last time!
. . . My father / Who loves me so much! And whom I have /
So much adored! . . .)

Or, finally, from *Cristina di Svezia*; Giulia is waiting in
the Park at Fontainebleu, to flee from Paris with Monaldeschi:

255

GIULIA
Posa la terra, già si mostra in cielo
Qualche romita stella. – È questa l'ora,
Questo il vial de' salici, ed ancora! . . . –
Sorgea forse un inciampo? . . . Ahimè! son lunghi,
Angosciosi gl' istanti
Che precedon la fuga! . . . I rami scuote
L'aura notturna, o fu mutar di passi
Il suon che intesi?
  (Act II scene 4)
(The earth is still, already some lonely star / Shows in the
heavens. This is the time, / This the avenue of willows, and
yet! . . . – / Perhaps some snag has arisen? Alas, they are long,
/ Distressing, the moments / Which precede flight! . . . The
nocturnal breeze / Rustles the branches, or was it the sound
of footsteps / That I heard?)

Such passages show that when Cammarano wanted to,
he could write simple and effective lines. Significantly, all
of these passages come in *versi sciolti*, presumably since
the additional freedom allowed him to write in a more
direct style. The constraints and conventions of the set
verse seem to have led him into the standard style and
language of the libretto.

Nevertheless, it was on his flowing verses that his reputation largely rested. That these verses employ exaggerated
language and patterns of word use is not important; the
point is that even using this language his verses *do* flow
smoothly, and sound well when read aloud. The sound of
the text is of prime importance, since – and this must
never be forgotten – they were written to be set to music,
and if they read and sound well, and flow on without
interruption, they will be that much easier to set. Cammarano's verses have an intrinsically musical quality that
must have made them attractive to his composers.

It is hard to define the particular qualities which contributed to the success of Cammarano's best verses. It is
not the sentiments expressed, since these are, for the most
part, stereotyped if not trite – love, self-pity, anger, jealousy – using time-worn similes and constructions. Any
examples must be arbitrary, accepting that what seems
flowing and successful to one pair of ears may well not

seem so to another. Since it is the sound and the flow
which is important, I have in this coming section refrained
from adding any translations. The test of the verses are
how they sound *when read aloud*. Since *Saffo* was frequently held up as his masterpiece, a few examples can be
taken from it for analysis, even if the first one (from Act II
scene 3) had been lifted from *Poliuto*.

> Di quai soavi lagrime
> Aspersa è la mia gota! ...
> Qual mi ricerca l'anima
> Dolce potenza ignota! ...
> Somiglia una speranza. ...   5
> L'umana gioja avanza. ...
> Par che involato bene
> Amico Iddio mi renda! ..
> Par che il mio core intenda
> I moti del tuo cor!   10

This passage – part of a duet for Saffo and Climene – is in
settenarii, with the first and third lines *sdrucciolo*, creating an added sense of forward movement (see the appendix
for an explanation of the terms used). The only *tronco* line
is the last, but this is quite usual, being the metrical equivalent of a full stop (though often the final four lines
rhyme XYXY, where both Y lines are *tronco*). The rhyming
scheme in these lines is ABCBDDEFFG, not an unusual
pattern for one of Cammarano's ten-line stanzas. There is
no full stop or other pause in the middle of any line. (This
is a general rule: there is only a handful of internal stops in
all of Cammarano's verses, and these are often for dramatic
effect. Verdi was later to draw attention to one of Cammarano's few lapses, in a line from *Belisario*.)

The primary stress in *settenario* lines such as these falls
naturally on the penultimate (sixth) syllable, leaving the
rest of the line relatively fluid and unstressed, though a
secondary stress can usually be felt. Cammarano avoids
metrical monotony by varying the position of this secondary stress, offering the composer opportunities for moving
away from a regular, four-square setting if he wished to
take advantage of them. Thus in line 1, a secondary stress
is felt on the fourth syllable (so*a*vi); in line 2, on the
second (As*pe*rsa); in line 3, on the fourth (ri*ce*rca); in line

4, on either the first or the fourth; in line 5 and 6, on the second; in lines 7, 8 and 9, on the fourth; in line 10, on the second. In this way, Cammarano has maintained variety in the pulse of the lines, without in any way departing from the integrity of the *settenarii*. This, and the use of *sdrucciolo* lines at the beginning of the stanza, keep the verse moving.

So much for the versification and the flow of the lines. The sound of the passage depends more on a careful choice of words. Firstly there are very few 'hard' sounds, or awkward juxtapositions of consonants – only *gota* (line 2) *ricerca* (3), *che* (7 and 9), *core* (9) and *cor* (10). All the rest are fluid and soft. Secondly the various vowel sounds are distributed in such a way as to achieve maximum variety – so that when a line is met which has a preponderance of the same sound this is immediately apparent – L'um*a*n*a* gioj*a* *a*v*a*nz*a* (line 6). Thirdly there is a widespread use of *sinalefe* (lines 2, 4, 5, 6, 7, 8 and 9). This helps to keep the sound soft, avoiding too many juxtapositions of consonants at the ends and beginnings of adjacent words. Since Italian is rich in words beginning and ending with vowels, this is a general feature of the language, but one which Cammarano exploits carefully. He was certainly conscious of the need to achieve sonority. Commenting on changes made by someone else to the third act of *L'assedio di Calais*, he wrote sarcastically: 'Note that the juxtaposition of the sounds "ime" (in "sublime") and "ine" (in "crine") makes exquisite consonance'.

A second, and quite different example is Alcandro's aria in *Saffo*, Act I scene 2:

> Di sua voce il suon giungea
> Dolce all' alma e conosciuto!
> Come in segno mi parea
> Quel sembiante aver veduto!
> E che palpito mi scosse, 5
> Quale affetto mi commosse
> Nè può dir linguaggio umano,
> Nè pensiero intender può . . .
> Ah! d'amarla un senso arcano,
> Una forza il cor provò! 10

This passage is in *ottonarii*, a much more difficult metre

to keep moving, firstly because Cammarano never uses a *sdrucciolo* line in it and secondly because there is a strong secondary stress falling normally on the third syllable, a stress which is less easily shifted. Nevertheless, in line 2 there is a suggestion of stress on the first syllable (Dolce all' alma) and in line 7 the first three syllables all seem to require some stress. The verse form is regular: again it is a ten-line stanza, and because there are no *sdrucciolo* lines (which Cammarano very rarely rhymes), there is a simple pattern, ABABCCDEDE, both lines E being *tronco*. Again there is a marked absence of hard sounds and a careful distribution of vowels. In the ten lines of the passage there are eleven *sinalefe*. I have the impression that Cammarano attempted to use more *sinalefe* in passages of *ottonarii* to compensate for the more rigid distribution of stress.

Some effective and well-sounding lines come in Act I scene 6 of *Pia de' Tolomei*, when Pia's ladies are inviting her to sit by the window:

Qui posa il fianco. È vivida
Quest' ora del mattino,
Imbalsamata è l'aura
Che move dal giardino:
Di vaghi fior smaltato   5
Ve' come ride il prato,
Qui tutto spira e parla
Celeste voluttà . . .
(È vano! A confortarla
Uman poter non v'ha!)   10

Here again is a passage in *settenarii*, with lines 1 and 3 *sdrucciolo* − 'aura' at the end of line 3 must be sounded here − as usual at the end of the line − as a three-syllable word. The stanza is ten lines long, rhyming ABCBDDEFEF, lines 8 and 10 being *tronco*. There are no hard sounds (except perhaps for vaghi) in the whole passage, and only the word 'Imbalsamata' (otherwise splendid in the context) has any repetition of vowel sounds, and even this is mitigated by the succeeding *sinalefe*. The secondary stress moves between the second and fourth syllables, and this, with the two *sdrucciolo* lines, keeps the verses flowing, as do the six *sinalefe*. One point is of great interest: in the first line there is an internal full stop, but the effect of this is totally lost, since it occurs in the middle of a *sinalefe* (fianco. È). The composer could thus choose to set the words without regard to the full stop, or to ignore the *sinalefe* (as was frequently done) and break the phrase at that point. In fact, Donizetti followed the former path. Incidentally, it is hard to believe that Solera did not have this passage in mind when he wrote in *Ildegonda*, for which he also wrote the music:

> Qui posa il fianco! E balsamo
> Quest' aura mattutina;

To take a passage in *ottonarii* from the same act of *Pia de' Tolomei*, we can turn to the trio between Pia, Nello and Ghino in scene 13. Pia's lines are:

> Egli asconde un rio furore
> Sotto il vel di finta calma!
> Ah! d'ambascia, di terrore
> Circondata, ingombra ho l'alma!...
> Odo un gemito... un lamento!...
> Veggo oggetti di spavento!...
> Un avello insanguinato
> Par che s'apra innanzi a me!

Here the same features emerge; an eight-line stanza, ABABCCDE (with the D and E lines rhyming with the equivalent lines in the two verses for Nello and Ghino). There is a subtle variation in stress, but rather more hard sounds, though a wide distribution of vowels. There is a high proportion of *sinalefe* – eleven in eight lines.

Perhaps some of Cammarano's most beautiful *ottonario* lines are the two *quartine* of Edgardo's final cabaletta at the very end of *Lucia di Lammermoor*:

> Tu che a Dio spiegasti l'ali,
> O bell' alma innamorata,
> Ti rivolgi a me placata...
> Teco ascenda il tuo fedel.
> Ah! se l'ira dei mortali
> Fece a noi si lunga guerra,
> Se divisi fummo in terra,
> Ne congiunga il Nume in ciel.

The rhyming pattern is, again, one of Cammarano's

favourites, ABBCADDC, with lines 4 and 8 *tronco*. Despite the occasional hard sound, and the bunching of vowel sounds in the second line, the verses are successful by virtue of the most subtle variations of stress and sound, and a high incidence of *sinalefe* (nine in eight lines).

As an example of a passage in *ottonarii* that does not read well, here is one from *Alzira* (Act II scene 6):

> Irne lungi ancor dovrei
>   Carco d'onta e fuggitivo? ..
>   Separarmi da colei
>   Onde sol respiro, e vivo?
>   Io guardai la morte in viso,
>   La guardai con un sorriso! . . .
>   Ma spezzar mi sento il core! . . .
>   Ma non reggo a tal pensier! . . .
> Ahi, che debil rende amore
>   Anche l'alma del guerrier!

This seems to me to be less successful for several reasons: an accumulation of awkward words and phrases ('Irne lungi', 'Io guardai', 'La guardai', 'Ma spezzer', for instance); a failure to vary the stress between the lines; a low count of *sinalefe*. The test is in the sound, admittedly a matter of personal opinion, and in my submission it is rough. There is no doubt that Cammarano's verses could be inelegant, despite his attempts to polish them. Perhaps I should end this section by quoting the verses which Cammarano used four times in various libretti, choosing the first version that appeared (in *La sposa*) as a fine example of his mellifluous work:

> O giovinetta sposa,
>   Soave sei, gentile!
>   Gentil come la rosa
>   D'un bel mattin d'aprile,
>   Soave come un'aura
>   Che spirar dal giardin!

Cammarano's *versi sciolti* is always accurate and economical, as the *Folco d'Arles* excerpts show, and his set-piece verses smoothly flowing and well sounding. He was weakest in open verse sections of dialogue, connective tissue set in verse rather than in *versi sciolti*, though in a continuous, seamless pattern. Usually this is in *settenarii* (though there are passages in *ottonarii* and some interesting ones in *decasillabi*), with alternating *sdrucciolo* and *piano* lines, which at its worst and most routine degenerates into a banal jog-trot, as in this excerpt from *Virginia*, Act I scene 7:

APPIO
    Non mai!... Qual lampo orribile
    Balena al mio pensiero!
    Solo un rival può rendere
    Tuo cor cotanto altero...
    Dilegua il fero dubbio...
VIRGINIA
    (Dei!...)
APPIO   Quale in te pallore?...
    Vacilli?... Or più non dubito:
    Arde tu d'altro amore.
VIRGINIA
    (Ah!)
APPIO   Del rival pronuncia
    L'odiato nome...
VIRGINIA   (Ahimè!)
APPIO
    Quale s'appella?
VIRGINIA   Lasciami...
APPIO
    Donna, il palesa a me.

This pattern is usually rounded off by a *tronco* line, or a *quartina* ABAB with both B lines *tronco*, but can immediately reassert itself, continuing for several pages at a time.

In passing it may be added that Cammarano was very careful with his rhyming patterns, and unlike many of his contemporaries, rarely broke the pattern or left a succession of lines unrhymed (a serious fault, for instance, in the verses of Rossi and Gilardoni). His choice of rhymes was usually good, being unforced, though there are some rhymes which seem rather too facile – *padre/madre*, for instance, or *sangue/esangue* – but it should be remembered that Italian is very well provided with words which rhyme, though the librettists were perhaps fortunate in having available such pairs as *core* (heart)/*amore* (love), *sorriso* (smile)/*viso* (face), *gloria* (glory)/*vittoria* (victory), *bella* (beautiful)/*stella* (star) and the like, which they certainly overused.

One way in which the librettist provided the composer with opportunities for varying the musical treatment of the text was by using a range of different metres, and a short excursion into this aspect of the libretto is required in order to establish Cammarano's own position.

The division of a libretto between *versi sciolti* and rhymed verse changed steadily during the nineteenth century. At the beginning of the century, around 60 per cent of the whole text was in *versi sciolti*, and this proportion fell steadily till at the middle of the century it had reached 30 per cent or less. Obviously these are average figures, and in any one librettist's work there will be marked variations, depending on the way the text is organized. In the libretti of Gaetano Rossi, which cover a sixty-year period from 1795 to 1855, there is a steady decline in the proportion of *versi sciolti*, but those of Cammarano (whose work, after all, spanned less than twenty years) show no such trend. *Versi sciolti* accounts for, at the most, 42 per cent of the text (all percentages are based on the number of lines) in *Il vascello de Gama* to 21 per cent (*Il reggente*), the average being about 30 per cent. These percentages are not in themselves of any importance – what is important is that there is no evidence of any connection between the amount of *versi sciolti* and the type of subject or the composer for whom he was writing.

There were changes during the century, too, in the verse lengths used. The two main types were always *settenario* and *ottonario*; a preference for the latter at the beginning of the century changed in favour of the former as the century went on, though with all librettists successive texts vary greatly. Two trends are, however, very clear: the first is a very marked decline in the use of 'mixed' line lengths, the use of lines of different lengths in the same stanza – for instance, a quartina of three *settenarii* and one *quinario*. The second trend was a shift from short lines (*quinarii* and *senarii*) to long ones (*decasillabi, quinarii accoppiati* and *senarii accoppiati*). The ten-syllable lines (of both types) were always used, but became more common as the century wore on, but the twelve-syllable lines seem to be rarely used before about 1825 (Rossi's *Semi-*

ramide of 1823 was one of the earliest known to me to contain a significant number of them). Although any one text is likely to depart from the average, a comparison is helpful: contrast a typical libretto of the turn of the century (Butturini's *Merope*, written for Nasolini, 1796) with a typical one of the 1860s (Bolognese's *Virginia*, written for Petrella, 1861):

	Merope	Virginia
Percentage of	(1796)	(1861)
Quinarii	14	—
Senarii	25	—
Settenarii	28	53
Ottonarii	28	21
Decasillabi	5	4
Quinarii accoppiati	—	19
Senarii accoppiati	—	3

As it happens, Butturini's libretto contained no 'mixed line' verse, but I cannot recall that Bolognese ever wrote any. The overall effect of these changes was an impoverishment in the variety of verse forms used, and the replacement of *ottonarii* by *settenarii* and longer lines, as the very short lines disappeared from use.

Cammarano made little use of the *quinario*. There is quite an amount in his early texts, but thereafter it is rarely used, except in *Non v'è fumo senza fuoco*. It was, in fact, more generally used in comedies than in serious works; Ferretti was a master in its use. *Senarii* are always rare in Cammarano's work (and by the 1830s had fallen out of fashion). He only used this line in six texts, with the largest proportion (10 per cent of the text) in *Malvina di Scozia*, right at the end of his career, in sections which were not common to *Ines de Castro*.

The proportions of *Settenarii* and *ottonarii* in his works vary, but together form about 80–85 per cent of all lines (discounting, as always, *versi sciolti*). Some of the libretto are predominantly in *settenarii* (e.g. *Saffo, Bondelmonte, Alzira, Orazi e Curiazi* and *Virginia*, all with nearly 60 per cent of the lines of verse in this length), others contain a high proportion of *ottonarii* (e.g. *Cristina di Svezia*, 60 per cent). There is clear evidence of a decline in the extent to which Cammarano used the *ottonarii* – early works have a consistently higher proportion than later ones, the lowest being *Orazi e Curiazi* and *Virginia*, both with less than 20 per cent. This was a line which Verdi, at least, disliked – 'I do not much like the *ottonarii* rhythm because of the two damned notes on the upbeat' he wrote to Boito in 1881, when they were working on the revision of *Simon Boccanegra*, referring to the way the stress falls on the third syllable.

On the other hand, Cammarano was constant in his use of *decasillabi*, which always accounted for 5–10 per cent of the verse lines of a libretto, but the amount of *quinarii accoppiati* rose steadily, reaching 22 per cent of all lines in *Luisa Miller*, though this was exceptionally high: 10 per cent in the middle-period works was about usual. The amount of *senarii accoppiati* was consistently less – usually a few per cent only, presumably for the sake of variety, though *Poliuto* had, exceptionally, 9 per cent in this line, as did *La vestale*. If there is a trend, it is for a slight increase in this line as time went on. It was not a form familiar in Naples; Tottola and Gilardoni used it rarely, at least in their tragic works. Romani had begun to use it consistently in the libretti he wrote in the early 1830s, and since those which were set by Donizetti were played in Naples, it was probably from them that Cammarano adopted it.

By and large, Cammarano's libretti display the same features as the general trends – a reduction in the shorter lines and an increase in the longer. None of his texts use less than four line lengths, while five are the average and six are frequent. A high number offered the composer more variety and greater flexibility in his settings (the series of essays by Lippmann in *Analecta Musicologica* for 1973, 4 and 5 should be consulted by anyone wishing to see how line lengths influence the melodic pattern of composers of this period).

The other way of avoiding monotony was by the use of stanzas of mixed line lengths, or unusual metres such as the *endecasillabo*. This seems to have been very much a matter of personal taste. Romani used mixed lines fairly frequently, usually mixtures of five and seven syllables, but earlier in his career, four and eight. Similarly, Rossi's libretti are rarely without mixed lines, and he employed a number of different types. (Rossi's sense of theatre was splendid, and his technical ability in versification secure, but the absence of any sense of poetry and the haste with which he obviously wrote made his work crude and less than gratifying to the ear). Tottola made very occasional use of mixed lines, but Gilardoni was more enterprising – *Il paria*, for instance (Donizetti, Naples 1829) has passages in lines of five and seven syllables; seven and eleven; and five, seven and eleven.

Cammarano's use of mixed lines is interesting, since after two early libretti he reserved them for set pieces of unusual significance: In *L'assedio di Calais*, Act III scene 4, when the English soldiers hear the victims from Calais approaching; in *Il reggente* Act I scene 6, the sorcerer's invocation (with its clear echoes of *Macbeth*); in *Il ravvedimento*, Act II scene 4, a benediction; in *Il vascello de Gama*, Act II scene 1, a notturno, scene 2, a drinking song; in *Merope*, Act III scene 4, a hymn (a fascinating piece of writing: the Priests sing in mixed six- and twelve-syllable lines, the People in five and ten, the shorter lines of each section rhyming throughout); in *La battaglia di Legnano*, the chorus of the Knights of Death as they assemble; in *Luisa Miller* there is an unusual instance in Act II scene 7: Rodolfo's aria 'Quando le sere placido' (in *settenarii*) has after each verse the same *quinario* 'Ah! . . . mi tradia', perhaps indicating an obsessive image; in *Folco d'Arles* Act II scene 4, a chorus of victory.

All this makes no mention of *Il trovatore*, which is, from the point of view of versification, quite the most virtuoso performance before Boito's *Amleto* of 1863 (where the important characters are differentiated by the type of verse used for each). In *Il trovatore* there is no verse in *quinarii* or *senarii*, an average content of *settenarii*, some *ottonarii*, making up 62 per cent together; some *decasillabi*, a great deal of *quinarii accoppiati*, some *senarii accoppiati*, but altogether some 8 per cent of the verse is in mixed lengths. The rest is in a form not previously used in libretti, as far as I can discover, the *settenarii accoppiati*.

The mixed forms are: five and seven syllables; seven and eleven; and five and ten; and it is worth while examining how they are used. The first to be met with is the seven and

eleven, used for Ferrando's spine-chilling narrative in the
first scene of all, a few moments after the curtain goes up:

> Di due figli vivea, padre beato,
> Il buon Conte di Luna;
> Fida nutrice del secondo nato
> Dormia presso la cuna. *etc.*

Two such verses of eight lines each, separated and followed
by twelve lines of *quinarii accoppiati*, make up his story.

The second usage is in five and seven, and is Manrico's
off-stage serenade in Act I scene 3. The first of the two
verses is:

> Deserto sulla terra,
> Col rio destino in guerra,
> È sola speme un cor,
> Al trovator!

The third passage in mixed lines comes in Act II scene 1,
in five and ten – the famous Anvil Chorus:

> Quale a voi splende propizia stella?
> La Zingarella.

Again, each time the mixed verse is used in exceptional,
set-piece situations. So too are the *settenarii accoppiati*,
which Verdi was later to hold up to Ghislanzoni (the
librettist of *Aida*) as an example of versification. This is
Azucena's narrative, Act II scene 1, the recollection of
seeing her mother burn to death at the stake: 'Condotta
Ell' era in ceppi, al suo destin tremendo / Col figlio... teco
in bracchio io la seguia piangendo / Infino ad essa un varco
tentai, ma invano, aprirmi . . . / Invan tentò la misera
fermarsi, e benidirmi!' etc.

In these four lines, note in the first line the absence of a
sinalefe across the 'join' between the two *settenarii* ('. . .
ceppi al . . .'). In the fourth line, the first *settenario* is
sdrucciolo ('misera'), as is the sixth, not quoted above. In
line three, although the two *settenarii* abut at 'varco –
tentai', the natural break in the line as written occurs after
'tentai', so that Cammarano has run on the first in an
unusual and sensitive way. This is something he exploits
still further in the later lines: 'Scalza, discinta!... il grido,
il noto grido ascolto... / Mi vendica!... La mano convulsa
tendo . . . stringo'. Altogether a versatile and sensitive
piece of writing.

So too is the famous Miserere, with its eleven-syllable lines having subtle variations in stress. Cammarano wrote to Verdi on 9 August 1851 about this piece in the following terms: 'I have written for this last piece lines of eleven syllables, none of them *tronco*, as these are better adapted to musical setting'. He clearly knew what he was doing.

At the very end of his career, almost on his death-bed Cammarano was still prepared to experiment with new forms and to perfect his verse techniques. There is no evidence – either from correspondence or from the texts themselves – that he chose different verse types (or, for that matter, different forms of language) to suit the composer he was writing for. If the Donizetti libretti have an above-average proportion of *ottonarii*, it is because they were all written early in his career, and as he progressed he moved away from this rather rigid form to those of greater flexibility. Had he been writing for Donizetti later in his life, I believe there would have been fewer *ottonarii* in the libretti. It was, indeed, his last libretto for Donizetti – *Poliuto* – that set a pattern for the future, with 20 per cent of its verse lines either *quinarii accoppiati* or *senarii accoppiati*.

No two libretti are the same, and variety was obtained by maintaining a range of metres, as well as varying the pattern and the construction of the individual lines. There is no one 'finger-print' by which Cammarano's work can instantly be recognized, and some libretti are more interesting from a technical point of view than others: but few betray signs of undue haste or shoddy workmanship.

Appendix. Italian Versification

The Italian word for a line of poetry is *verso*, but I will use 'line' to avoid confusion with the familiar use of the English 'verse'. A line is categorized by the number of syllables it contains, so it is advisable to begin with what makes a syllable for this purpose. Most words present no trouble to the reader: *che* is obviously one, *core*, two: similarly, *immenso* and *momento* are equally obviously three-syllable words. The first problem comes when there are two adjacent vowels in a word – what are we to do with *Io*? There can be no absolute rule as to whether such words are to be counted as one or two syllables, since much depends on context, but some general rules-of-thumb can be offered. Assume that when the second of two vowels is normally accented, count as two syllables (e.g. *beàtò*); also as two, the vowel combinations *ae, ao, oa; ia, ie, io* and *iu*. Note, however, that with *ie* and *uo*, where the first vowel is not present in the parent language, the two vowels count as one syllable (*cielo, piede* and *buono* are therefore two-syllable words, not three). *Ia, io* and *iu* similarly count as one syllable when following *c, g, gl* or *sc* (as in *giovane, figlio*). One important exception: at the end of a line of poetry, two unaccented vowels (or pairs of vowels where the first is accented) are counted as two syllables. Thus *mio* counts as one syllable in the middle of a line, but two if it comes at the end.

The other factor affecting vowels and syllable counts is the *sinalefe*, the slide that occurs between two vowels, one at the end of one word, and the other at the beginning of the next. While the two vowels may just be heard separately, they merge in such a way as to form almost one sound, so that they are counted as one syllable:

> Chi mi frena in tal momento?...
> (*Lucia di Lammermoor*, Act II scene 6).

Having clarified the nature of the syllable, we can examine the line. The line is categorized by the number of syllables it contains: thus *quinario* (five), *senario* (six), *settenario* (seven), *ottonario* (eight), *novenario* (nine; rare in libretti), *decasillabo* (ten), *endecasillabo* (eleven). A second type of line is made up of two shorter lines abutting at the centre: in libretti of this period the *quinario accoppiato* (two times five syllables, ten altogether in the line) the *senario accoppiato* (two times six) are common while the *settenario accoppiato* (two times seven) occurs just once.

For each category of line there are three varieties which, confusingly, differ in the number of syllables. The standard line is *piano*: that is, it ends with the stress on the penultimate syllable, and, if a *settenario*, will have seven syllables:

<pre>
1   2 3 4 5 6 7
Raggio di tetra lŭnă . . .
</pre>
(Act I scene 4).

The second type of line is *sdrucciolo*, and has an extra syllable added to the end of the *piano* line, making eight in all:

<pre>
1   2 3   4 5 6 7 (8)
Quando sommesso gèmĭtŏ
</pre>

The third type is *tronco*: here the last, unaccented syllable is omitted, so that the line ends on the stressed syllable:

<pre>
1 2   3   4 5 6
Fra l'aure udir si fè.
</pre>

Thus a *settenario* can have on a count of syllables six, seven or eight, but the stress invariably falls on the sixth. While most stanzas are written in *piano* lines, *sdrucciolo* lines are used for variety and to give forward motion, while *tronco* lines tend to occur at the end, being the verse equivalent of the full stop.

We can now quote examples from Cammarano's works of all the line lengths he used, quoting always *piano* lines, but remembering that *sdrucciolo* and *tronco* lines may appear to have different numbers of syllables:

a) *Quinario*
<pre>
1   2   3   4 5
S' innalzi un grido:
</pre>
(*Lucia di Lammermoor*, Act III scene 3)

b) *Senario*
<pre>
1   2 3 4   5   6
Il cielo rimbomba! . . .
</pre>
(*Belisario*, Act III scene 6)

c) *Settenario*
<pre>
1 2 3 4   5   6 7
Alta la notte e bruna
</pre>
(*Lucia di Lammermoor*, Act I scene 4)

d) *Ottonario*
<pre>
1   2 3 4 5   6   7 8
Come vinti da stanchezza
</pre>
(*ibid.*, Act I scene 3)

e) *Decasillabo*
<pre>
1   2   3 4 5   6   7 8 9 10
Percorrete le spiagge vicine
</pre>
(*ibid.*, Act I scene 1)

f) *Quinario accoppiato*

1 2 3 4 5 = 6 7 8 9 10
Di quella pira l'orrendo fuoco
(*Il trovatore,* Act III scene 6)

g) *Endecasillabo*

1 2 3 4 5 6 7 8 9 10 11
Miserere d'un' alma già vicina
(*ibid.,* Act IV scene 1)

h) *Senario accoppiato*

1 2 3 4 5 6 = 7 8 9 10 11 12
Morì di paura un servo del Conte,
(*ibid.,* Act I scene 1)

i) *Settenario accoppiato*

1 2 3 4 5 6 7 = 8 9 10 11 12 13 14
Condotta Ell' era in ceppi, al suo destin tremendo
(*ibid.,* Act II scene 1)

Note that in *accoppiato* lines, there is never a *sinalefe* between the two half lines, and that the first half can be *sdrucciolo,* but never *tronco*:

1 2 3 4 5 6 * 7 8 9 10 11 12
O sole, piu rapido a sorger t'appresta...

Versi sciolti was a major component of a libretto; free verse, unstressed, basically lines of eleven syllables with some of seven. The syllable count in all Cammarano's *versi sciolti* is invariably accurate, and his lines are always *piano.* Occasionally the lines may rhyme, in particular a seven-syllable line may rhyme backwards or forwards with an adjacent eleven-syllable one, or the last two eleven-syllable lines of a passage may rhyme.

CHAPTER FIFTEEN

Cammarano's Duties as Producer

The part played by the librettist in the production of operas of this period has been little studied, though later in the century it became the custom for a publishing house like Ricordi's of Milan to issue detailed staging instructions along with the musical material. Putting operas on the stage was part of Cammarano's duties, and was recognized in the title of *Poeta e concertatore* which he held from 1834 till his death. We know that it was usual for the theatre poet to carry this double function at that time – Calisto Bassi held a similar post at La Scala, Milan, as did Piave later – so that the practice was not peculiar to the S. Carlo.

Fortunately, some autograph papers about Cammarano's production duties have survived, and there are scattered references in correspondence between composers and impresarios which fill out the picture. There are also the stage directions which he inserted in his own libretti. Some instructions which Verdi sent him when he was entrusted with the production of the Neapolitan premiere of *Macbeth* in 1849 have often been quoted.

It is clear from the Donizetti-Lanari correspondence that Cammarano's involvement with the production of an opera for which he was providing the libretto began at an early stage in the collaboration. Even before the actual libretto was completed, he was asked to supply details of the costumes which would be required – in August 1836 Lanari pressed for a note about the wardrobe of *Pia de' Tolomei* at the same time as he sent the libretto, or, if that couldn't be ready, the synopsis. This provision of production details seem to have extended at times to productions in other theatres of works originally staged under his own direction at the S. Carlo, as when Mercadante wrote to the authorities of the Fenice theatre in Venice in June 1847, six months after *Orazi e Curiazi* had first been given in

Naples, saying that he would ensure that Cammarano sent a note of the wardrobe, the properties and the scenery for this opera (which was given there three months later, in September). Some notes Cammarano provided for the staging of *Lucia di Lammermoor* were probably intended for a production at some other theatre.

As Cammarano had begun life as an art student, had spent some years as an artist before turning to the writing of libretti, and had come from a highly professional theatrical family, these duties probably came easily to him. Some of his costume and scenery specifications have survived, and those for Donizetti's *Anna Bolena* are worth reproducing, if only for the light they shed on operatic production of the period. The preparation of this opera was one of the first tasks which came his way after being taken onto the staff of the Royal Theatres. The document is dated June 1834, though by this time the opera had been in the S. Carlo repertoire for two years. Whether these notes were put down for a new production (Cammarano had also to make a few small changes to the text) or for the use of a colleague in another theatre cannot now be determined, but they clearly reflect S. Carlo practice. There are two documents, one of the wardrobe, the other of the scenery:

Royal Theatres   S. Carlo
————————————

ANNA BOLENA
Wardrobe

The action takes place in England – the period is 1536

ACTORS

Sigr: Henry VIII – Court dress, with a rich loose-fitting cut-away coat. Cloak, knitted stockings and hat with feathers. Hunting dress, with simple loose coat and hat.

Siga: Anna – rich court dress with train, crown with short head-bands. A plain dress for the prison scenes.

Siga: Giovanna – a rich dress with train, a veil for her head.

Sigr: Rochefort – court dress, loose-fitting coat, cloak, knitted stockings and a hat with feathers.

Sigr: Percy – loose-fitting coat, cloak, knitted stockings and a hat with feathers.

Siga : Smeton – as a page, loose coat, cape, knitted stockings and a cap with feathers.
Sigr : Hervey – as an officer. Loose coat, knitted stockings, breastplate and helmet with a plume.

CHORUS

Men (　) As knights in indoor dress, that is loose coat, cape, knitted stockings, shoes, hat with feathers and gloves. Another costume for the hunt, that is plain loose coat and boots.
Women (　) As Ladies, with rich clothes, veils for the head and gloves.

SUPERS

Boys (4) As pages, much the same as Smeton, with gloves.
(8) As pages in hunting costume, that is simple loose coat, knitted stockings, cap, shoes and gloves.

EXTRAS FROM THE ARMY

(40) As soldiers.

LOCAL EXTRAS

(2) As sheriffs – loose coat, wool cloak, shoes and black cap, with gloves.
(8) As servants – with simple loose coats, stockings and shoes.
(1) Officer with uniform similar to the soldiers', knitted stockings, hat and boots.

Naples – June 1834　　Cammarano

Royal Theatres　　S. Carlo

ANNA BOLENA
Scenery

The action takes place in England – the period is 1536

Act I
1. Room in Windsor Castle, in the Queen's apartments. It is illuminated as it is night-time.
2. Park of Windsor Castle, at the back are two walls with a gate in the middle.
3. Lobby in the Queen's apartments with an entrance in the centre – on the left (stage-left) a door, and a window with a curtain, behind which a person can conceal himself.

Act II
4. Lobby with two side doors.
5. Entrance-hall leading to the room where the Council have gathered – a door at the back which when needed can be opened to permit a view of the Council Room.
6. Hall in the prison of the Tower of London – four side doors leading to various prison cells.

Naples – June 1834   Cammarano

It is a pity that in providing these details for *Anna Bolena* Cammarano did not indicate how many members of the chorus had to be provided for. In 1848, as we know from Torelli's draft budget for the Royal Theatres, there were fifty of them, and it is likely that there were about the same number in 1834. With the various extras, and seven principals, there would have been about 120 people on the stage for, say, the central finale, not counting any stage band that may have been used – later notes indicate that the stage band at the S. Carlo was thirty strong, and was probably a regular feature of the performances there. (At the bottom of another list of costumes, this time for another Donizetti opera, *La regina di Golconda*, Cammarano wrote a reminder to himself, 'ask the Director of Music if there is a stage band').

Rather surprisingly, Cammarano's involvement in planning performances seems to have gone beyond drawing up lists of costumes and scenery and directing the movements of the cast, and included specifying how the chorus were to be used. In 1848, when he was collaborating with Verdi in writing *Luisa Miller*, he told the composer in a letter, 'The Archers will be the basses of the chorus, the tenors and the women will be the peasants' – an allocation which one might have expected the composer to have made in the light of the musical design he had in mind. There is no suggestion in the letter that in writing in this way Cammarano was going beyond what was expected of him, and the clear implication is that the responsibility for the distribution of roles among the chorus was the librettist/*concertatore*'s, not the composer's.

Naturally, the principal role of the *concertatore* was to see the operas safely onto the stage, and the evidence

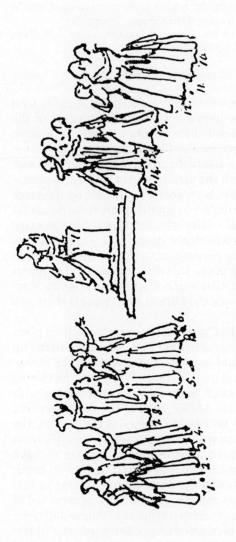

Figure 1

1. Gioja	5. Speranza A	7. Venturini	A. Barbieri	10. Paoletti	13. Della Torre
2. Farina	6. Sant	8. Speranza R	B. Salvetti	11. Nuzzi	14. Checcherini
3. Parisi		9. Cortiggiani		12. Scala	15. Lambati
4. Chiaradini					16. Dervoux

reviewed in the earlier chapters makes it all too clear that the time devoted to rehearsals was short, usually only a couple of weeks. The many practical problems – entrances, exits, groupings and movements; coordination of technical support; props and scene shifting – all had to be thought out and imparted to the cast and to the stage crew. Probably a great deal was left to convention and to experience, at least as far as the principals were concerned. To assess how Cammarano viewed this part of his duties we have the benefit of a number of documents, in particular some sketches and the text that accompany them. Two of these sketches from the Lucchesi-Palli library in Naples were reproduced by di Giacomo in 1904, but without the notes which Cammarano had appended to them. As the article in which they appeared is not readily accessible, I reproduce them again, adding his notes. The first of these (Figure 1) is labelled by di Giacomo as being a sketch for the production of *Saffo*, and it could indeed be taken as representing the moment at which Saffo upsets the altar when she discovers that Climene's bridegroom is none other than Faone. There is nothing on Cammarano's sketch to identify it, but as most of the documents in the collection come from the last few years of his life, I am inclined to suspect a later work.

The sketch is accompanied by a list of names identifying the number in the sketch. The main figure A is labelled 'Barbieri', presumably the soprano Maria Anna Barbieri-Nini, who sang at the S.Carlo in 1847 and 1848. B is Salvetti, the seconda donna who sang all the supporting mezzo roles there from 1838 to 1856. The other numbers on the sketch are identified by name, from 1 to 16, in two sequences, each beginning at the wings and going towards the centre of the stage. Number 1 is Gioja, number 2 Farina, etc. Speranza A is differentiated from Speranza R, and we are clearly dealing with a listing of the women of the S.Carlo chorus, and the places they were to take up at a climatic moment in the opera, with the prima donna surrounded by her women. The sketch is noteworthy not only for Cammarano's effective and economical penmanship but also for the care with which each of the figures was identified and placed in the group. There is no way of

Figure 2. Largo del Finale

3	Paoletti	4	Gioja
	Scala		Farina
	Nuzzi		Parisi
			Chiaradini
2	Della Torre	2	Speranza R
	Checcherini		Sant
2	Lambati	3	Speranza A
	Dervoux		Venturini
			Cortiggiani
6	Bassi	6	Tenori
4	Bassi	5	Tenori

knowing now whether the individual members of the chorus were expected to take up the precise attitudes and gestures of the sketch, but there could have been little point in Cammarano's careful placements if he had not intended to arrange some such picture on the stage.

A similar sketch, also reproduced by di Giacomo without comment, was labelled by Cammarano 'Largo del Finale' and is given as Figure 2. The sketch appears to comprise two separate incidents, and it is the lower part which is the more interesting, as it is this to which the labelling refers. I think this is probably a sketch for the second act finale of *Merope*, given at the S. Carlo in November 1847.

The scene for the finale was a woody place, with the entrance to Cresfonte's tomb at one side. Both Barbieri-Nini and Salvetti appeared in *Merope*, and I suspect that the other sketch is also of that opera and not *Saffo*, which was not performed at the S. Carlo between 1845 and 1849. Certainly the costumes would be appropriate. In this sketch, too, the women of the chorus are identified, by their groups, three names bracketed, then two, and two more; then the other side of the stage, a group of four names and finally one of three. The sixteen names given are identical with the sixteen on the other sketch, though on the second sketch the principals are not named. With the names of the women on the left of the sketch is written 'six basses, four basses', and on the right side,'six tenors, five tenors', suggesting a total of sixteen women and twenty-one men in a chorus of thirty-seven, though of course some members of the chorus may have been used in other roles and were not on the stage at this point. It is interesting that the men are not separately labelled in this sketch, but as they were grouped behind the women it may not have been so important to place them individually. Note that all the tenors were on one side of the stage and all the basses on the other.

Further detailed sketches, this time for *Poliuto* (first produced in Italy in Naples on 30 November 1848), are bound up with one of the autograph copies of the libretto, the one with Donizetti's scribbled marginalia, in the Conservatorio S. Pietro a Majella. There are six pages of notes,

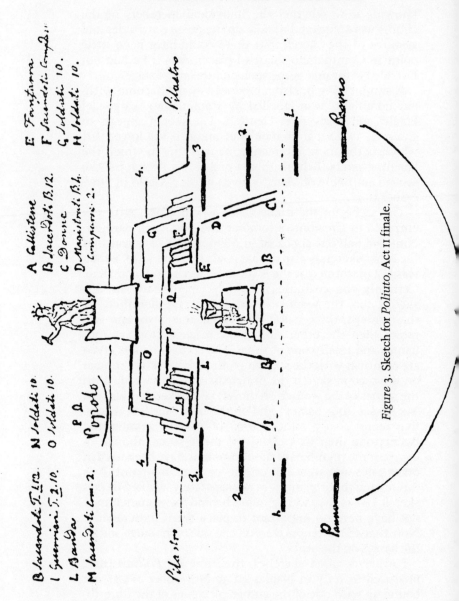

Figure 3. Sketch for *Poliuto*, Act II finale.

presumably for this production. The first page has a list of the individual male members of the chorus, and the parts they were to play in each act. In the introduction, all the men were to be Christians. In the next scene, the triumphal entry of Severo, the tenors were to be warriors, six basses (named) were to be magistrates, the rest priests. There was a note against the tenors who were to be priests – 'very rapid change of costume'. In Act II, the first tenors were to be priests, and two basses, previously named as magistrates, were marked down as priests. The end of Act III had four men of the chorus named as Christians (presumably those who were to be thrown to the lions with Poliuto and Paolina); one of them had previously been a magistrate. All the other tenors were to be warriors, and the rest of the basses, priests. The second sheet contains details of all of these scenes, such as the distribution of the non-singing extras, of whom there seem to be no less than sixty. The third sheet is reproduced in Figure 3, and seems to show the grouping for the finale of Act II. The libretto describes this scene as the Temple of Jove, with a large representation of the god in the middle, and a burning altar before it, and this seems to match what is shown. The letters and the key to them at the top locate the High Priest, Callistene, at the altar. This was only a small part, and none of the principals are shown on the sketch, even though they were on the stage throughout the scene. It may be adduced from this that Cammarano may not have had the same authority over the principals as he had over the chorus, though, as we will see, this is not borne out by other documents. For this scene he certainly did not seem to find it necessary to mark their positions on the sketch. The cast is divided into left and right, in a symmetrical grouping, and the notes at the top can be translated thus:

B	Priests, 1st tenors, 12.	A	Callistene.
I	Warriors, 2nd tenors, 10.	B	Priests, basses, 12.
L	Stage band.	C	Women.
M	Priests, extras, 2.	D	Magistrates,
N	Soldiers, 10.		basses 4, extras 2.
O	Soldiers, 10.	E	Trumpeters
P	Populace	F	Priests, extras, 2.
Q		G	Soldiers, 10.
		H	Soldiers, 10.

It seems a very formal grouping, static and balanced, with the tenors on one side of the stage and the basses on the other, as in the sketch believed to be for *Merope*, and a line of forty soldiers right across the back, on a raised platform. With a stage band of thirty (the number given in another list for *Poliuto*) and, say, eight trumpeters, there must have been about 150 people on the stage. This is confirmed by another sketch in the *Poliuto* series, with a similar formalized grouping – this time for the end of Act I. On this sketch, Cammarano noted down very carefully the number of people on each side of the stage, and added them up – fifty on the 'Temple' side, seventy-six on the 'Town-Hall' side (including thirty quoted for the stage band). In addition, there are thirty-eight placed centrally, giving a total, without the principals, of 164, or 168 with the four principals. Of these, as we know from other *Poliuto* sheets, there were twenty women in the chorus, nine first and seven second tenors, and twelve basses, making a total chorus of forty-eight; thirty in the stage band; four principals – all the rest non-singing extras, of whom there were about eighty-five.

The impression given by these various sketches and documents is one of careful individual placement and the allocation of the various members of the chorus to their roles, but of a static and formal approach to grouping and 'tableaux'. This is not, however, borne out by what is by far the most interesting of Cammarano's production documents, the notes he wrote for putting *Lucia di Lammermoor* on the stage. I have reproduced these notes in full, with a translation and commentary, in the fourth issue of the *Journal of the Donizetti Society*, for 1980. This document is apparently in draft form – it contains many abbreviations, and would surely have been corrected. It is also in a very hurried hand, quite unlike any of Cammarano's 'fair copies' (though unquestionably in his distinctive handwriting). It gives detailed instructions on how to stage this opera, and would seem to have been written for the benefit of a *concertatore* in another city. Cammarano states that he doesn't know who was to take the part of Raimondo, also suggesting a production somewhere else. It runs to about 750 words, on four sheets of paper.

These notes show Cammarano to have been a much more imaginative and flexible producer than might be suggested by the other diagrams. Above all, there is overwhelming evidence that he was anxious to maintain dramatic consistency and truth. For instance, each side of a set is associated with a particular place – a room, the park and so on – and the entrances of the characters are carefully regulated accordingly. There are many instructions of practical significance – at the beginning of the contract scene, for instance, the inhabitants of Lammermoor (non-singing extras) are to remain at the back of the stage, 'without, however, blocking the door' (through which Edgardo has later to erupt); after the sextet, Edgardo must put down his hat and cloak on a chair, but when he is hustled out he must leave them there, 'it being unlikely that he would think of picking them up in a moment of such desperation'. At this point Cammarano advises his colleague to ensure that the action of the chorus is very animated. Similarly, when Lucia enters to begin what we now call the mad scene, the chorus are to show themselves full of pity and terror; Alisa is to follow her all the time with her eyes 'as we usually do with unfortunate people who have gone out of their minds'. At the end of her aria, the women of the chorus are to group themselves around her, hiding her from the audience, while she can be carried off. There are many practical points like this, which give a very good picture of how Cammarano saw his role as a producer, and what was expected on the stage. One other point of practical significance is mentioned: since in an early scene the inhabitants of Lammermoor are represented by extras, but in the final scene by the chorus, they must wear the same clothes, so as to appear to be the same people – though it would be appropriate to provide two sets of costumes so that they didn't have to share the same ones. The document shows that Cammarano was steeped in the practice of the theatre, and was concerned to provide a convincing and consistent staging. He had obviously assumed control over the movements of the whole cast, including the principals – where and when they were to put their hats down, etc. Naturally it would not be possible to give complete production instructions for an opera like

Lucia di Lammermoor in 750 words, but given these notes and the details in the stage directions in the libretto, another *concertatore* would find that he had an adequate guide to the problems of staging it, and how they should be met. Despite the speed with which these operas were put onto the stage, Cammarano's approach was well thought out, logical and practical, even if he was not able to work at a level of detail which a modern producer might expect.

The other source of Cammarano's ideas on the production of opera is the evidence that can be found in the libretti themselves. This falls into various categories: footnotes, descriptions of settings, stage directions for the behaviour of the various characters and matters of technical detail.

There are only four footnotes in the whole of Cammarano's work, but their very presence confirms that he expected his libretti to be read and studied. In *Lucia di Lammermoor*, there is one in the fountain scene, when Lucia and Edgardo exchange tokens. It explains that in Scotland at that time such an exchange had the force of an unbreakable oath – 'the most usual ceremony was for two lovers to break a coin, each keeping a part, but here an exchange of rings is substituted, as being more appropriate on the stage'. A second footnote comes at the beginning of *La fidanzata corsa*: 'It was the custom of the Corsican people for everybody to carry with him his own musket at all times: so in the course of the opera the characters never lay aside their fire-arms'. The other two footnotes refer to the use of cannons by the English troops under Edward III (*L'assedio di Calais*, Act I), and to the temple of Dodona (*Saffo*, Act III). Three of these are clearly aimed at the reader, as they are of no assistance to the producer or the actor, the text being self-sufficient on the points mentioned, but the note in *La fidanzata corsa* is a matter of guidance for the proper staging of the work.

The extent to which the settings are described in the libretti varies greatly, though by and large descriptions are more detailed than in the texts of other librettists. Sometimes, it is true, they are as bald as could be – the first scene of *Medea* is described simply as 'Royal Palace' (even Romani's old text, which Cammarano was adapting, said

'Hall in Royal Palace'). 'The Marascialla's Room in the Louvre' (*Elenora Dori*, Act I scene 1), 'A Room in Rivers' Mansion' (*Folco d'Arles*, Act I scene 4) are unusually brief. Many include some guidance for the designer, such as *Poliuto*, Act II scene 1 – 'Hall in Felice's house: delightful gardens at the back'. 'Gallery hung with portraits in Sigifredo's palace' (*Elena da Feltre*, Act III scene 1). More typical is 'Gallery in the Appiani mansion – On one side, the door leading to Eleonora's rooms, the main entrance on the other side, closed balcony at the back' (*Luigi Rolla*, Act II scene 4). 'Room in Chevreuse's house. Entrance facing the audience: a side door: a large clock at the back: a small table with two chairs' (*Il conte di Chalais*, Act III scene 1). Others are complex and detailed: 'Gardens gaily illuminated: on one side the magnificent steps to the castle, before which is a platform with an orchestra, a lake at the back, covered with boats, from which alight ladies and gentlemen, the relatives of Murray: The Ruthvens come from the castle, by way of festive greeting: Osvaldo is amongst the guards, who surround the area' (*Il proscritto*, Act I scene 1). 'Horrible prison in the Tower of London, intended for the last dwelling place of guilty people condemed to death: it is illuminated by a little gloomy light which finds a way in through a window fashioned high up in the wall, and secured with great bars of iron: a closed door on one side' (*Roberto Devereux*, Act III scene 4). 'Ground-floor room in the Louvre. On the left side a magnificent staircase, which leads to the rooms of the king; a similar staircase on the right, leading to those of the Queen; side doors: at the back an arched vestibule, hung across with silken, embroidered curtains. Night is falling: graceful candelabra are alight'. (*Il conte di Chalais*, Act I scene 1). 'Inside the great temple of Leucado – festoons of flowers hang from the columns, and flowers are scattered over the steps up to the altar; a flame burns in front of an image of Hymen' (*Saffo*, Act II scene 4). 'Part of Zampardi's house, which opens on to the garden; luxuriant vines are clinging to the wall, which forms a corner – the side best seen by the spectator is broken by a balcony, a little off the ground, below which there is a stone seat: on the other side is a door: here and there are thick groups of trees: at the back an open gate, at a little distance from the edge of the lake, in the water of which the rising moon is reflected' (*La fidanzata corsa*, Act I, scene 4). Not surprisingly, *Il reggente*, which depends greatly on the atmosphere of the settings, provides some detailed descriptions: 'The habitation of the fortune-teller: on the right a fireplace with a cauldron on a tripod: a few torches burn around the room; on one side, the entrance to another room: on the opposite side, a secret entrance at the top of a small flight of steps: the door is at the back and a window, through which can be seen the gates of Edinburgh' (Act I, scene 6); 'A wild place on the outskirts of Edinburgh: at the back, in a valley formed from the bare rock, can be seen the burial ground of those condemned to the extreme penalty; a little way off is the winding river: the sky is covered with thick clouds, which move in the wind, now showing, now hiding the moon' (Act II, scene I). Finally, a description from *Luisa Miller*, Act I, scene 8, which again shows Cammarano's concern for detail – 'Inside Miller's house. Two side doors; one leads to Miller's room, the other to Luisa's: near the first hangs a sword and a soldier's old uniform: facing is the entrance and a window, through which can be seen part of the church'.

The actual locations of the scenes betray Cammarano's place in the romantic movement and the sources he drew upon for his plots – tombs, secret doors, prisons galore; all manner of caves and other subterranean places, figuring in at least a dozen of the libretti; and many scenes played at night. Some of his instructions – like the clouds moving over the moon in *Il reggente* – must have made heavy demands on the stage staff, but none more so than *Il vascello di Gama*, with its captain's cabin on a ship at sea; a discharge of artillery; a harbourside with a ship at the back; a storm at sea, with the mainmast breaking off and felling the captain; a raft adrift on the ocean and its rescue. Unfortunately, critical reception indicated that Cammarano's demands on this occasion were not successfully met. *Luigi Rolla* calls for a fully equipped sculptor's studio (the terminology of which was well known to the librettist). *Stella di Napoli* ends with the clouds clearing away to reveal a ship out at sea – an essential element in the story, allowing Stella to die knowing that her lover had escaped. Often the view through windows is important, as when Bondelmonte is murdered just outside Beatrice's house. Some of his demands must have been difficult to make convincing, for instance, the bloody hand-print on top of the railings around the park at the opening of *Folco d'Arles,* vital to the recognition of Folco as the person who had thrown a bunch of flowers to the Countess. It is clear that where Cammarano's pictorial imagination was caught up in a plot, he was able to conjure up an economical thumb-nail sketch of what he required.

This involvement of his eye for the stage picture is even more evident in the stage directions added to the text. They are very much more numerous than is usual with libretti of the period; only the very theatrically conscious Gaetano Rossi consistently provided as many as did Cammarano. To illustrate this point, Cammarano's treatment of a few plots can be compared with those of other librettists working at about the same time, the assumption being that the same plot is likely to require more or less the same stage directions.

Cammarano's *Pia de' Tolomei* (1837) can be compared with Marini's of 1835. Cammarano's text is 695 lines long (excluding directions, descriptions of scenes etc.); Marini's is 760; yet Cammarano has more than three times as many stage directions, as revealed by a count of words. *Lucia di Lammermoor,* in Cammarano's version of 1835, is 690 lines long, in Beltrame's of 1834, 521, but Cammarano prints five times as many stage directions. Similarly Cammarano has twice as many stage directions in his *Luigi Rolla* of 1841 as compared to Rubini's of the same year, though both were the same length. A qualitative examination of other pairs of libretti shows the same result, that Cammarano went to greater length to specify the theatrical action than did the majority of his contemporaries.

Stage directions fall into two main groups, those which indicate what the characters do, and those which indicate how they are to appear. In the first group comes all the straightforward entrances and exits, which door to use, etc., and essential actions such as 'rapidly plunges the dagger into her heart' (*Virginia*, closing scene). 'A cannon shot echoes from the ship' (*Cristina de Svezia*, Act I scene 7). These are all essential, prescriptive directions, and naturally abound in all the libretti, being vital to the process of the drama. The more interesting directions are, however, those which are descriptive: they are not essential to the action, and might perhaps have been left to the imagination of singer and producer – but they weren't. They are so numerous that it is hard to know which to choose in order to illustrate their use. Some contain elements of prescription and description – 'Throwing away the wreath, and the lyre, and with an expression of the most terrible desperation' (*Saffo*, Act III, closing scene), but most are basically descriptive – 'All present take off their hats. The King is wrapped up in his thoughts; sitting, resting his elbow on a table, with his forehead in his hand: after a moment of silence he raises his head and turns to Gonzales' (*Ines de Castro*, Act I, scene 3).

The last act of *Il conte di Chalais* contains a passage with four long stage directions for as many lines of verse:

MARIA

(*comes forward with uncertain and hesitant steps; her face is marked by extreme pallor, her eyes are fixed and full of terror: she remains a long time in silence, as if stupefied, then she rouses herself, looks around and exclaims*):
My punishment is at hand!

CHEVREUSE

(*Comes back in, unseen by Maria, who is at the front of the stage: he has a dagger in his right hand, and his fury is clearly seen in his eyes, but seeing the state Maria is in, he is moved to pity*)
(Oh! cruel sight!..
It would be easier for me to plunge it
Into my own heart!) – (*letting the dagger fall on the table*)
(*Coming forward he makes his wife sit close to him: at a sign from him the servant leaves them alone. A moment of silence. Maria turns to look at the clock*)
How restlessly
You watch the time! Ah, you have good reason: The Queen is waiting for you!

Descriptions like this, which do not have their origin in the source play, show that as he wrote Cammarano had a clear picture in his mind of how the work would look on the stage. Almost every libretto furnishes examples of this, but a few more must suffice. Here is Rosa, in *La fidanzata corsa* (a libretto which is full of evocative stage directions), about to elope, as she thinks, with Alberto: 'Cautiously she opens the door of her father's room: a night-light only just reveals the outline of the old man. She goes over to her father, hesitates a moment, then she bends over and kisses his hand: she draws back a little, terrified, but having made certain that he was still asleep, closes the door again. Meanwhile a figure, wrapped up to the eyes in Alberto's cloak, is visible in the window' (Act II, scene 2).

Two more examples of straight description may be quoted: *Lucia di Lammermoor*, Act III scene 5, the entry of Lucia at the beginning of the 'mad' scene: 'Lucia is wearing a scanty white garment: her hair is dishevelled and her face, being covered by a deathly pallor, makes her look more like a ghost than a living person. Her expressionless gaze, her convulsive movements and even her stony smile indicate not only a fearful insanity, but also the signs of a life already moving towards its end'. Similarly, in *Il reggente*, there is a stage direction which is purely descriptive. Hamilton, in Act III scene 3, is faced by the suspicion that his wife is in love with the Regent. He is suddenly struck by the possibility that her son is not his, but the Regent's: 'The convulsive shudder with which he pronounced these words, and his ravaged features, disclose how horrible a suspicion is upsetting him: he covers his face with trembling hands, and a stifled groan escapes from his breast'.

The closing scene of *Saffo* provides the last example. Here are the stage directions which precede and follow the cabaletta of Saffo's aria finale, as she prepares for, and takes, the fatal leap from the Leucadian cliffs:

> (*At the sound of the trumpet, an involuntary shudder is seen in Saffo's limbs: her fury is exhausted, and a flood of tears runs down her face: she throws herself at the feet of Alcandro, who is struck dumb by such great grief. She places her father's right hand on her own head, as if to obtain his blessing; she then gets up, and leads Climene to Faone's arms*).
> [At this point comes the cabaletta]

(*Saffo, escorted by the Aruspici, climbs to the top of the cliff.
Alcandro kneels, all eyes are fixed immovably on the dangerous summit: a fearful silence everywhere. Saffo, having
taken a look at the precipice, pulls back for a moment, but
then raises her eyes and arms to the sky and throws herself
into the waves. From the beach below comes the sound of
confused voices, crying out:*)

CHORUS
We are hurrying . . . She is dead!

(ALL ON STAGE)   Dead!

ALCANDRO
Daughter!

CLIMENE   O Heavens!

FAONE   I must follow her!

(*Alcandro falls face down on the ground, Climene faints in
Dirce's arms, Faone tries to throw himself into the sea, but is
held back. Everyone is overcome with horror and extreme
grief*).

THE END

There is no evidence from a study of Cammarano's libretto
that he provided fuller notes and directions for those that
were written for other theatres, where the first performance would not be under his own direction, than he did for
those which he would himself have seen onto the stage.
Some texts are certainly fuller than others, but these seem
to be the most colourful – in a way, the ones which least
needed them. There can be little doubt that as Cammarano
worked on his libretti, he had in his mind's eye a picture of
how the action would go on the stage, and took the trouble
to write it down. The sketches and groupings – to say
nothing of the notes for the performance of *Lucia di Lammermoor* – indicate a strong visual imagination, developed, no doubt, in the studio as much as by his artistic and
theatrical family inheritance. He was, indeed, a librettist
of the theatre, well able to sustain the double duties of his
appointment.

CHAPTER SIXTEEN

Assessment

Cammarano's career as a librettist spanned the years from
1834 to 1852, eighteen years which more or less covered
the last half of the period which saw the flowering of the
Italian romantic opera, which we can date from the early
1820s till about 1850. It would be fruitless to attempt to set
a firm date at which such a period began: it was not
ushered in by any one new work which suddenly revealed
that a new genre had arrived, in the way we associate the
beginning of the *verismo* period with the production of
Cavalleria rusticana in 1890. The romantic style crept in
gradually, overtaking the old *opera seria* and uniting elements from comic opera, making slow headway against
the conservatism of governments, managements and singers. Its architect, however unwillingly, was Rossini, as
Julian Budden has pointed out in the introductory chapter
to Volume I of his *The operas of Verdi*, essential reading for
anyone interested in this period. If one has to pin-point a
work which, even in retrospect, can be seen to have confirmed a new style, it could be *Semiramide*, first given in
Venice in 1823, with a libretto by Gaetano Rossi, but many
of the operas written between 1815 and 1825 looked forwards as well as backwards – Romani's libretto for Mercadante's *Amleto* of 1822 used a typical romantic subject,
but Hamlet was sung by a soprano and survives, having
killed his mother (off stage) and received her forgiveness
(on stage). Even as late as 1830, in Bellini's *I Capuleti e i
Montecchi* (libretto again by Romani), Romeo was sung by
a woman.

The period ended, stylistically at least, with Verdi's three
great operas of 1851–3, *Rigoletto* (1851), *Il trovatore* and
La traviata (both 1853). This is not to say that operas of
the great romantic style were not written thereafter, but
theatrical effectiveness and sentimentality began to replace true tragic feeling, and the increased watchfulness of

the authorities following the uprisings of 1848 made librettists more wary of the sentiments they depicted. The years from 1855 to 1890 produced few works other than those of Verdi (which in any case became increasingly international in outlook) which have stood the test of time – perhaps only Boito's *Mefistofele* and Ponchielli's *Gioconda*, which appeared in 1868 and 1876 respectively. For the lover of Italian opera, it is a sad and chastening experience to leaf through the pages of Loewenberg's *Annals of Opera* for these years. The records of the great Italian opera houses show, as expected, plenty of new works, but they came to rely more and more on French (and later even on German) works. Composers like Petrella who wished to keep the older forms alive found themselves saddled with texts by librettists such as Domenico Bolognese, Cammarano's successor at the S. Carlo – texts which were pale shadows of what had gone before, with facile dramatic writing and jog-trot, insipid verse. As Julian Budden has pointed out (in Volume II of his great book on Verdi) there was increased interest in theatrical effect – floods, volcanic eruptions and the like – though these were by no means unknown earlier, as *Il vascello de Gama* bears witness. Theatrical effects for their own sake only serve to betray the absence of an underlying commitment to the drama, and Italian opera had to wait for the arrival of *verismo* to overcome the poverty of ideas of the intervening years.

Cammarano arrived on the scene when the form of the Italian romantic opera was already settled. The early 1830s had seen the masterpieces of Bellini (*Norma*, 1831; *I puritani*, 1835) and Donizetti (*Anna Bolena*, 1830; *Parisina* and *Lucrezia Borgia*, 1833), four of which were written to libretti by Felice Romani. Other composers of the period, if they did not write works which have survived as have the greatest productions of Bellini and Donizetti, continued to fill out the form with popular and successful operas – Mercadante (e.g. *I Normani a Parigi*, 1832, libretto by Romani), Persiani, (e.g. *Eufemio di Messina*, 1829, Romani), Pacini (e.g. *Gli Arabie nelle Gallie*, 1827, Romanelli) or Luigi Ricci (e.g. *Chiara di Rosembergh*, 1831, Rossi).

Cammarano's working life was brief – only eighteen years, as compared with Romani's forty-two (from 1813 to

1855) or Rossi's incredible sixty (from 1797 to 1855). At the outset of his career he had the great good fortune to fall in with Donizetti, then at the height of his powers, and their collaboration over *Lucia di Lammermoor* projected him immediately into the front rank of librettists. This brought him continuing work with Donizetti, though none of the other operas they wrote together achieved the same success. After Donizetti left Naples in 1838 for Paris and Vienna, contracts for Mercadante and Pacini followed, with *La vestale* and, in particular, *Saffo* becoming two of the most popular works in the Italian operahouses. Finally came collaboration with the rapidly-maturing Verdi. Had Cammarano lived, he would undoubtedly have written more with Verdi, though whether he would have been able to keep pace with the composer's developing ideas is another matter. Cammarano had no real successors, not so much because there were no other librettists ready to take his place but because the genre had changed. For all that, there is no evidence that any of those who followed him, either at Naples or elsewhere, had his vital combination of theatrical understanding and expressive ability with the Italian language. What, then, did Cammarano bring to the romantic opera libretto, and how is his contribution to be assessed?

The two librettists who, above all the others working in the theatres of Italy, moulded the form of the romantic libretto were Romani and Rossi. These two were very different in their approach, and in the type of text they turned out. Both were prolific and both worked in the north, Romani principally in Milan and Rossi in Venice and Milan, though both accepted commissions for other theatres. Nevertheless their work became known up and down the peninsula through the way that successful operas moved from theatre to theatre, often within circuits controlled by influential impressarios. While Romani's work is generally well known and recognized through his association with Bellini and Donizetti, Rossi has never been given his proper due.

As Patrick J. Smith has pointed out in his book *The Tenth Muse*, one of the few books to have attempted a comprehensive account of the libretto, Romani was a romantic *malgré lui.* He was a man of literary aspirations and taste, whose roots were well grounded in the classics and mythology (he contributed to a large dictionary of mythology) and he published volumes of poetry in his own right. Although he continued to write a few libretti after 1834, he became then the editor of the *Gazzetta* in Turin and devoted himself almost exclusively to journalism. He himself stated that he was neither a classicist nor a romantic, but rather pursued the beautiful wherever it might take him. His great ability with words enabled him to write verses of economy and elegance, easy to read and fluent. He had an unusual ability (unusual in librettists, that is) to understand human nature and to capture feelings and emotions in a few well-chosen words and expressions. He always wrote under pressure, and caused enumerable delays to the composers he was working with. Such was his reputation that he was always in demand, and many of his libretti were set to music several times over, one (*Francesca da Rimini*) eleven times, and there are about 240 settings of his texts. Classicist, romanticist or whatever, he certainly had the ability to use the developing form of the libretto in a way that proved stimulating to the composer.

Rossi, on the other hand, made no claims to being a poet, describing himself rather as a word-smith, and a study of his libretti certainly bears this out. His language is crude and unfeeling, his verses rough and his language stilted and laboured. He had, however, a highly-developed sense of the theatre, and recognized and exploited strong and colourful situations. His particular contribution to the development of the romantic libretto was his choice of subjects for his operas, and many of the important themes entered the genre through his work. He clearly had a wide knowledge of European dramatic literature and pillaged it remorselessly for appropriate subjects. His 160 libretti contain many inconsequential farces, but in sixty years of productive libretto-writing, from 1795 onwards, he remained at the front of the scene. Significantly, he was the librettist of Rossini's *Semiramide.*

Of the many other librettists writing in this period, only two of the non-Neapolitans are worth a mention: Romanelli, of Milan, whose writings were old-fashioned but well-turned, whose outlook was conservative and severe, the only librettist to achieve a 'collected edition', and Ferretti, of Rome, who like Romani was an educated man of literary sensibilities. In particular his comic verse was facile and individual. As a Vatican employee he turned his pen to all literary purposes, but held no post in a theatre.

If Cammarano had to hand a language and a form for his work, inherited from Romani, and a quarry of subjects, from Rossi, it is likely he was more conscious of the work of those living and writing in Naples itself. Although the successful and popular works of opera houses elsewhere all found their way, sooner rather than later, onto the stages of the S. Carlo or the Fondo, the emphasis was always on the Neapolitan school itself. It was the work of local poets which he grew up with, and with his theatrical family background it is likely that he knew many of them personally. There had, however, been a serious dearth of good librettists in Naples for some decades. The years following the re-opening of the S. Carlo in 1817 were dominated by the work (and pretty miserable work it was) of two men, Tottola and Schmidt. Tottola was a hanger-on in Barbaja's entourage, and wrote altogether about a hundred libretti, starting in 1786. These included a number for Rossini, whose fortunes took him to Naples in 1815, including *La donna del lago* (1819) and *Zelmira* (1822), but his most successful work was in the comic vein, for composers such as the two Fioravanti. His work could be well-made from a dramatic point of view, though it is usually slip-shod and superficial. He could write effective scenes, such as the ending of *Imelda da' Lambertazzi* quoted in Chapter 12, but his verse is usually most unrewarding – though again Imelda's death scene reads well. He was certainly catholic in his choice of subjects, and was, for instance, the first to use the novels of Sir Walter Scott for operatic purposes in Italy (*La donna del lago*, 1819; later, *Il castello di Kenilworth*, 1829). Ashbrook in his book on Donizetti describes him as inept (or, to be precise, 'more inept than Schmidt') and 'inept' is probably just, though I have the feeling that a full study of his work (if anyone could be persuaded to undertake it) might well reveal unexpected strengths as well as all-too-expected weaknesses. Tottola dropped out of sight around 1830.

Giovanni Schmidt wrote about forty libretto between 1800 and 1835, again including some for Rossini (*Elizabetta Regina d'Inghilterra*, 1815 and *Armida*, 1817). He was still on the staff of the S. Carlo when Cammarano took up his duties there in 1834 and was, according to Pacini, a man of utter misery. Unlike Ashbrook, I am inclined to consider Schmidt to have been more inept than Tottola: his verse is certainly more pedestrian and I have not found anything to admire in it. The best work he did, I think, was the translation into Italian of the libretto of Spontini's *La vestale*. A study of his work would, I fear, prove almost entirely unrewarding.

In the mid-1820s another and far more interesting librettist entered the scene, Domenico Gilardoni, someone whose works would certainly repay attention. He produced some twenty libretti, starting in 1826 with *Bianco e Gernando*, one of Bellini's earliest operas, and his most frequently performed text was certainly the Goldonian *Il ventaglio* (1831: Raimondi) which for a couple of decades was rarely absent from the Neapolitan playbills. His work is exceptionally variable: some of it is empty and unpolished, often with pages of prose and making widespread use of Neapolitan dialect. Many of his libretti were comedies, semi-serias, 'romanticas' and even farces, and are for the most part devoid of interest, though containing scenes which have clarity and point. The serious works, such as *L'esule di Roma* (1828, Donizetti), *Il paria* (1829, Donizetti), *Edoardo Stuart Re in Iscozia* (1831, Coccia) or *Fausta* (1832, completed after his death by Donizetti himself) seem almost as if written by a different person, being on an altogether higher plain. I am inclined to think that *Il paria* was his best work, but it has to be admitted that Delavigne's tragedy gave him a head start. His language is vivid and even terse, but often strained, and even in his best works his verse is untidy and ill-judged, with a far higher proportion of lines lying unrhymed than is usual in this period, with unbroken series of *tronco* lines which interrupt the flow, and with a willingness to break the rules of metre. When Dalbono came to write Cammarano's obituary notice twenty years later, he began by bewailing the decline of the dramatic verse in the hands of Tottola and Schmidt (the last, he said, could have done better than he did) but singles out Gilardoni's role in the restoration of standards. Dalbono claims that Gilardoni worked with awareness and intelligence to reform poetry for music; he began to produce verses unlike his immediate predecessors, verses which harked back to Metastasio, particularly in recitative, where his verses had the same inflexions. The death of Gilardoni, Dalbono concludes, was a grave loss.

How much more Gilardoni would have produced had he lived longer is hard to say. His influence on Cammarano, too, is not easy to define: I doubt whether it was in his verses or language, from which it seems to me that Cammarano could learn little – less than he could learn, say, from Passaro, another contemporary Neapolitan librettist, who had a much more facile pen than Gilardoni, and whose comic work has some bite. Gilardoni's importance lay more in his willingness to treat deeply tragic subjects sincerely, without avoiding tragic conclusions. There is no direct influence of any of the Neapolitan librettists on Cammarano's style, where Alfieri was the obvious source, but however much he read and listened to the verses of other poets and librettists, he cannot have escaped the inherited atmosphere of the theatres in which he worked.

Where then did Cammarano's contribution lie? He added very little to what was available, though he certainly developed the use of the pathetic closing calabetta for the aria finale in a masterful way, and provided opportunities for composers in this respect which enabled Donizetti, if not to break entirely new ground, at least to cultivate it to a hitherto unknown extent. Unlike Romani, he obviously seized the romantic form wholeheartedly, without hesitation or scruple, and nothing in his work is insincere. If he lacked Romani's gift for thumb-nail sketches of human nature, he could exploit adequately the range of material open to him, even if his preferred range was narrow. He was fortunate in being present when he was needed, and he could offer what was wanted – in particular verses for music.

Where Cammarano scored over literary figures like Romani was in his keen sense of theatre. He is often blamed for reliance on stock situations, shoddy *coups-de-théâtre* and unlikely coincidences, muddled and incomprehensible plots and cardboard characters without individuality. All these criticisms have a grain – and often more than a grain – of truth in them, but it is as well to remember that librettists did not invent new plots, but adapted existing ones. Much of the crude theatricality which disfigures their libretti was taken from the source, and could not be avoided; indeed the condensation that was required was likely to concentrate the theatricality. The need to find a suitable 'trigger' with which to launch the central finale on its way required a situation of dramatic significance which all too easily degenerated into mere theatricality. Cammarano certainly never wrote a text so full of feeling as Romani's *Norma,* but equally he could not be accused of writing anything as crude as *Ugo Conte di Parigi* (Romani / Donizetti 1832). But his range was limited, and he never approached the subtlety of *La sonnambula* (Romani / Bellini, 1831) or *L'elisir d'amore* (Romani/Donizetti, 1832). His comedies are few and inconsequential.

The muddled and incomprehensible aspects of Cammarano's libretti are often over-emphasized. Some of this is of course due to condensation, but also because in those days the libretti were available for consultation during the performance itself. In any case, dramatic time moves more slowly in opera than on the legitimate stage, and the nature of Italian romantic opera was the creation of opportunities for lyrical display, not dramatic thrust and action. This is not of course to say that action was not required, or provided, but the clarity and 'well-made-ness' that we look for today was not expected by opera audiences of the 1830s. Even at a time in his career when Cammarano was striving to match the new dramatic requirements of Verdi, works he wrote for other composers reverted to the accustomed type.

It comes as rather a surprise to find that Cammarano regarded himself as an innovator, since it is not clear just what he contributed to the development of the libretto. On one occasion he pointed out to Verdi that he had swept away many of the conventions : 'I did not speak of essential cavatinas nor of other long-established, almost stupid requirements – I that have destroyed so many of them'. It is true that he succeeded in opening up the form, increasing the use of terzets and decreasing the number of double arias and duets, and if he saw this as an innovation, it can only emphasize the dead hold that conventional structures had on the libretto. He wrote these words at the time he was preparing *Luisa Miller*, and the more drastic innovations of *Il trovatore* were still to come; and even these were made in response to Verdi's insistence. It is greatly to Cammarano's credit that he was ready and willing to experiment with so basic a component of the libretto as the central finale in the last libretto he was destined to prepare, though he had already made one move in this direction, in the finale of *Pia de' Tolomei* (its first version). There are certainly unusually structured scenes in his libretti – the triple aria-finale of *Ines de Castro*, the duet/terzet finale of the third act of *Poliuto*, the scene of the Knights of the Death in *La battaglia di Legnano*, and the remarkable number structure of *Luisa Miller* for example, but these are all variations, however imaginative, within the accepted form. Cammarano cannot really be said to have contributed any significant new development to the form of the libretto, nor did his own technique or style change over the eighteen years of his working life. At the end of his life, setting aside the libretti he wrote for Verdi, texts such as *Folco d'Arles* and *Malvina di Scozia* are as unenterprising structurally as anything he wrote when he began. Apart from a move to a more fluid form and an increase in metrical sensitivity, it is hard to put a finger on any new development or evolution as his work proceeded. While this may in part be ascribed to the shortness of his working life, and to his relatively late start (he was in his early thirties when he began writing for the lyric stage), it is in my opinion more likely that by the time he wrote, the form was relatively secure; being suited to its purpose it was resistant to change. Cammarano's strength lay not in dramatic invention, which might have propelled him towards the development of new forms, but in his verses, and he was adept at fitting these into the standard mould.

Faced with a composer who made new and revolutionary demands on the form, he did his best to comply, and, no doubt, saw the point of what was being asked of him. The old forms still shine through, and it is one of the paradoxes of his work that the changes made, after he had died, to his most experimental text move it firmly back towards the traditional structures.

Cammarano's usefulness to the authorities of the Royal Theatres depended on a number of factors: his ability to negotiate with the censors, his ability to satisfy the composers for whom he wrote and his ability to get the operas onto the stage.

On the first point, there is as yet little evidence, though the correspondence which Jeremy Commons has unearthed in the State Archives in Naples is of the greatest interest and promise. One letter, quoted in Chapter 3, shows that the censors had a high opinion of his capabilities, and were not above claiming some credit for discovering and nurturing his talent. On the evidence that has come down to us, relatively few revisions were made to his texts. Admittedly two of his works were prohibited, *Poliuto* at the instance of the King, and against the recommendations of the censor responsible, and *Virginia*, which was perhaps too risky a subject in the years immediately following the uprisings of May 1848. To have piloted a *Ruy Blas* libretto through the censors not once but twice was no mean feat, and the number of explicitly nationalistic sentiments he had sung on the S. Carlo stage (not counting the patriotic fervour of *La battaglia di Legnano*, which was produced in Rome) pays tribute to his ability to walk the tight-rope between what could and could not be done. It is hard to understand why at so late a point in his career as *Folco d'Arles* (1851), he was still including instances of religious imagery which his long experience of the censor's requirements must have told him would be found objectionable. I think the reason must have been that the censor's stipulations referred only to performances in Naples, and that he was aware that a successful work would in due course be produced elsewhere, where other requirements prevailed. His familiarity with the censor's office and his experience of keeping on the right side of their requirements – such evidence as there is suggests face to face discussions – was of undoubted benefit to the management in ensuring trouble-free seasons.

On the second point, Cammarano's relationship with his composers seem to have been excellent, notwithstanding the continued delays which they all experienced in obtaining verses from him. He was obviously on the best of terms with Donizetti, and an informal, joking atmosphere is evident in their correspondence. After their successful collaboration over *Lucia di Lammermoor* in 1835, for as long as he continued to live in Naples, Donizetti turned to no other librettist (he himself wrote the words for the two slighter works for the Teatro Nuovo in 1836). Even after he left Naples, Donizetti still thought of him first for S. Carlo projects, as his abortive *Ruy Blas* opera shows. He remembered, too, the libretto for *Il conte di Chalais*, and had it rewritten for himself to use as *Maria di Rohan* – though he would probably have felt free to use in this way any 'old' text which took his fancy. In the event, this opera held the stage longer than some of his other 'Cammarano' operas.

The correspondence with Mercadante is not so extensive, but the student of the period is hampered by the absence of a critical study of this important composer, and few of his letters have been published. Such letters as exist suggest friendliness, even at times cordiality. Mercadante, as Director of the Conservatorio, was a respected and influential person, with a very considerable reputation as a composer. (There is an interesting sidelight in the letter Verdi wrote to Cammarano over the S. Carlo production of his *Macbeth* – that Mercadante would understand his ideas better than anyone else.) Since Mercadante lived in Naples, it is fair to assume that he and Cammarano would discuss their projects together rather than correspond about them. After Cammarano's death, his widow certainly felt able to ask Mercadante's advice on a career for one of the boys, and the old composer hung on to the Cammarano libretti of his unperformed opera *Virginia* and the unused *Caterina di Brono*.

The working relationship with Pacini again seems to have been good, and in his memoirs (however unreliable they may be on matters of fact) the picture of Cammarano which emerges is friendly – the story of the composition of *Saffo* is written in a way which suggests that Pacini respected his judgement. Later, when they collaborated over other works for the S. Carlo, there were the familiar complaints of delay, but equally Cammarano showed himself willing to go a long way to meet the composer's wishes, even to the extent of changing subjects at the last moment and using his influence to delay the date of production.

Verdi's relationship with Cammarano is better documented, since the two of them collaborated through the post rather than in person. His attitude started with unwonted respect due, I have suggested, to Cammarano being the first experienced librettist with whom he had worked (it must be said that the libretto of *Alzira* does nothing to deserve such respect). Even so, Verdi was always careful in his dealings with Cammarano, wrapping up his criticisms and not attempting to bully him as he did his faithful Piave. Verdi was even prepared to write an opera for Naples solely to get him out of trouble with the S. Carlo authorities, though he stressed that he felt under no legal obligation to fulfil that contract – a rare and even unexpected gesture from Verdi at the time of *Luisa Miller*, and certainly one which he was unlikely to have offered to a librettist he did not respect. His distress at Cammarano's death goes way beyond concern over the revision of *Il trovatore* or rescuing the synopsis of *Re Lear*, though typically these matters were at the forefront of his mind, and he went out of his way to assist Cammarano's widow financially. It was to Verdi that Cammarano turned at the end of his life when conditions in Naples became so intolerable that he contemplated launching himself on a career as a freelance librettist, and Verdi found himself in some difficulty in knowing how to dissuade him from such a course.

The usual complaint of all composers was of failure to deliver work on time. By and large, Cammarano's dilatoriness cannot be ascribed to excessive pressure of libretto writing, since he never turned out more than three or four in a year, and often fewer, unlike the six or seven that Romani or Rossi were regularly responsible for. There was, of course, other work to be done – rewriting old texts, providing words for interpolated arias and adjusting the words of others to suit the whims of singers on the one hand, and production duties on the other. How much time Cammarano would have had to spend actually in the theatre cannot now be determined, but Michele's story of being left in charge of the prompter is written in a way to suggest that his father used to attend all performances, though there is no real evidence of this. Although in his early years at the S. Carlo he was one of three or more *concertatori*, after about 1840 he seems to have been the only one and no doubt had an increased work load in the theatre. Obviously he would have to take rehearsals, but the impression is that these were hurried and probably relied on stock action, static groupings and exaggerated gesture. Equally, Cammarano was not to be hurried in his work, and he may well have been something of a perfectionist. His autographs show careful attention to layout and a delight in calligraphy, and his drafts give every indication of repeated polishing. All this took time, and with attendance at the theatre probably made it inevitable that his work would not be available by the due date.

On the third point, his usefulness as a producer, it is well to remember that he was first and foremost a practical man of the theatre, not a lawyer or goverment official writing for the stage in his spare time. His theatrical background, and the number of actors, singers and musicians in his immediate family conferred familiarity with the stage and an approach based on professional expertise. Coupled with this was his early training as a painter, leading to a clear visual imagination which manifested itself in his stage directions. The way he could see the action in his mind's eye as he wrote down the text would have been of direct value when he came to direct the staging, as he would only have to recreate what he had already visualized, rather than working out details of the production from the written text. His libretti are self-sufficient, not depending on preliminary explanation (though this is not to say that they can all be perfectly understood at first reading).

When all is said and done, Cammarano's place in the history of opera depends not on the introduction of any new development or any one outstanding text, but in his good fortune in arriving on the scene at the height of an epoch with an ability to draw all the threads together. He knew where to find the right subjects for the mood of the times, and to handle them in such a way as to keep out of trouble with the authorities. He had the theatrical acumen to articulate his plots in a straightforward and dramatic way, even if he was restricted by the need to condense and adapt a sometimes intractable source. Above all he had the great gift of writing limpid and economical verse which caught the imagination of his composers. Again he exploited existing verse forms rather than developing anything new, although an interest in metrical innovation pervades his last work. His verses were always carefully wrought and smoothly flowing, and were often very expressive: they sound well. His work was remarkably even: it did not develop, improve or decline with time. It is a constant mystery to me why he – and other librettists – should have taken such trouble to perfect their verses, in the face of the way composers set them, omitting words, repeating phrases *ad nauseam*, having several different verses sung simultaneously so that none could be properly heard, breaking *sinalefe* and in other ways showing such a fine disregard for the texts. But at the end of the day, libretti were written to be set to music, and in studying them we lose sight of this at our peril. It is no bad thing to go down in the history of opera as the author of the texts which gave birth to *Lucia di Lammermoor* or *Poliuto*, *Luisa Miller* or *Il trovatore*; or, his contemporaries would have added, *La vestale* and, above all, *Saffo*. The time may not be far off when a revival interest in the operas of Mercadante and Pacini brings about further opportunities to assess Cammarano's place in the history of Italian opera.

Cammarano's personality and character may not now be well documented, but one matter is beyond question, his artistic integrity. His dignified letter to Barbaja when he felt himself to have been unjustly accused of delay over the libretto of *Poliuto*, and his response to Pacini when the latter went behind his back to the S.Carlo management, and other references scattered throughout his letters, all demonstrate a determination not to compromise his principals for the sake of producing hasty or shoddy work. Far and away the most important statement on his artistic position was his letter to Verdi at the time of *Luisa Miller*, perhaps the most interesting expression on record of any Italian librettist of the period. This letter was quoted in Chapter 7, and it is worth turning back to page 123 and reading it again. The idea that, to obtain perfection, the same person should be responsible for both words and music was truly revolutionary in the world of Italian opera of 1848, though by this time Temistocle Solera had set four of his own texts to music. It is an idea that we are more likely to associate with Wagner, and a much more intellectualized concept of music drama. Cammarano's context makes it clear that he was not thinking of some vague intellectual unity but of the practical problems of bringing together words and notes, the problems of the appropriate words and the music to which they were to be united. His remark that he always consulted the composers with whom he shared his work ('i maestri co' quali ho diviso il lavoro') confirms that he saw himself as a partner, perhaps even an equal partner, in a joint enterprise.

If Cammarano was as sincere in this as his letter suggests – and there is nothing in any of his letters, nor in the circumstances of his life, to suggest that he was anything but sincere and truthful in his dealings with managements, publishers and composers alike – he must have found life truly frustrating. We are apt to look on these librettists as mere hacks, botchers-up of improbable plots using a sequence of hackneyed expressions and rubbishy verse. At the time, he was seen as the management's agent responsible for the practical tasks of guiding a work from the censor to the stage, providing at the same time suitable words for the composer to set to music. Yet for all that an opera would be billed as by Cammarano, with music by Donizetti; but literary sensibilities were not, I suspect, to be encouraged if they got in the way of quick and successful production. We cannot dismiss as a mere hack or a theatrical hanger-on someone who can express ideas on opera as an art form so out of tune with contemporary practice or conventions. He must have been constantly pulled two ways, between the pressing and importunate demands of the theatre and his own artistic conscience. It is not surprising that he sought to leave the rat race and become a freelance librettist. Buffetted by incomprehending managements, not properly paid and even threatened with imprisonment, he must have turned to his poetry for consolation. No wonder he haunted the peaceful colonnades of the church of S. Francesco. There we can leave him, dozing off against one of the pillars, his head full of the verses on which his reputation rested. Of one thing we may be certain: never would he have dreamed that 130 years after his death the first comprehensive study of his work should appear in Scotland, that remote and unknown territory to which he safely banished his more sensitive plots.

Appendix A

Operas to texts by Cammarano in order of appearance

1.   LA SPOSA i. Vignozzi, Naples (Fondo)   3.11.1834
     (LA FIDANZATA) ii. Miceli, Naples (Fondo)   2.8.1858

2a. INES DE CASTRO i. Persiani, Naples (S. Carlo) 28.1.1835
     INES DE CASTRO ii. Marchetti,
     Mantova (Sociale)   29.2.1840
     INES DE CASTRO iii. Coppola, Lisbon (S.Carlos) 26.12.1841
     (DON PEDRO DI PORTOGALLO) iv. Gibelli,
     Novara (Teatro)   30.12.1849
     (DON PEDRO DI PORTOGALLO) v. Drigo,
     Padova (Nuovo)   25.7.1868
2b. MALVINA DI SCOZIA Pacini, Naples (S. Carlo)   27.12.1851

3.   UN MATRIMONIO PER RAGIONE Staffa,
     Naples (Fondo)   8.7.1835

4.   LUCIA DI LAMMERMOOR Donizetti,
     Naples (S. Carlo)   26.9.1835

5.   BELISARIO Donizetti, Venice (Fenice)   4.2.1836

6.   L'ASSEDIO DI CALAIS Donizetti,
     Naples (S. Carlo)   19.11.1836

7.   PIA DE' TOLOMEI Donizetti, Venice (Apollo)   18.2.1837

8.   ROBERTO DEVEREUX Donizetti,
     Naples (S. Carlo)   28.10.1837

9.   MARIA DE RUDENZ Donizetti,
     Venice (Fenice)   30.1.1838

10. ELENA DA FELTRE Mercadante,
     Naples (S. Carlo)   1.1.1839

11. I CIARLATANI L. Cammarano, Naples (Fondo)   15.4.1839

12. IL CONTE DI CHALAIS i. Lillo, Naples (S. Carlo) 6.11.1839
     (MARIA DI ROHAN) ii. Donizetti,
     Vienna (Kärntnertor)   5.6.1843

13. LA VESTALE Mercadante, Naples (S. Carlo)   10.3.1840

14a. CRISTINA DI SVEZIA Nini, Genoa (Carlo Felice)   6.6.1840
14b. CRISTINA DI SVEZIA i. Lillo, Naples (S. Carlo)   21.1.1841
     CRISTINA DI SVEZIA ii. Fabrizi, Spoletto (Nobile)   1844

15. SAFFO Pacini, Naples (S. Carlo)   29.11.1840

16. LUIGI ROLLA F. Ricci, Florence (Pergola)   30.3.1841

17. IL PROSCRITTO Mercadante, Naples (S. Carlo)   4.1.1842

18. LA FIDANZATA CORSA Pacini, Naples (S. Carlo) 10.12.1842

19. IL REGGENTE Mercadante, Turin (Regio)   2.2.1843

20. ESTER D'ENGADDI Peri, Parma (Ducale)   19.2.1843

21. IL RAVVEDIMENTO L. Cammarano,
    Naples (Fondo)   16.5.1843

22. IL VASCELLO DE GAMA Mercadante,
    Naples (S. Carlo)   6.3.1845

23. BONDELMONTE Pacini, Florence (Pergola)   18.6.1845

24. ALZIRA Verdi, Naples (S. Carlo)   12.8.1845

25. STELLA DI NAPOLI Pacini, Naples (S. Carlo)   11.12.1845

26. ORAZI E CURIAZI Mercadante,
    Naples (S. Carlo)   10.11.1846

27. ELEONORA DORI Battista, Naples (S. Carlo)   4.2.1847

28. MEROPE i. Pacini, Naples (S. Carlo)   25.11.1847
    MEROPE ii. Zandomeneghi, Pesaro (Rossini)   16.3.1871

29. POLIUTO Donizetti, Naples (S. Carlo)   30.11.1848

30. LA BATTAGLIA DI LEGNANO Verdi,
    Rome (Argentina)   27.1.1849

31. LUISA MILLER Verdi, Naples (S. Carlo)   8.12.1849

32. NON V'È FUMO SENZA FUOCO i. L. Cammarano,
    Naples (Fondo)   3.8.1850
    (LO ZIGARO RIVALE) ii. Lauro Rossi, Milan
    (Canobbiana)   18.6.1867

33. FOLCO D'ARLES De Giosa, Naples (S. Carlo)   22.1.1851

34. MEDEA Mercadante, Naples (S. Carlo)   1.3.1851

35. IL TROVATORE Verdi, Rome (Apollo)   19.1.1853

36.   VIRGINIA Mercadante, Naples (S. Carlo)   7.4.1866

N.B. 2a, with Bidera; 14a, Act III by Saccherò; 34, original
text by Romani, almost completely rewritten.

Known reworkings of older libretti

by Tottola
LA DONNA DEL LAGO Rossini, Naples (S. Carlo) 1834.
Four new scenes

by Romani
ANNA BOLENA Donizetti, Naples (S. Carlo) 1834. One new scene
EUFEMIO DI MESSINA Persiani, Naples (Fondo) 1836. Rewritten
FRANCESCA DONATO Mercadante, Naples (S. Carlo) 1845.
New 3rd Act

Appendix B

Act titles of Cammarano's libretti

Many of Cammarano's texts have titles for each act. This list is compiled from first printings of his texts; sometimes variations are introduced in later printings. The texts are listed in order of production, and if one is not included, it is because no sub-titles were given.

LUCIA DI LAMMERMOOR part 1, La Partenza (in one act)
part 2, Il Contratto Nuziale
(in two acts)

BELISARIO part 1, Il Trionfo
part 2, L'Esilio
part 3, La Morte

MARIA DE RUDENZ part 1, Il Testamento
part 2, Un Delitto
part 3, Lo Spettro

IL CONTE DI CHALAIS act 1, Triste Conseguenze de' Duelli
act 2, Non Amore, ma Riconoscenza
act 3, Una Cieca Vendetta

LA VESTALE act 1, Il Serto Trionfale
act 2, La Fiamma Sacra
act 3, Il Campo Scellerato

CRISTINA DI SVEZIA part 1, L'Abdicazione
(Naples version) part 2, Il Paggio
part 3, Un' Ora Tremenda

SAFFO part 1, La Corona Olimpica
part 2, Le Nozze di Faone
part 3, Il Salto di Leucade

LUIGI ROLLA act 1, La Statua
act 2, Il Verone
act 3, Il Lauro

LA FIDANZATA CORSA act 1, La Disfida
act 2, La Fuga
act 3, La Vendetta

IL REGGENTE act 1, Il Sortilegio
act 2, La Dama Velata
act 3, Il Ballo in Maschera

IL RAVVEDIMENTO act 1, Eduardo Stuard
act 2, La Chiave
act 3, Lo Scoprimento

IL VASCELLO DE GAMA prologue, La Nave Africana
part 1, L'Imbarco
part 2, Il Naufragio
part 3, La Zattera

BONDELMONTE part 1, Cosa Fatta Capo Ha
part 2, La Demente
part 3, Vendetta Memorabile

ALZIRA prologue, Il Prigioniero
act 1, Vita per Vita
act 2, La Vendetta d'un Selvaggio

STELLA DI NAPOLI part 1, La Zingana
part 2, Il Padre
part 3, Amor Senza Pari

ORAZI E CURIAZI act 1, Alba e Roma
act 2, L'Oracolo
act 3, La Pugna

MEROPE act 1, L'Ucciso e l'Uccisore
act 2, Il Cinto
act 3, La Bipenne

POLIUTO act 1, Il Battesimo
act 2, Il Neofito
act 3, Il Martirio

LA BATTAGLIA DI LEGNANO part 1, Egli Vive!
part 2, Barbarossa
part 3, L'Infamia
part 4, Morire per la Patria

LUISA MILLER act 1, Amore
act 2, Intrigo
act 3, Veleno

FOLCO D'ARLES part 1, Il Cavaliere
part 2, Il Duce
part 3, Il Servo

IL TROVATORE part 1, Il Duello
part 2, La Gitana
part 3, Il Figlio della Zingara
part 4, Il Supplizio

Selected Background Reading

This list is not intended as a full statement of references supporting every point made in the text of this book, but rather as a list of
books and articles which may be consulted to give further information on the various subjects touched upon. There is, of course,
a very large number of books on composers like Verdi and Donizetti, but the ones mentioned are those particularly relevant to
the work of their librettists in the period 1830-50.

REFERENCE BOOKS

Caselli, A. *Catalogo delle Opere Liriche Pubblicate in Italia.*
Florence, 1969.

Dassori, C. *Opere e Operisti (Dizionario Lirico, 1541-1905).*
Genoa, 1906.

Loewenberg, A. *Annals of Opera 1597-1940.* 2 Volumes.
Geneva, 1955.

Manferrari, U. *Dizionario delle Opere Melodrammatiche.*
3 Volumes. Florence, 1954, 1955.

Regli, F. *Dizionario Bibliografico dei piu Celebri Poeti e Artisti
Melodrammatici in Italia, 1800-1860.* Turin, 1860.

Salvioli, G. and C. *Bibliografia Universale del Teatro
Drammatico Italiano.* Volume 1 (all published).
Venice, 1903.

Schmidl, C. *Dizionario Universale dei Musicisti.* 2 Volumes.
Milan, 1926.

Sesini, U. *Catalogo della Biblioteca del Liceo Musicale di
Bologna.* Volume 5 – Libretti d'Opera in Musica.
Bologna, 1943.

Stieger, F. *Opernlexikon.* Tutzing, 1975.

NAPLES – HISTORY AND BACKGROUND

Acton, H. *The Bourbons of Naples.* London, 1956.

―――― *The Last Bourbons of Naples.* London, 1961.

Cione, E. *Napoli Romantica, 1830-1848.* Naples, 1957.

313

« SELECTED BACKGROUND READING »

NAPLES – THEATRES

Alberti, A. *Quarant' Anni di Storia del Teatro de' Fiorentini in Napoli. Memorie.* 2 vols. Naples, 1878.

Black, J. *Donizetti's Operas in Naples.* London, 1982.

De Filippis, F. *Napoli Teatrali.* Milan, 1962.

De Filippis, F. and Arnese, R. *Cronache del Teatro di S. Carlo.* 2 vols. Naples, 1961.

De Filippis, F. and Mangini, M. *Il Teatro 'Nuovo' di Napoli.* Naples, 1967.

Scalera, A. *Il Teatro dei Fiorentini (dal 1800 al 1860).* Naples, 1909.

Schletterer, H. M. *Die Opernhäuser Neapels. Monatschefte für Musikgeschichte, 14* and *15,* 1882 and 1883.

Viviani, V. *Storia del Teatro Napoletano.* Naples, 1969.

THE OPERATIC WORLD IN GENERAL

Commons, J. *Maria Stuarda* and the Neapolitan Censorship. *Journal of the Donizetti Society,* 1977.

Cottrau, G. *Lettres d'un mélomane.* Naples, 1885.

Dent, E. J. (ed. W. Dean) *The Rise of Romantic Opera.* Cambridge, 1976.

Florimo, F. *La Scuola Musicale di Napoli.* 4 vols. Naples, 1881-3.

Jarro (Giulio Piccini) *Memorie d'un Impresario Fiorentino.* Florence, 1892.

Il Melodramma Italiano dell' Ottocento *Studi e Richerche per Massimo Mila.* Turin, 1977.

Monaldi, G. *Impresari Celebri del Secolo XIX.* Rocca S. Casciano, 1918.

Schlitzer, F. *Il Mondo Teatrale dell' Ottocento.* Naples, 1954.

COMPOSERS

Vincenzo Bellini

Bellini, V. (ed. Cambi, L.) *Epistolario.* 1943.

Lippmann, F. *Vincenco Bellini und die Italienische Oper seria seiner Zeit. Analecta Musicologica,* 1969.

Weinstock, H. *Vincenzo Bellini.* London, 1971.

Gaetano Donizetti

Ashbrook, W. *Donizetti.* London, 1965.

Ashbrook, W. *Donizetti and his Operas.* Cambridge, 1982.

314

Commons, J. Una Corrispondenza tra Alessandro Lanari e
Donizetti. *Studi Donizettiani*, 1978.

Dent, E. J. Donizetti: and Italian Romantic, in *Fanfare for Ernest
Newman* (ed. Van Thal). London, 1955.

Weinstock, H. *Donizetti*. London, 1964.

Zavadini, G. *Donizetti. Vita-Muische-Epistolario*. Bergamo,
1948.

Saverio Mercadante

Comitato pro Mercadante di Altamura *Saverio Mercadante,
Notizie e Documenti*. Bari, 1945.

De Napoli, G. *Le triade melodrammatica altamurana*. Milan,
1834.

Notarnicola, B. *Saverio Mercadante nella gloria e nella luce*.
Rome, 1951.

Schlitzer, F. Mercadante e Cammarano, in *Numero Unico,
S. Mercadante*. Bari, 1945.

Giovanni Pacini

Pacini, G. *Le Mie Memorie Artistiche*. Florence, 1875.

Giuseppe Verdi

Abbiate, F. *Verdi*. 4 vols. Milan, 1959.

Budden, J. *The Operas of Verdi*. 3 vols. London, 1973–81.

Cesari, G. and Luzio, A. *I Coppialettere di Giuseppe Verdi*.
Milan, 1913.

Luzio, A. *Carteggi Verdiani*. Vol. 1. Rome, 1935.

Noske, F. *The Signifier and the Signified*. The Hague, 1977.

Osborne, C. *Letters of Giuseppe Verdi*. London, 1971.

THE LIBRETTO IN GENERAL

Baldacci, L. *Libretti d'Opera e altri saggi*. Florence, 1974.

Bragaglia, L. *Storia del Libretto*. 3 vols. Rome, 1970.

Miragoli, L. *Il Melodramma Italiano nell' Ottocento*. Rome,
1924.

Rolandi, U. *Il Libretto per Musica*. Rome, 1951.

Smith, P. J. *The Tenth Music. A Historical Study of the Opera
Libretto*. London, 1971.

LIBRETTISTS

Salvadore Cammarano

Checchi, E. Librettisti e Libretti di Giuseppe Verdi. *Nuova
Antologia*, 1913.

Dalbono, C. T. Salvatore Cammarano. 3 parts. *Poliorama
Pittoresco*, 1853.

Di Giacomo, S. Salvatore Cammarano, il Libretto del 'Trovatore'
e Giuseppe Verdi. *Musica e Musicisti*, 1904.

Lanfranchi, A. Salvatore Cammarano, in *Dizionario Biografico
degli Italiani*. Vol. 17. Rome, 1974.

Martorano, P. *Notizie Biografiche e Bibliografiche degli Scrittori
del Dialetto Napoletano*. Naples, 1874.

Torelli, V. Salvatore Cammarano. Necrologia. *L'omnibus*, 21
July 1852.

Viviani, V. Libretti e Librettisti, in *Cento Anni di Vita di San
Carlo* (ed. F. de Filippis). Naples, 1848.

Jacopo Ferretti

Cametti, A. *Un Poeta Melodrammatico Romano. Appunti e
Notizie. Jacopo Ferretti*. Milan, n.d. but 1898.

Felice Romani

Branca E. *Felice Romani ed i più Riputati Maestri di Musica del
suo Tempo*. Turin, 1882.

Rinaldi, M. *Felice Romani*. Rome, 1965.

LIBRETTI
Literary Influences and Sources

Arruga, F. L. Incontri fra Poeti e Musicisti nell'Opera Romantica
Italiana. *Contributo dell' Istituto di Filologia Moderna,
Serie Storia del Teatro*, 1968.

Cella, F. Indagini sulle Fonte Francesi dei Libretti di Gaetano
Donizetti. *Contributo dell' Istituto di Filologia
Moderna, Serie Francese*, 1966.

—— Indagini sulle Fonte Francesi dei Libretti di Vincenzo
Bellini. *Contributo dell' Istituto di Filologia Moderna,
Serie Francese*, 1968.

—— Prospettive delle Librettistica Italiana nell' Eta
Romantica. *Contributo dell' Istituto di Filologia
Moderna, Serie Storia de Teatro*, 1968.

Cisotti, V. *Schiller e il Melodramma di Verdi*. Florence, 1975.

Mitchell, J. *The Walter Scott Operas*. Alabama, 1977.

Wicks, C. B. *The Parisian Stage, 1800-1875*. 4 vols. Alabama,
1950-67.

« SELECTED BACKGROUND READING »

Language and Verse

Bentivogli, B. Preliminari sul linguaggio dei Libretti nel Primo Ottocento. *Italianisca*, 1975.

Dallapiccola, L. Parole e Musica nel Melodramma, in *Appunti, Incontri, Meditazioni*. Milan, 1970.

Fabrizi, A. Riflessi del Linguaggio Tragico Alfieriano nei Libretti d'Opera Ottocentechi. *Studi e Problemi di Critica Testuale*, 1976.

Lippmann, F. Der Italienische Vers und der Musikalische Rhythmus. 3 parts. *Analecta Musicologica*, 1973, 1974, 1975.

Index